My Second Pictionary

ABCDEFGHIJKLMNOPQRSTUVWXYZABCDE

Marion Monroe
W. Cabell Greet

SCOTT, FORESMAN AND COMPANY

FGHIJKLMNOPQRSTUVWXYZ

2

Contents

About This Book

My Second Pictionary is an intermediate step between *My Little Pictionary* and the *Thorndike-Barnhart Beginning Dictionary*. Here children will find words alphabetized within each classification. Illustrations in color are included for many of these words. Here, also, children will become familiar with the format of a dictionary. When they go on to the *Beginning Dictionary*, learning to interpret pronunciations will be the only new major step.

There are 3818 entry words in *My Second Pictionary*. Included are (1) most of the words in The New Basic Readers, the *Learn to Listen, Speak, and Write* series, and books for other curriculum areas through third grade; (2) words common to other readers and spellers through third grade; (3) words familiar to second-graders and likely to be used by them, such as names of months, holidays, and the ordinal numbers; (4) words of special interest, which include the names and abbreviations of the states, state birds, state trees, state flowers, state animals.

My Second Pictionary has three parts. Part One: **How to Use This Book**; Part Two: **Words and Pictures**; Part Three: **Words and Meanings.**

Part One contains exercises that help a child understand and use the book. Some children will be able to do the exercises independently. Many will need direction and help.

Part Two contains words classified by meaning and function and arranged in alphabetical order within each classification. Pictured words are printed in blue.

Part Three contains the same words as Part Two but in alphabetical order and with definitions (in roman type) and/or illustrative sentences (in italic type). Irregular verb forms are separate entries. Words printed in blue in Part Two are printed in blue in Part Three. A blue numeral before a definition or illustrative sentence in Part Three indicates that there is a picture in Part Two for that use of the word. The way entry words are printed indicates where they may be divided at the end of a line in writing.

How to Use This Book

ABCDEFGHIJKLMNOPQRSTUVWXYZABCDEFG

Before You Begin

Before you begin to use this book,
you will want to know what
My Second Pictionary is like.

My Second Pictionary has three parts.

Part One is **How to Use This Book.**
There are exercises in this part that
will help you understand this book
and teach you how to use it.

Part Two is **Words and Pictures.** There
are twelve groups of words in this part.
The name of each group tells you what the
words in that group are for or what they
can do. The Color Key will help you find
each group quickly. The words that have
pictures are blue.

Part Three is **Words and Meanings.** This
part will help you understand the meaning
of each word. The words that are blue in
Part Two are blue here, also. A blue
numeral before one meaning of a word
shows you that there is a picture for that
meaning of the word in Part Two.

Read the sentences in the box. Then do
each thing you are asked to do.

---

1. Turn to page 3. Find the number of the
   page on which each part begins.
2. Turn to the page on which Part Two
   begins. Then look at the first few
   pages in that part.
3. Do the same for Part Three.

After you have looked at your book, write
the answers to the questions below.

Number your paper from 1 to 5. Put one
numeral under the other and put the
numerals on the left side of your paper.

1. How many parts are there in the book?
2. What is the name of the part in which
   you find a Color Key?
3. In which part would you look first
   to find a picture of an alligator?
4. In which part would you look to find
   the meaning of the word *alligator?*
5. In which part is the page you are
   reading now?

Words and Pictures

The Color Key

It is easy to learn to use the Color Key. You will find it very easy if you have used *My Little Pictionary*.

Read the sentences in the box. Then do each thing you are asked to do.

1. Turn to page 40. Look at the Color Key and the name of each group of words on pages 40 and 41.
2. What is the name of the group of words that begins on page 42? What color is the half circle at the left of it?
3. Turn to page 42 and then look at each page on which you find a green half circle.
4. On what page does Words for People end?
5. Use the colored half circles to find the pages on which each group of words begins and ends.

See how many ways you can find to tell
where a new group of words begins.

After you have looked at all twelve groups
of words, turn back to this page and write
the answers to these questions.

Number your paper from 1 to 5.

1. How many groups of words are there?
2. What color in the Color Key goes with
   Words for Animals?
3. What color are the words that go with
   the pictures?
4. With what letter does the first word in
   each group begin?
5. With what letter does the last word in
   Words for Places begin?

Words and Groups of Words

Read the sentence below. Then read the two questions in the box and answer them.

We watched the ____ cut Dad's hair.

<blockquote>
1. What is the word that has been left out?
2. In which group of words will you find it?
</blockquote>

Write your answers on one line. They should look like this:

barber – Words for People

Number your paper from 1 to 15. Read each sentence on page 11 and write the answers to the two questions in the box.

1. The name of our state is _____.

2. My birthday comes in _____.

3. There are _____ people in our family.

4. You can see an _____ at the zoo.

5. We are at _____ now.

6. A turtle moves _____.

7. A _____ has two wheels.

8. Some children _____ bikes to school.

9. Some children never have _____ a bike to school.

10. Patty has a new _____ dress.

11. We _____ inside at recess time on rainy days.

12. He reads very _____.

13. He has two brothers but only one _____.

14. He hung his hat on a _____.

15. She _____ gone to school.

The Alphabet

Before you can find a word quickly in any group, you must know the alphabet.

The alphabet is these 26 letters in this order:

A B C D E F G H I J K L M N O P Q R S T U V W X Y Z

In the alphabet, B always comes after A; C always comes after B; and so on. This is called *alphabetical order*.

Number your paper from 1 to 10 and write the answers to these questions.

1. What letter comes after C?
2. What letter comes after D?
3. What letter comes after E?
4. What is the next letter in the alphabet?
5. What letter comes after I?
6. What letter comes before K?
7. What letter comes between L and N?
8. What letter comes between R and T?
9. What are the first three letters in the alphabet?
10. What are the last three letters in the alphabet?

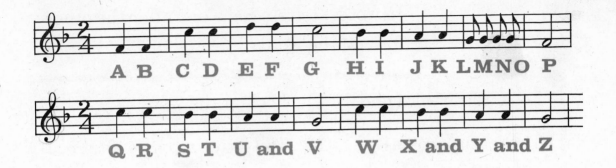

Number your paper from 1 to 26. Without
looking at your book, see if you can
write the letters of the alphabet in
order beside the numerals.

Number your paper from 1 to 8 and write
the answers to these questions.

1. What is your first name?
2. With what letter does it begin?
3. What letter comes just after the first
   letter in your first name?
4. What letter comes just after that letter
   in the alphabet?
5. What is your last name?
6. With what letter does it end?
7. What is the letter just before that letter?
8. In the alphabet, what letter comes just
   before the last letter in your name?

In words, letters come one after the other to spell the word.

Look at the word *and*. The letter *n* comes after the *a*. The letter *d* comes after the letter *n*.	Look at the word *on*. The letter *n* comes after *o*. If the letter *o* came after *n*, what word would the letters spell?

Number your paper from 1 to 10 and write the answers to these questions.

1. Write the word *saw*.
2. What letter comes after *s*?
3. What letter comes after *a*?
4. What other word can you make by changing the order of these letters?
5. What is the first letter in the new word?
6. What is the last letter?
7. Write the word *ten*.
8. What letter comes after *t*?
9. What letter comes after *e*?
10. What other word can you make with these same three letters?

You will use each word in the box to answer the questions on this page.

Number your paper from 1 to 26. Write the answers to the questions below. Your first answer should look like this:

1. a — arm

1. With what letter does the first word begin? What is the word?
2. With what letter does the second word begin? What is the word?
3. What are the next four letters in the alphabet that go beside the next four numerals on your paper?
4. What word in the box goes beside the last letter you wrote?
5. What letters go beside the other numerals? What words in the box go beside the letters?
6. What word can you write beside each letter for which there is no word in the box?

arm
back
farm
girl
home
jam
laugh
name
picture
rake
saw
town
wagon
yard
zoo

The Same First Letter—
Different Second Letters

about
again
air
all
am
an
are
as

Look at the words at the left. With what letter does each word begin?

Look at the second letter in each word. *About* comes before *again* because *b* comes before *g* in the alphabet. Why does *air* come after *again?*

Number your paper from 1 to 6. Beside each numeral write the two letters that should go in the blank spaces below.

1. *Again* comes before *air* because _____ comes before _____.
2. *Air* comes before *all* because _____ comes before _____.
3. *Am* comes before *an* because _____ comes before _____.
4. *Are* comes before *as* because _____ comes before _____.
5. *Am* comes after *all* because _____ comes after _____.
6. *An* comes after *am* because _____ comes after _____.

Look at the words in the box. How many words begin with *b?* How many begin with *f?*

Look at the second letters of the words that begin with *b.* Why does *baby* come before *bed?* Why does *bed* come before *big?* Why does *black* come after *big?* Should *brown* come before or after *book?*

Number your paper from 1 to 5. Write the correct letters and the word *before* or *after* beside the numerals.

1. *Clown* comes _____ *coat* because _____ comes _____ _____.
2. *Dog* comes _____ *duck* because _____ comes _____ _____.
3. *Food* comes _____ *find* because _____ comes _____ _____.
4. *Fun* comes _____ *from* because _____ comes _____ _____.
5. *Game* comes _____ *fun* because _____ comes _____ _____.

baby
bed
big
black
book
brown
but
by
cat
chair
clown
coat
dark
dear
did
dog
duck
feed
find
food
from
fun
game

17

bag
bait
bake
balance
coat
coin
color
could
eleven
elf
elm
family
farm
fast
fat
he
head
help
hen
said
sang
sat
saw

Looking Beyond the Second Letter

Look at the first letter of each word in the box. Look at the second letter of each word that begins with *b*. What is the third letter? Why does *bag* come before *bait?* Why does *balance* come after *bake?*

Number your paper from 1 to 7. Write the correct letters beside each numeral.

1. *Coat* comes before *coin* because ＿＿ comes before ＿＿.
2. *Could* comes after *color* because ＿＿ comes after ＿＿.
3. *Family* comes before *farm* because ＿＿ comes before ＿＿.
4. *Fat* comes after *fast* because ＿＿ comes after ＿＿.
5. *Help* comes after *head* because ＿＿ comes after ＿＿.
6. *Sang* comes before *sat* because ＿＿ comes before ＿＿.
7. *Saw* comes after *sat* because ＿＿ comes after ＿＿.

Looking Beyond the Third Letter

You will use the words in the box to answer the questions on the page.

In an alphabetical list would the word *chicken* come before or after the word *chickadee?* Why? How many letters did you look at before you knew? Would *angrily* come before *angry?* Why? Should *cabbage* come before *cabin?* Why?

Number your paper from 1 to 6. Write the correct letters beside each numeral.

1. *Balcony* comes before *ballerina* because _____ comes before_____.

2. *Busily* comes before *busy* because _____ comes before _____.

3. *Daisy* comes after *daffodil* because _____ comes before _____.

4. *Gallop* comes after *gallon* because _____ comes after _____.

5. *Tricycle* comes after *trick* because _____ comes before _____.

6. *Winter* comes after *window* because _____ comes after _____.

angrily
angry
balcony
ballerina
busily
busy
cabbage
cabin
chickadee
chicken
daffodil
daisy
gallon
gallop
trick
tricycle
window
winter

Using What You Have Learned

Look at the pictures on page 21. Look at the story below. In each blank where a word or words have been left out, there is a numeral. Number your paper from 1 to 18. Write the words that go in the blanks and the name of the group of words in "Words and Pictures" in which you found each one.

Blast Off!

One day in spring two astronauts were walking out to the ____ 1 ____. One __ 2 __ was wearing his ____ 3 ____. The other __ 4 __ was wearing a __ 5 __ coat. There were __ 6 __ getting __ 7 __ for their newspapers. One man was talking into a __ 8 __.

When the two __ 9 __ came to the ____ 10 ____, they stopped. The one wearing the ____ 11 ____ got in the elevator to go up to the __ 12 __.

After a while the count down __ 13 __. 10-9-8-7-6-5-4-3-2-1-Blast off! Everyone looked at the __ 14 __ zooming off toward __ 15 __.

Before long the astronaut in the __ 16 __ said, "Everything is A.OK!"

Then someone shouted, "He is in orbit. He will __ 17 __ the __ 18 __ many times."

Words and Meanings

Finding Entry Words

Read each sentence in the box.

1. The words in "Words and Meanings" for which meanings are given are called *entry words*.

2. Entry words are either black or blue. A blue entry word tells you that you will find a picture for that word in "Words and Pictures."

3. The entry words in "Words and Meanings" are arranged in alphabetical order. All the words that begin with the letter *a* come first in "Words and Meanings." All words that begin with the letter *b* come next, and so on.

Number your paper from 1 to 14 and write the answers to the questions on page 23.

1. On what page does the part of your book called "Words and Meanings" begin?
2. What is the first entry word?
3. How many pages of entry words begin with the letter *a?*
4. On what page is the first entry word that begins with *b?*
5. On what page do the entry words that begin with *m* start?
6. How many pages have entry words that begin with *m?*
7. How many pages have entry words that begin with *w?*
8. What is the first word beginning with *a* that is printed in blue?
9. In "Words and Pictures," in which group of words is this word found?
10. On what page did you find the picture for the word?
11. On what page is the entry word *Eskimo?*
12. In "Words and Pictures," in which group of words will you find a picture of an Eskimo?
13. What entry word comes just before *rhinoceros?*
14. What entry word comes after *zebra?*

Dividing Words

John was writing a story about rabbits. When he came to the end of the line, he did not have enough room to write *rabbits*.

Look at *rabbit* in "Words and Meanings." It is written *rab bit*. The space between the *b*'s means you can divide the word there.

This is the way John should write the word:

I like to see the rab-
bits playing in the woods.

Sometimes there are no spaces between letters in an entry word. This means you cannot divide the word at the end of a line.

Number your paper from 1 to 6. Look up each word below in "Words and Meanings." Write each word, leaving a space at each place where it can be divided.

1. blacksmith
2. Halloween
3. idea
4. among
5. cafeteria
6. balloon

Using Guide Words

Read the sentences in the box and
do what the directions tell you.

1. The two words at the left near the top
   of page 184 are called *guide words*.
2. Find the entry word *apple*.
3. Find the entry word *around*.
4. All the other entry words on page 184
   come in alphabetical order between
   apple and *around*.
5. Look at the guide words and the first
   and last entry word on each of the first
   ten pages of "Words and Meanings."
6. The entry words on each page in
   "Words and Meanings" come in
   alphabetical order between the two
   guide words.

Turn to page 289. What are the guide
words? Would you look for the word
Mexico on this page? Why?

Turn to page 327. What are the guide
words? Would you look for the word
raw on this page? Why?

Finding Root Words

Words from which other words are made are called *root words*. The word *book* is the root word from which the word *books* is made.

Most words to which the ending *s, es, ed, ing, er,* or *est* has been added are not entry words in "Words and Meanings." If you want to find one of these words, you will need to look up the root word.

Number your paper from 1 to 15. Look up the words in the box. Beside each numeral write the root word from which the word is made.

Do it like this: _____ 1. baby _____

1. babies	6. cried	11. looked
2. bigger	7. finer	12. named
3. boxes	8. prettiest	13. running
4. ponies	9. hoped	14. slower
5. coming	10. hopped	15. wanting

An *entry* is the entry word and everything that is told about the entry word to help you understand it.

Find the entry for the root word *baby* in "Words and Meanings." Find the word *babies* at the end of the entry. Find the entry for *big*. What words do you find at the end of the entry? Write all the words you find at the end of the entry for each root word you have written on your paper.

If only *s* is added to a root word, you will not find the new form at the end of an entry.

Find the entry for *deer* and the word at the end of the entry. Do you know why the word *deer* is at the end? This means that you use the word *deer* even when you are writing about more than one deer.

Number your paper from 1 to 10. Beside the numerals write the ten words that are in the box. Now look up each word. Write the word or words in each entry that mean more than one.

1. aircraft
2. cactus
3. elf
4. fish
5. goose
6. man
7. mouse
8. potato
9. sheep
10. woman

Learning More About an Entry

Words that tell what something is or what a word means are called a *definition*. Read the sentences in the box.

1. In some entries there is just a definition.
2. In some entries there is a definition, and the entry word is used in a sentence to help you understand it.
3. In some entries the entry word is just used in a sentence to help you understand it.

Number your paper from 1 to 12. Find each word below in "Words and Meanings " and read the entry. Write the word and the number of the sentence in the box that tells what you find.

1. eraser   5. acrobat   9. am
2. drip   6. large   10. camel
3. instantly   7. except   11. completely
4. its   8. excitedly   12. barge

Look up the word *end* and read all of the entry. There are five numbered parts in this entry. In each of the first two parts there is a definition, and *end* is used in a sentence. In each of parts 3, 4, and 5, the word *end* is just used in a sentence.

Find *end* in five groups of words in "Words and Pictures." Number your paper from 1 to 5. Beside each numeral write the name of one group of words in which you found the word *end*.

Read the sentences below. The same word will fit in all of them. What is the word?

Look up the word and read all of the entry. How many numbered parts are in the entry? Number your paper from 1 to 5. Beside each numeral write the number of the part of the entry that fits in each sentence.

1. The _____ of my head hurts.
2. Do not _____ the car into the street now.
3. Get in the _____ seat.
4. Go _____ to your seat.
5. It happened _____ in the fall.

You know that pictures help you understand the meaning of a word. Even though there are some pictures in "Words and Meanings," you may want to turn back and look at a picture in "Words and Pictures." This is why some entry words and some numerals in an entry are blue.

Look up *horn* in "Words and Meanings." What color is the entry word? What color are the numerals? Will you find a picture of a horn in "Words and Pictures"? In how many groups of words will you find *horn*?

Look up the word *dive*. What color is the entry word? What does this tell you? What color is the numeral 1? What color is the numeral 2? What does this tell you? In which group of words in "Words and Pictures" will you find a picture for the word *dive*?

Now look up the word *joke*. In which groups of words will you find *joke* in "Words and Pictures"? Will you find a picture in either group? How can you tell?

Number your paper from 1 to 24 and write
the words in the box beside the numerals.
Then look up each word and read all of the
entry. How many numbered parts are there
for each word? Write your answer. Then
write *yes* if there are one or more pictures
for the word in "Words and Pictures."
Write *no* if there is no picture.

Your answer should look like this:

1. aquarium — 2 — yes

1. aquarium	9. judge	17. bend
2. column	10. America	18. allow
3. danger	11. watch	19. plain
4. earth	12. daily	20. zigzag
5. elm	13. behind	21. dial
6. garden	14. dart	22. ask
7. happy	15. jacket	23. dance
8. interest	16. paper	24. kick

Using Directions in an Entry

When you look up an entry word in "Words and Meanings," you may see a direction telling you to see another word.

Look up the word *caught*. What are you told to do? You will see the word *caught* at the end of the entry for *catch*, because it is a form of the root word *catch*.

1. fought
2. grown
3. had
4. knelt
5. laid
6. written

Number your paper from 1 to 6. Write the word you are told to see when you look up each word in the box.

When you look up an entry word, you may find one or more pictures near the entry. Sometimes you will find a picture with different parts named. There is an entry in "Words and Meanings" for each part of a picture that is named.

Look up the word *bulb*. What are you told to do? How many pictures do you find? Look up the word *wing*. What are you told to do?

Number your paper from 1 to 12. Write the number or word that is missing in each of these sentences.

1. The word *wheel* is on page ____.
2. The picture of a wheel has ____ parts.
3. The names of these parts are ____, ____, and ____.
4. You can find out more about these parts on pages ____, ____, and ____.
5. Find *ankle*. You must find the word ____ to see a picture of an ankle.
6. You can find *baseball* on page ____.
7. You can find out about an umpire on pages ____ and ____.
8. The second entry for *bill* tells you to see the picture under ____.
9. There are ____ pictures for the entry *bulb*.
10. Find the word *nail*. There are ____ pictures for the word *nail*.
11. Find the word *body*. The drawing for the entry *body* has ____ parts.
12. Find the word *leg*. You are told to look for the word ____ to see another picture.

Finding Special Meanings

You know what the words *do* and *up* mean. Do you know what *do up* means? Find *do up* in "Words and Meanings." Look up the word *do*.

What word in "Words and Meanings" would you look up to find *in charge of?* What does it mean? What page did you find it on? Find *on account of.* What word did you look up? What page was it on?

What words will you look up to find the special meanings of the words in the box?

Number your paper from 1 to 10. Beside each numeral write the entry word you would look up. Then find the word. Put the number of the page where you found it next to the word you found it under.

1. all at once
2. as a rule
3. bring up
4. strike out
5. a Western
6. of course
7. department store
8. over and over
9. every now and then
10. excuse me

Choosing the Right Entry

Sometimes two or more different words have the same spelling. Find the two entry words spelled *b-a-t*. Look at the small numeral after each entry. When you see a small numeral after an entry word, you know there is at least one more entry word spelled this same way.

Number your paper from 1 to 6. Read the sentences below. Write the correct entry word and its small numeral for each underlined word. The first one is done for you.

1. bear¹

1. I saw a <u>bear</u> in the woods.
2. We saw <u>palm</u> trees in Florida.
3. The bird can <u>fly</u> swiftly.
4. Mother wants us to <u>rest</u> after lunch.
5. <u>Jam</u> is good to eat.
6. We bought six <u>ears</u> of corn.

Using All of This Book

All the words in "Words and Pictures" can
be found in "Words and Meanings."

In "Words and Pictures," in which
groups of words is the word *crane* found?

As you look through "Words and Pictures,"
you can tell how the words are grouped.
In what order are the words in each group
arranged? In what order are the words in
"Words and Meanings" arranged?

How does knowing the alphabet help you
find a word quickly in either part of
your book?

Number your paper from 1 to 8. Choose
eight words from "Words and Meanings"
and write them next to the numerals.
Find each word in "Words and Pictures."
Next to each word on your paper write the
name of the group or groups of words
in which you found it.

Do it like this: 1. king — Words for People

Number your paper from 1 to 12 and write the answers to the questions below.

1. How many parts are there in *My Second Pictionary?*
2. What is each part called?
3. In which part would you look to find entry words?
4. In which part would you look to find sentences that help tell what a word means?
5. What color is an entry word in "Words and Meanings" if there is a picture for it in "Words and Pictures"?
6. In which part do you find the Color Key?
7. What color goes with Words for Animals?
8. Could the word *party* be a guide word on page 308? Why?
9. Would the word *asked* be an entry word?
10. What is the root word in the word *asked?*
11. What does a large blue numeral in an entry tell you?
12. What does a small numeral after an entry word tell you?

Words and
Pictures

ABCDEFGHIJKLMNOPQRSTUVWXYZAB

Color Key

Words for People

A

acrobat

agent

Air Force
airman
airmen
amateur
American
announcer

archaeologist

Army

artist

astronaut

athlete
audience

aunt
author

B

baby
baker

ballerina

band
banker

barber

Words for People

batter

blacksmith

Blue Bird

boss

boxer

boy

Boy Scout

brakeman

bride
bridegroom
brother

Brownie
butcher

C

Camp Fire Girl
Canadian
captain
carolers

carpenter

cashier

catcher

center
chairman
character

43

Words for People

chauffeur

checker

chief

child

children

choir

citizen

class

classmate

clerk

clown

club

coach

Coast Guard

Coast Guardsman

Coast Guardsmen

cobbler

collector

committee

company

conductor

council

couple

cousin

coward

cowboy

creature

crew

crowd

Cub Scout

custodian

customer

Words for People

D

dad
dancer
daughter

drummer

Eskimo

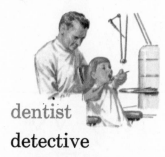
dentist
detective

duchess
duke

F

fairy
family
farmer
father
fellow
female
fireman
firemen

diver

E

editor

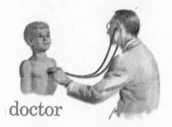
doctor

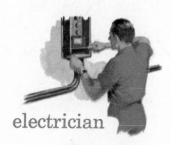
electrician

druggist

elf
enemy
engineer

forward
friend

Words for People

G

ghost

giant

girl

Girl Scout

goblin

governor

grandchild

grandchildren

granddaughter

grandfather

grandmother

grandson

grocer

group

grown-up

guard

guest

guide

H

he

her

herself

him

himself

husband

I

I

Indian

inventor

J

janitor

judge

K

king

knight

L

lad

lady

landlord

lass

lawyer

Words for People

librarian

M

magician
maid
majesty
male
mama
man

Marine Corps
marine
master

mate
mayor
me

mechanic
member
men
messenger
Mexican

miner

minister
Miss
mom

mother
Mr.
Mrs.
musician
myself

N

narrator
nation

Navy
neighbor
nephew
niece

nurse

Words for People

O

officer
operator

orchestra
ourselves

P

painter
papa

papoose
parent
partner
passenger
pastor
patient
people
person

photographer
picket

Pilgrim
pilot
pioneer

pirate

pitcher
playmate

plumber
police
policeman
policemen

postman

preacher
president

priest

48

Words for People

prince
princess
principal

printer
pupil

Q

queen

R

rabbi

ranger

referee
refugee
relative

reporter
ruler

S

sailor

Santa Claus
scientist

scoutmaster
self
servant
settler
she

sheriff
sir
sister

Words for People

soldier
son
spy
star
superintendent
supervisor
sweetheart

swimmer

T

teacher
team
them
themselves
they
trapper
troll

trooper

twins

typist

U

umpire
uncle
us

V

visitor

W

waiter
waitress
we
who
whom
wife

witch
wizard
woman
women

wrestler
writer

Y

you
yourself

50

Words for Animals

A

alligator
amphibian
animal
ant

antelope

armadillo

B

badger

bass

bat

beagle
bear

Black Bear

California
Grizzly
beast

beaver
bee

beetle
bird

bluebird

bluejay

bobolink

buffalo
bug

bulldog

bumblebee

Words for Animals

bunny

bunting

burro

butterfly

C

calf

camel

canary

cardinal

cat

caterpillar

cattle

chickadee

chicken

Blue Hen
Chicken

Rhode Island
Red

Chihuahua

chimpanzee

chipmunk

clam

cockatoo

cocker spaniel

52

Words for Animals

cod

collie

colt

cow

coyote

crab

crane

crayfish

creature

cricket

crow

cub

D

dachshund

deer

dinosaur

doe

dog

dolphin

donkey

dove

dragon

Words for Animals

dragonfly

duck

E

eagle

eel

elephant

elk

ewe

F

falcon

fawn

finch

Goldfinch

Purple Finch

firefly

fish

flamingo

flounder

fly

flycatcher

fowl

fox

frog

G

geese

giraffe

goat

goldfish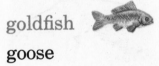

goose

54

Words for Animals

gopher

gorilla

grasshopper

greyhound

grouse

guinea hen

guinea pig

gull

guppy

H

halibut

hamster

hare

hawk

hedgehog

hen

heron

hippopotamus

hog

honeybee

hornet

horse

hound

hummingbird

Husky

I

insect

it

itself

55

Words for Animals

J

jaguar

K

kangaroo

katydid

kid

kingfisher

kitten

koala

L

ladybug

lamb

leopard

lion

lizard

lobster

loon

M

mackerel

magpie

mallard

mammal

mammoth

marlin

Words for Animals

meadow lark

mice

mink

mockingbird

mole

mongrel

monkey

moose

mosquito

moth

mouse

mule

muskie

N

nene

newt

O

octopus

opossum

oriole

ostrich

otter

owl

Words for Animals

ox
oxen

pelican

pointer

oyster

P

penguin

police dog
pony

panda

perch
pet

poodle

parakeet

pheasant
pig

parrot

pigeon

porcupine

peacock

pike

porpoise
poultry

Words for Animals

prairie dog

ptarmigan

puppy

Q

quail

R

rabbit

raccoon

rat

reindeer

reptile

rhinoceros

road runner

robin

rodent

rooster

S

salmon

Scotch terrier
Scotty

sea horse

seal

setter

shark

sheep

sheep dog

Words for Animals

shrew

shrimp

skunk

snail

snake

sparrow

spider

squirrel

starfish

starling

steer

stork

swallow

swan

T

tadpole

tarpon

thrasher

thrush

tiger

toad

tortoise

Words for Animals

trout

California
Golden

Cutthroat

tuna

turkey

turtle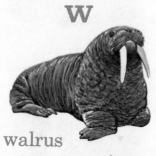

W

walrus

wasp

weasel

whale

whippoorwill

wolf

woodchuck

woodpecker

worm

wren

Cactus Wren

Carolina Wren

Y

yellowhammer

Z

zebra

Words for Things

A

abbreviation
accent
accident
account
ache

acorn

act
address
adventure
advice
aerial
afternoon
age
air
aircraft
airplane
aisle
alarm

alfalfa

allowance

A B C D E F G
H I J K L M
N O P Q R S T
U V W X Y Z
alphabet
amount
amusement
ankle
answer

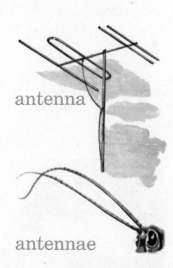
antenna

antennae

antlers

apartment
apostrophe

apple
apple blossom

apricot

apron

aquarium

arbor

Words for Things

arithmetic

arm

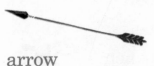

arrow

art

artichoke

ashes

asparagus

attention

audiometer

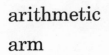

autograph

automobile

auto

avenue   Ave.

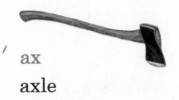

ax

axle

azalea

B

back

bacon

bag

baggage

bait

balance

balcony

bale

ball

balloon

banana

band

bandage

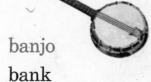

bangs

banjo

bank

Words for Things

bar

barbecue

bargain

barge

bark

barley

barn

barrel

base

baseball

basket

basketball

bat

bath

baton

batter

battery

beach

beads

beam

bean

beard

beauty

bed

beef

beet

bell

belt

bench

bend

berry

bib

Bible

bicycle

bike

bill

bin

biography

birch

64

Words for Things

birth

biscuit

bit

bite

bitterroot

blackberries

black-eyed Susan

blade

blame

blank

blanket

---

blaze

bleat

blind

blizzard

block

blood

bloom

blossom

blouse

blow

blueberries

bluebonnet

board

boat

body

boil

---

boiler

bone

book

bookcase

boom

boots

bother

bottle

bottom

bouquet

bow

bowl

box

bracelet

braid

brain

brake

branch

brand

brass

Words for Things

bread
break
breakfast
breath
breeze
brick
bridge
broadcast
brook
broom

brownie
brush

bubble

bucket

buckeye

buckle
buckskin
bud

buggy

bugle

building
bulb

bulletin board
bump

bun
bunch
bundle
burn

burrow
bus
bush
business
butter

button
buzz

C

cab

cabbage
cabin

66

Words for Things

cable

caboose

cactus

cafeteria

cage

cake

calendar

calf

calves

call

camellia

camera

camp

can

candle

candy

cane

canoe

cantaloupe

canvas

canyon

cap

cape

capital

Capitol

capsule

67

Words for Things

car
card
care

carnation

carpet

carrier

carrots

cart

carton

cartoon

case
cash

castle

catsup

cauliflower

cause

cave

cavity

cedar
ceiling
celebration

celery
cell

cello
cement
cent
cereal
chain
chair
chalk

Words for Things

chance
change
chapter
charm
chart
chat
check
cheek
cheer

cheese

cherries

chest

chestnut

chill

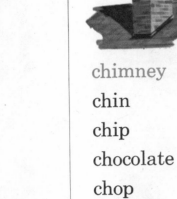

chimney
chin
chip
chocolate
chop
chuckle

church

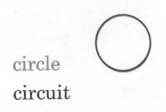

churn

circle
circuit

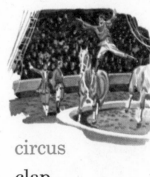

circus
clap

clarinet
class
claw
clay
clearing

cliff
clip

clippers

Words for Things

clock
closet
cloth
clothes
clothing

clouds

clover
club
clue
coach
coal

coast

coat

cobbler
cocoa

coconut

cocoon
code

coffee
coin
cold

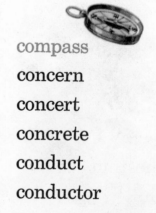
collar
collection
color

columbine

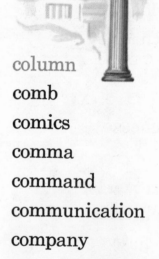
column
comb
comics
comma
command
communication
company

compass
concern
concert
concrete
conduct
conductor

Words for Things

cone
conservation
consonant

constellation
contest
contraction
control
cookies

coop
copper
copy
coral
cord
corduroy

cork

corn
corner

cornet

corral
corridor
cost
costume
cot

cottage

cotton

cottonwood
cough

counter
courage
course
court

courthouse
cover
crack

Words for Things

cracker

cradle

crane

crash

crate

crayons

cream

creek

crib

croak

crocus

crop

cross

crown

crumb

crust

cry

cube

cup

cupboard

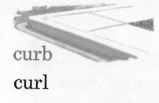

curb

curl

currants

current

curtain

curve

cushion

cut

cyclone

cymbal

72

Words for Things

D

daffodil

daisy

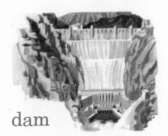

dam

dance

dandelion

danger

dare

dark

darkness

dart

dash

date

dawn

day

daybreak

deal

deck

defense

definition

delay

delight

den

dent

department

depot

desert

desire

desk

dessert

detour

dew

dial

diamond

dictionary

difference

dime

dinner

diplomacy

dipper

Words for Things

directions
dirt
dishes
distance
ditch
dive

dock

dogwood
doll

dollar
door
dose

dot

doughnut
down
drain

drawer
dream
dress

dresser
dressing
drift

drill
drink
drive

drop
drug
drum

dryer
dump
dust
duty

E

ear
earth

easel
edge
education
egg
elbow
electricity

Words for Things

elevator

elm

end

enemy

engine

entrance

envelope

eraser

escalator

escape

eve

evening

event

evergreen

example

excitement

exclamation

excuse

exercise

experiment

expressway

eye

F

face

fact

factory

faint

fair

fall

fan

fancy

fare

farm

fashion

fat

fault

fear

feast

feather

feed

feet

felt

fence

Words for Things

fender

fern

ferry

festival

field

fife

fight

figs

figure

file

film

fin

fine

finger

fir

fire

fireworks

fist

fit

flag

flake

flame

flap

flare

flash

flashlight

flat

flight

float

flock

flood

floor

flour

flower

flute

fog

fold

food

76

Words for Things

foot
football

footprints
force
forehead
forenoon
forest

forget-me-not
fork
form

fort
fortune

fountain

frame

frankfurter

freight train
friction
fright

fringe
front
frost

frown
fruit

fulcrum
fun

funnel

fur
furnace
furniture

G

gallon
game

garage

77

Words for Things

garbage

garden

gardenia

gas

gasp

gate

gears

geography

germ

gift

gingerbread

gingham

gladiolus

glass

glider

globe

glory

gloves

glow

glue

gobble

gold

goldenrod

goodness

gourd

government

grade

grain

grandstand

grapefruit

grapes

grass

grate

gravy

grease

grin

groan

groceries

ground

group

grove

growl

grunt

78

Words for Things

guess

guitar

gum

gun

gym

gymnasium

H

habit

hail

hair

ham

hamburger

hammer

hammock

hand

handkerchief

handle

handwriting

hangar

happiness

harm

harp

haste

hat

hawthorn

hay

hayloft

haymow

head

headquarters

health

heap

heart

hearth

heat

hedge

Words for Things

heel

helicopter

helmet

help

hemlock

herd

hibiscus

hiccups

hickory

hide

highway

hike

hill

hinge

hint

hip

history

hit

hive

hoe

hold

hole

holiday

hollow

holly

honesty

honey

hood

hoof

hook

hoop

hoot

hop

hope

horn

hose

hospital

Words for Things

hotel
hour
house
howl
hub
hug
hum
hunger
hurricane
hurry
hurt
husk
hut

hyacinth

hydrant

I

ice

ice cream

icicle
idea
inch
index

Indian
  Paintbrush

ink
inn
inside
instant
instrument
insurance
interest
invention
invitation

iris

iron

island
it
item
itself

J

jacket

jack-o'-lantern
jacks
jam
jar
jasmine
jaw

jeans

81

Words for Things

jeep
jelly

jessamine
jet
jewel

jewelry

jigsaw
jingle
job
joint
joke

Joshua tree
journey
joy
juice
jump
jungle

juniper

K

kettle

key

kick

kimono
kind
kiss

kitchen
kite
knee

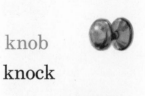

knife

knob
knock

knot

82

Words for Things

kukui

kumquats

L

lace
ladder
lake
lamp
land
lane
language

lantern

lariat
latch
laugh
laughter

launch

launching pad
laundry

laurel

law
lawn
layer
lead

leaf
leaves
leak
leap
leather
leave
leg

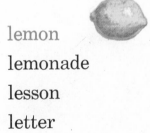

lemon
lemonade
lesson
letter

lettuce

Words for Things

level

lever

library

licorice

lid

lie

life

light

lightning

lilac

lily

limb

lime

limestone

limp

line

linen

lip

liquid

list

load

loaf

lock

locket

log

look

loop

lot

love

low

luck

lumber

lump

lunch

lung

M

macaroni

machine

magazine

magic

magnet

84

Words for Things

magnifying glass

magnolia

mail

main

mandolin

mane

mango

manners

map

maple

marble

march

marionette

mark

market

mask

mass

mat

match

mate

material

matter

mattress

mayflower

Mayflower

meadow

meal

measles

measure

meat

medicine

melon

menu

Words for Things

merry-go-round

mesquite

message

metal

meteor

microphone

mike

microscope

might

mile

milk

mill

mind

mine

mineral

mint

minute

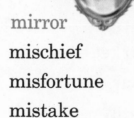

mirror

mischief

misfortune

mistake

mistletoe

mittens

moat

moccasin flower

moccasins

model

molasses

moment

money

month

moon

mop

morning

motel

motion

motor

motorcycle

Words for Things

mound

mount
mountain
mouth
movie

mower
mud
muff

muffler
mumps
muscle

museum

mushroom
music

mustache
mustard
mystery

N

nail
name
nap

napkin

nature
neck

necklace

necktie

needle
nest
net
news
newspaper
nickel
night
noise
nonsense
nose
note
notice

Words for Things

notion

noun

nozzle

number

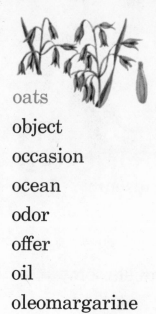

oats
object
occasion
ocean
odor
offer
oil
oleomargarine

orbit

orchard

1 2 3 4 5
6 7 8 9 10
numerals

nut

O

olive

one

orchestra

order

oak

onion

opera

operation

organ

outfit

outside

oven

oar

oatmeal

orange

orange blossom

P

pack

Words for Things

package

pad

paddle

page

pail

pain

paint

pair

pajamas

palace

palm

palmetto

paloverde

pan

pane

pansies

pantry

pants

papaya

paper

parachute

parade

paragraph

parcel

pardon

park

parlor

part

party

Words for Things

pasqueflower

pass

paste

pasture

patch

path

patio

pause

paw

pay

pea

peace

peach

peach blossom

peak

peanut

pear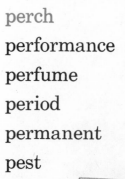

pearl

pecan

pedal

peel

peep

pen

pencil

penny

peony

pepper

perch

performance

perfume

period

permanent

pest

photo

photograph

piano

90

Words for Things

pick
picket

pickle
picnic
picture
pie
piece
pile
pill

pillow
pin
pinch

pine

pineapple

piñon
pipe
pit
pitcher

pitchfork

pizza
place

plaid

plan
plane
planet
plank
plant
plate

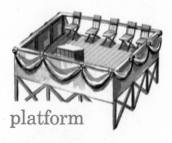

platform

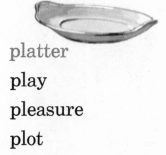

platter
play
pleasure
plot

plow

plum

91

Words for Things

plural
pneumonia
pocket
poem
point
poke
pole
pond
pool
popcorn

poplar

poppy
porch
pork
position

92

post

poster
posture
pot

potatoes

pouch
powder
power

power shovel

practice

prairie
praise
prayer
prefix
present
pressure
price
pride

primrose
print
prize
problem
production
program
promise

Words for Things

proof

propeller
property
protection
puff
pull

pulley
pump

pumpkin
punctuation
pupil

puppet

purse

puzzle

Q

quack
quarrel
quarter
question

quill

quilt
quotation

R

race

radio

radish
rag
rage
rail
railroad
rain

rainbow

raisin
rake
ranch
rap

93

Words for Things

raspberries

rattle

razor

reader

reason

recess

recipe

record

recreation

redbud

redwood

reel

refrigerator

remainder

remark

rent

reply

report

reservoir

respect

rest

restaurant

return

reward

rhododendron

rhyme

rib

ribbon

rice

riddle

Words for Things

ride
ring
river
road
roar
roast
robe
rock
rocket
rod

rodeo

roll
roof
room

roost

root
rope

rose

row

rubbers

ruffle
rug
rule

ruler
rumble
run
rung
rush

rust

rye

S

sack

saddle
safe
safety

sagebrush

sail

95

Words for Things

salad

sale

salt

sand

sandals

sandwich

satellite

satin

sauce

saucer

sausage

saw

saxophone

scale

scalp

scarecrow

scarf

scarves

scene

scent

school

science

scissors

scoop

scooter

scowl

scrap

scratch

scream

screen

screw

sea

seal

search

96

Words for Things

seat
second
secret
seed
seesaw
segment

semaphore
sense
sentence
sewer

sewing machine
shade
shadow
shame
shape
share

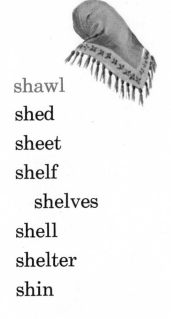

shawl
shed
sheet
shelf
  shelves
shell
shelter
shin

ship

shirt
shock
shoelace
shoes
shoot
shore

shot
shoulder
shout
shove

shovel
show

shower
side
sigh
sight
sign
signal
silk

sill

Words for Things

silo
silver
sink
siren
size
skates

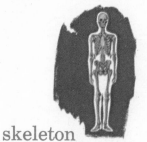

skeleton
skill
skin

skirt

skis

slacks
slap
sled
sleep

sleeve

sleigh
slice
slide
sling
slip

slippers
slope
smell
smile
smog

smoke
snap
sneeze
sniff

snorkel
snow
soap
sob
social
socks
soda
soil
somersault
song
sore
sound
soup
source

Words for Things

soybean

space

space helmet

space ship

space suit

spade

spaghetti

spark

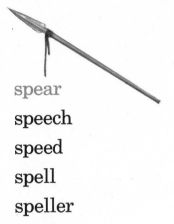

spear

speech

speed

spell

speller

spice

spike

spire

spite

splash

spoke

sponge

spool

spoon

sport

spot

sprain

spray

spread

spring

sprinkler

sprout

spruce

spur

square

stable

Words for Things

stack

stage

stagecoach

stairs

stake

stalk

stall
stamp
stand
stars
start
state

stationery

steak
steam
steel

steeple
stem
step
stew

stick

stilts
sting
stock

stockade

stockings
stole
stomach
stone
stool
storm
story

100

Words for Things

stove

strap

straw

strawberries

streak

stream

street

strike

string

strip

stripes

struggle

stuff

stump

stunt

subject

success

suffix

sugar

suit

suitcase

sum

sun

sundae

sunflower

supper

surface

surprise

swamp

sweat

sweater

sweeper

swing

swish

switch

syllable

syringa

T

table

tablet

Words for Things

tack
tag
tail
tale
talk
tallow

tambourine
tank
tape
tar
task

tassel
taste
tax

taxi
tea

team
tear
tease
teeth

telegram

telephone
  phone

telescope
television TV
temperature
tennis
tension
tent
terminal
test

that

thatch
thaw
theater
them

thermometer
these
they
thigh
thing
this
thorn
those
thought

thread

Words for Things

thrill
throat

throne
thumb
thunder

ticket
tide
tie
timber
time
tin
tip
tire
title

toast

toaster

toe

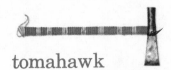

tomahawk

tomato
tone
tongue
tonsils
tool
tooth
top

torch
tornado
touch

towel

tower
toy
track

tractor
trade
traffic
trail
train
tramp
transom
transportation
trap
trash
tray
treasure
treat

Words for Things

tree

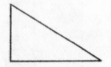

triangle

trick

tricycle

trip

trombone

trouble

trousers

truck

trumpet

trunk

trust

truth

tub

tuba

tube

tuck

tulip

tulip tree

tumble

tune

tunnel

turn

turnip

typewriter

typhoon

U

umbrella

104

Words for Things

uniform

urn

use

V

vacation

vacuum cleaner

valentine

valley

van

vase

vegetable

vehicle

velvet

verb

verse

vest

vibration

view

vine

vinegar

violet

violin

visit

voice

vote

vowel

W

wafer

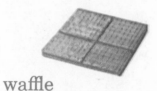

waffle

wagon

walk

walkie-talkie

wall

Words for Things

walnut

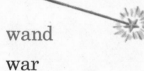

wand

war

wash

washer

waste

watch

water

wave

wax

way

weather

weather vane

wedding

wedge

weed

week

weight

well

wharf

wheat

wheel

whiskers

whisper

whistle

wick

wiener

willow

wind

Words for Things

window
wing
wink
wire
wish
wonder
wood

woods
wool
word
work
wound
wrap

wreath

wrench
wrinkle
wrist

X

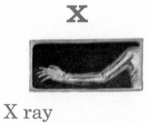

X ray

xylophone

Y

yard

yarn
yawn
year
yeast
yell

yew

yoke

yolk

yucca

Z

zero

zipper
zoo

107

Words for Places

A

Africa
airport

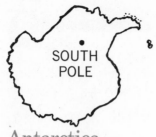

Antarctica
apartment

aquarium

Asia
Atlantic
attic

auditorium

Alabama Ala.

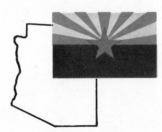

Arizona Ariz.

Australia

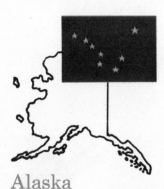

Alaska
America

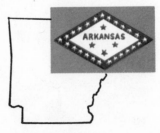

Arkansas Ark.

B

bakery
bank
barn
basement

Words for Places

bedroom

block

capital

city

closet

cafeteria

Capitol

coast

California Calif.

camp

castle

cathedral

cellar

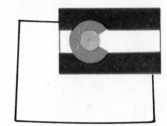

Colorado Colo.

community

Canada

church

Connecticut
Conn.

corner

Words for Places

corral

corridor

cottage

country

county

court

courthouse

D

dairy

deck

Delaware Del.

department store

depot

District of
Columbia D.C.

drugstore

dump

E

Earth

entrance

Europe

Words for Places

F

factory

fairgrounds

farm

firehouse

Florida Fla.

fort

G

garage

Georgia Ga.

grocery store

gym
gymnasium

H

hall

hangar

harbor

Hawaii

Words for Places

hayloft
haymow
headquarters
hill
home

hospital
hotel
house

Idaho

Illinois Ill.

Indiana Ind.
inn

Iowa

island

jail
Jamestown

Kansas Kans.

Kentucky Ky.

kitchen

112

Words for Places

L

laboratory

library

Louisiana La.

lumberyard

M

Maine

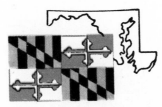
Maryland Md.

Massachusetts
Mass.

Mexico

Michigan Mich.

mill

mine

Minnesota
Minn.

Words for Places

Mississippi
Miss.

mosque
motel

Nebraska Nebr.

neighborhood

Missouri Mo.

mount
mountain

Nevada Nev.

Montana Mont.

museum

N

nation

New Hampshire
N. H.

Moon

New Jersey N. J.

Words for Places

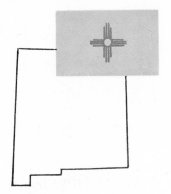

New Mexico
N. Mex.

New York N.Y.

North America

North Carolina
N.C.

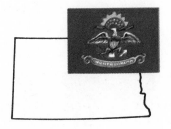

North Dakota
N. Dak.

North Pole

O

observatory

office

Ohio

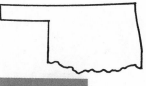

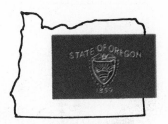

Oklahoma Okla.

Oregon Oreg.

Words for Places

P

Pacific

palace

pantry

parlor

patio

Pennsylvania
  Pa.

place

playground

Plymouth

porch

post office

R

ranch

restaurant

Rhode Island
R. I.

S

school

schoolroom

settlement

shelter

shop

shopping center

sky

South America

Words for Places

South Carolina
S.C.

South Dakota
S. Dak.

South Pole

space

spot

square

stable

stage

stall

state

station

store

studio

study

suburbs

supermarket

synagogue

T

tabernacle

tannery

temple

tenement

Tennessee
Tenn.

terminal

Texas Tex.

Words for Places

theater

town

U

United States
of America
U.S.A.

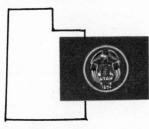

Utah

V

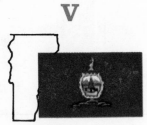

Vermont Vt.

village

Virginia Va.

W

Washington
Wash.
Washington, D.C.

West Virginia
W. Va.

Wisconsin Wis.

world

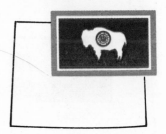

Wyoming Wyo.

Y

yard

Z

zoo

118

Words for What We Do and Did

A

accent accented
accuse accused
ache ached
act acted
add added
address
  addressed
admire admired
admit admitted
advertise
  advertised
agree agreed
aim aimed
alarm alarmed
allow allowed
amuse amused
announce
  announced
annoy annoyed
answer answered
appear appeared
approach
  approached

arrange arranged
arrive arrived
ask asked
attack attacked
attract attracted
autograph
  autographed

B

back backed

bait baited
bake baked

balance
  balanced

bale baled

bandage
  bandaged
bang banged
bank banked
barbecue
  barbecued
bark barked

bat batted
bathe bathed
bear bore
beat beat
become became
beg begged
begin began

Words for What We Do and Did

behave behaved
believe
 believed
belong belonged

bend bent
bet bet

bind bound
bite bit
blame blamed
blaze blazed
bleat bleated
bleed bled
bless blessed
blink blinked
block blocked

bloom bloomed
blow blew
board boarded
boast boasted
boil boiled
boom boomed
bore bored
borrow
 borrowed
boss bossed
bother bothered

bounce bounced
bound bounded

bow bowed

bowl bowled

box boxed
braid braided

brand branded

break broke

Words for What We Do and Did

breathe
 breathed
bring brought

brush brushed
buckle buckled

build built
bump bumped

burn burned
burst burst
bury buried

butt butted

button buttoned
buy bought
buzz buzzed

C

call called
camp camped
can canned
care cared
carpet carpeted
carry carried

carve carved
cash cashed
cast cast

catch caught
cause caused
celebrate
 celebrated
chain chained
change changed
charge charged
charm charmed

chase chased
chatter
 chattered
check checked
cheer cheered
chew chewed
chill chilled

Words for What We Do and Did

chin chinned

chip chipped

choke choked

choose chose

chop chopped

chuckle
  chuckled

churn churned

circle circled

clap clapped

clean cleaned

clear cleared

clerk clerked

climb climbed

cling clung

clip clipped

clog clogged

close closed

coach coached

coast coasted

coax coaxed

collect
  collected

color colored

comb combed

come came

command
  commanded

compare
  compared

compete
  competed

complain
  complained

122

Words for What We Do and Did

complete
  completed
compose
  composed
compute
  computed
concern
  concerned .
conduct
  conducted
confess
  confessed
confuse
  confused
connect
  connected
contain
  contained
continue
  continued
control
  controlled
cook cooked
copy copied

correct
  corrected
cost cost
cough coughed
count counted
cover covered
crack cracked
crash crashed
crate crated

crawl crawled
creak creaked
creep crept
croak croaked
cross crossed
crow crowed
crowd crowded
crunch
  crunched
crush crushed

cry cried
curb curbed
cure cured
curl curled
curve curved
cut cut

D

dance danced
dare dared
dart darted
dash dashed
decide decided
declare
  declared
delay delayed

Words for What We Do and Did

delight
  delighted
deliver
  delivered
demand
  demanded
dent dented
depend
  depended
describe
  described
desire desired
destroy
  destroyed
detour
  detoured
develop
  developed

dial dialed
die died

differ differed

dig dug
dine dined

dip dipped
direct directed
disappear
  disappeared
discover
  discovered
dismount
  dismounted
disturb disturbed

dive dived

divide divided
do (does) did
dock docked
dot dotted
double doubled
doubt doubted

drag dragged
drain drained

draw drew
dream dreamed

Words for What We Do and Did

dress dressed
drift drifted

drill drilled

drink drank
drip dripped
drive drove
drop dropped
drown drowned
dry dried
duck ducked
dump dumped
dust dusted

E

earn earned

eat ate
edit edited

empty emptied
end ended
enjoy enjoyed
enter entered

erase erased
escape escaped
examine
  examined
exclaim
  exclaimed

excuse excused
exercise
  exercised
expect
  expected
experiment
  experimented
explain
  explained
explore
  explored
express
  expressed

F

face faced
fade faded
fail failed
faint fainted
fall fell
fan fanned
farm farmed
fashion
  fashioned

Words for What We Do and Did

fast fasted

fasten fastened
fear feared
feast feasted

feed fed
feel felt
ferry ferried

field fielded
fight fought

figure figured

file filed

fill filled
find found
fine fined
finish finished

fish fished
fit fitted
fix fixed

flap flapped
flare flared
flash flashed
flicker
 flickered
fling flung
flip flipped
float floated
flock flocked
flood flooded
flop flopped
flow flowed

fly (flies) flew

fold folded

126

Words for What We Do and Did

follow followed
fool fooled
force forced
forget forgot
form formed

frame framed
free freed
freeze froze
frighten
 frightened
fringe fringed
frost frosted

frown frowned
fry fried

G

gallop galloped
gasp gasped
gather gathered
gaze gazed
get got
giggle giggled
give gave
glance glanced
glare glared
gleam gleamed
glitter glittered
glow glowed

glue glued
gnaw gnawed
go (goes) went
gobble gobbled
grab grabbed
grade graded

grant granted

grate grated
graze grazed
grease
 greased
greet greeted

grin grinned

grind ground
groan groaned

Words for What We Do and Did

group grouped
grow grew
growl growled
grumble
 grumbled
grunt grunted
guard guarded
guess guessed
guide guided
gulp gulped

H

hail hailed
halt halted

hammer
 hammered
hand handed
handle handled
hang hung

happen
 happened
harm harmed
hatch hatched
hate hated
haul hauled
have (has) had
head headed
heap heaped
hear heard
heat heated
help helped
herd herded

hide hid
hike hiked
hint hinted
hire hired
hit hit
hitch hitched

hoe hoed
hold held
hollow
 hollowed
honk honked
hook hooked
hoot hooted

hop hopped
hope hoped
howl howled

hug hugged

Words for What We Do and Did

hum hummed
hunt hunted
hurry hurried
hurt hurt
husk husked

I

ice iced
imagine
  imagined
improve
  improved
incline
  inclined
inquire
  inquired
insist insisted
interest
  interested
introduce
  introduced
invent
  invented
invite invited

iron ironed
itch itched

J

jam jammed
jar jarred
jerk jerked
jingle jingled
join joined
joke joked
judge judged

juggle juggled
jump jumped

K

keep kept
kick kicked
kill killed
kiss kissed

kneel knelt

knit knitted

knock knocked
knot knotted
know knew

Words for What We Do and Did

L

lace laced

land landed

last lasted

latch latched

laugh laughed

launch
 launched

lay laid

lead led

leak leaked

lean leaned

leap leaped

learn learned

leave left

lend lent

let let

lick licked

lie lay

lie lied

lift lifted

light
 lighted lit

like liked

limp limped

line lined

list listed

listen listened

live lived

load loaded

loaf loafed

locate located

lock locked

long longed

look looked

loop looped

loosen
 loosened

lope loped

lose lost

love loved

low lowed

lumber
 lumbered

M

mail mailed

make made

manage
 managed

Words for What We Do and Did

march marched

mark marked

marry married

mash mashed

match matched

mate mated

matter

mattered

mean meant

measure

measured

meet met

melt melted

mend mended

mention

mentioned

milk milked

mind minded

miss missed

mistake

mistook

mix mixed

model modeled

mop mopped

mount mounted

move moved

mow mowed

multiply

multiplied

N

nail nailed

name named

need needed

nibble nibbled

nod nodded

notice noticed

number

numbered

nurse nursed

O

obey obeyed

Words for What We Do and Did

object
  objected
offer offered

oil oiled

open opened
operate
  operated
orbit orbited
order ordered
organize
  organized
outfit outfitted
owe owed
own owned

P

pace paced
pack packed
pad padded

paddle paddled

paint painted

pardon
  pardoned
park parked
part parted
pass passed
paste pasted
pat patted

patch patched

patter pattered
pause paused
pay paid

pedal pedaled

peddle peddled
peek peeked

peel peeled

peep peeped
pen penned
perch perched
perform
  performed
pet petted

Words for What We Do and Did

pick picked
picket picketed
pickle pickled
pile piled
pilot piloted
pin pinned
pinch pinched
pit pitted
place placed
plan planned

plot plotted

plow plowed
pluck plucked
plunge plunged

plane planed

plant planted
play played
please pleased

point pointed
poke poked
pop popped
pot potted

pound pounded

pour poured
practice
  practiced
praise praised
prance pranced

pray prayed
prepare
  prepared
present
  presented
press pressed
pretend
  pretended
prey preyed

133

Words for What We Do and Did

print printed

produce
  produced
promise
  promised
protect
  protected
prove proved
provide
  provided
puff puffed

pull pulled
pump pumped
punish
  punished

push pushed
put put
puzzle puzzled

Q

quack quacked
quarrel
  quarreled
quit quit

R

race raced
rain rained
raise raised

rake raked

rap rapped
rattle rattled
reach reached
read read
realize
  realized
rear reared
receive
  received
recognize
  recognized
record
  recorded
reflect
  reflected
refuse refused
release
  released
remain
  remained
remark
  remarked
remember
  remembered

Words for What We Do and Did

rent rented

reopen
  reopened

repair repaired

repeat repeated

reply replied

report reported

request
  requested

require
  required

rescue rescued

respect
  respected

rest rested

return returned

revolve
  revolved

reward
  rewarded

rhyme rhymed

rid rid

ride rode

ring rang

rise rose

roar roared

roast roasted

rob robbed

rock rocked

roll rolled

roost roosted

rope roped

rotate rotated

row rowed

rub rubbed

rule ruled

rumble
  rumbled

run ran

rush rushed

rust rusted

s

saddle saddled

sail sailed

satisfy
  satisfied

135

Words for What We Do and Did

save saved

saw sawed

say said

scalp scalped

scamper

  scampered

scare scared

scatter

  scattered

scold scolded

scoop scooped

scorch

  scorched

scowl scowled

scramble

  scrambled

scrape scraped

scratch

  scratched

scream

  screamed

scrub scrubbed

scurry

  scurried

seal sealed

search

  searched

season

  seasoned

seat seated

see saw

seed seeded

seem seemed

sell sold

send sent

separate

  separated

serve served

set set

settle settled

sew sewed

Words for What We Do and Did

shake shook
shame shamed
shape shaped
share shared

shave shaved

shell shelled

shine shined
shine shone
ship shipped
shiver shivered

shock shocked

shoot shot
shop shopped
shout shouted
shove shoved

shovel
   shoveled
show showed
shrink shrank
shut shut
side sided
sift sifted
sigh sighed
sign signed

signal signaled
sing sang
sink sank
sip sipped
sit sat

skate skated

ski skied
skid skidded
skim skimmed
skip skipped
slam slammed

Words for What We Do and Did

slant slanted
slap slapped
sleep slept

slice sliced

slide slid
sling slung
slip slipped
slow slowed
smack
  smacked
smart smarted
smash
  smashed
smell smelled

smile smiled
smoke smoked
smooth
  smoothed
snap snapped
snatch
  snatched
sneeze sneezed
sniff sniffed
snow snowed
soar soared
sob sobbed
soil soiled
solve solved
sound sounded

sow sowed

spare spared
sparkle
  sparkled
speak spoke

spear speared
speed sped
spell spelled
spend spent

spill spilled

spin spun

Words for What We Do and Did

splash
 splashed

spread spread
 spring sprang

squeeze
 squeezed
stack stacked
stake staked

split split
spoil spoiled
sprain
 sprained

sprinkle
 sprinkled
sprout
 sprouted
spy spied
squawk
 squawked
squeak
 squeaked
squeal
 squealed

stalk stalked
stall stalled

stamp stamped
stand stood
stare stared
start started
starve starved

spray sprayed

139

Words for What We Do and Did

stay stayed
steady steadied
steal stole

steer steered
step stepped
sterilize
 sterilized
stew stewed
stick stuck
sting stung

stir stirred
stop stopped
store stored
stray strayed

streak
 streaked

stretch
 stretched
stride strode
strike struck

string strung
strip stripped
struggle
 struggled
study studied
stuff stuffed
stumble
 stumbled

stutter
 stuttered
subtract
 subtracted
succeed
 succeeded
suffer suffered
suggest
 suggested
suit suited
sulk sulked
suppose
 supposed
surprise
 surprised
surround
 surrounded
suspect
 suspected
swallow
 swallowed
sway swayed
sweat
 sweated

Words for What We Do and Did

sweep swept

swim swam

swing swung

swish swished

switch switched

swoop swooped

T

tack tacked

tag tagged

take took

talk talked

tame tamed

tan tanned

tap tapped

tape taped

taste tasted

tax taxed

teach taught

tear tore

tease teased

telephone
 telephoned

tell told

terrify
 terrified

test tested

thank thanked

thaw thawed

think thought

thread
 threaded

thrill thrilled

throw threw

thump thumped

thunder
 thundered

tickle tickled

tie tied

time timed

tinkle tinkled

141

Words for What We Do and Did

tip tipped
tire tired

toast toasted
toss tossed
touch touched
track tracked
trade traded
trail trailed

train trained
tramp tramped
trap trapped
travel traveled
treat treated
tremble
 trembled

trick tricked

trim trimmed
trip tripped

troll trolled
trot trotted
trudge trudged
trust trusted
try tried
tuck tucked
tug tugged
tumble tumbled
tune tuned
turn turned
twinkle twinkled

twirl twirled
twist twisted

U

unbuckle
 unbuckled
unbutton
 unbuttoned
unchain
 unchained
uncover
 uncovered
understand
 understood
unfasten
 unfastened
unhitch
 unhitched
unload
 unloaded

Words for What We Do and Did

unlock unlocked

unpack
  unpacked

unpin unpinned

unroll unrolled

unseal
  unsealed

untie untied

unwind
  unwound

unwrap
  unwrapped

use used

V

vibrate
  vibrated

view viewed

visit visited

vote voted

W

wade waded

wag wagged

wail wailed

wait waited

wake woke

walk walked

wander
  wandered

want wanted

warn warned

wash washed

waste wasted

watch watched

water watered

wave waved

wear wore

weave wove

wedge wedged

weed weeded

weep wept

weigh weighed

welcome
  welcomed

wheel wheeled

whimper
  whimpered

whine whined

Words for What We Do and Did

whirl whirled
whisper
  whispered

whistle
  whistled
wiggle wiggled
win won

wind wound

wink winked

wipe wiped
wire wired
wish wished
wonder
  wondered
work worked
worry worried
worship
  worshiped
wound wounded

wrap wrapped

wrestle
  wrestled

write wrote

Y

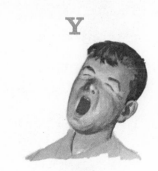

yawn yawned
yell yelled

Z

zigzag
  zigzagged

zip zipped

Words For What We Have Done

Most words for what we have done are the same as words for what we did, used with the word *have*. The words on this page are not like the others. These are never used as words for what we did. These words can also be used with *had*, *is*, and *has* to tell what we had done, what is done, what someone has done, or with *are* and *were* to tell what things are or were done.

have beaten

have become

have begun

have bitten

have blown

have borne

have broken

have chosen

have come

have done

have drawn

have driven

have drunk

have eaten

have fallen

have flown

have forgotten

have frozen

have given

have gone

have grown

have hidden

have known

have lain

have mistaken

have ridden

have risen

have run

have rung

have seen

have shaken

have shown

have shrunk

have spoken

have sprung

have stolen

have stridden

have sung

have sunk

have swum

have taken

have thrown

have torn

have worn

have woven

have written

Words That Tell What Kind or Color

A	B	
		blackberry
able	baby	blank
absent	backward	blind
afraid	bad	blue
alike	ball	blueberry
alive	barbecue	boiled
alphabetical	barbecued	bold
amateur	bare	braided
American	barley	brass
amiable	bass	brave
angry	bathing	brick
animal	bean	bright
anxious	beaten	broad
apple	beautiful	broken
apricot	beef	brown
armed	bent	buckeye
artichoke	best	buckskin
ashamed	better	buried
asleep	big	bushy
asparagus	bigger	busy
autumn	biggest	
awake	birch	C
away	birthday	cactus
awful	black	calm

Words That Tell What Kind or Color

Canadian

canned

canvas

capital

car

careful

careless

cedar

cement

charming

cheerful

cheese

cherry

chestnut

chicken

chief

chilled

chipped

chocolate

chopped

Christmas

circus

city

clay

clean

clear

clever

close

closed

cloth

cloudy

clover

coarse

coconut

cold

colored

common

community

complete

concrete

confused

connected

contented

contrary

control

cooked

cool

copper

coral

corduroy

corn

corner

correct

corrected

cotton

cottonwood

country

county

covered

cracked

crazy

creaking

cream

crisp

crooked

cross

crowded

cruel

crushed

cunning

curious

curly

Words That Tell What Kind or Color

curved
cut
cute

D

daily
dairy
damp
dangerous
dark
date
day
dead
deaf
dear
deep
delicate
delicious
delighted
deserted
diamond
diesel
different
dirt

dirty
distant
divided
dizzy
dog
dogwood
dotted
dreary
dress
dressed
dried
dry
dumb
dusty

E

eager
early
earth
Easter
easy
electric
elm
empty

end
enemy
enormous
entry
Eskimo
even
evergreen
exact
excellent
excited
express
extra

F

faded
faint
fair
fairy
fall
family
famous
fancy
farm
fast

Words That Tell What Kind or Color

faster
fastest
fat
favorite
feather
feeble
felt
female
field
fierce
fig
figure
final
fine
fir
fire
firm
first
fish
fit
fixed
flat
flower
flowering

fond
foolish
forest
forgotten
forward
fragrant
framed
free
freight
fresh
fried
friendly
frightened
fringed
frisky
front
frosted
frozen
fruit
funny
fur

G

garbage

garden
gardenia
gas
gay
gentle
ghost
giant
gingerbread
gingham
glad
glass
gloomy
gold
golden
good
grade
grand
grape
grapefruit
grassy
grated
gray
great
green

Words That Tell What Kind or Color

ground
grown-up
gruff
guide
gum

H

hand
handsome
handy
happy
hard
hawthorn
hay
head
heavy
helpful
helpless
hemlock
hickory
hidden
high
higher
highest

hind
hoarse
hollow
holly
home
honest
honey
hopeless
hot
hourly
huge
human
hungry
husky

I

ice
iced
impatient
impolite
important
impossible
Indian
instant

interesting
invisible
iron

J

jelly
jet
jolly
joyful
juniper

K

kind
kindly
knit
knotted
kukui
kumquat

L

lace
lamb
lame
land

150

Words That Tell What Kind or Color

large
late
lavender
lazy
lead
leaky
lean
leather
left
lemon
lettuce
level
licorice
light
lilac
lily
lime
limp
linen
liquid
little
live
loaded
local

log
lonely
lonesome
long
loose
lost
loud
lovely
low
lower
lowest
lucky
luscious
lying

M

mad
magic
magnificent
main
male
mammoth
mango
maple

marble
married
mashed
master
mean
meat
melted
merry
metal
Mexican
middle
milk
mineral
mint
mischievous
model
molasses
monthly
mother
motor
mountain
mounted
musical
mysterious

Words That Tell What Kind or Color

N

narrow
naughty
navy
neat
necessary
neighborhood
new
nice
nickel
night
noisy

O

oak
oat
oatmeal
obedient
odd
oil
oily
old
olive
open

opposite
orange
other
own

P

padded
paint
painted
palm
palmetto
paloverde
papaya
paper
park
party
past
patient
pea
peach
peanut
pear
pearl
pecan

perfect
permanent
pet
picture
pine
pineapple
pink
piñon
pizza
plaid
plain
pleasant
plum
plump
pocket
pointed
police
polite
pony
poor
poplar
pork
possible
potato

Words That Tell What Kind or Color

potted
power
present
pretty
prim
primary
principal
prize
probable
proud
public
pure
purple

Q

queer
quick
quiet

R

raisin
rapid
rare
raspberry

raw
ready
real
record
red
redbud
redwood
refreshing
remarkable
rice
rich
right
ripe
roast
rock
rocky
rose
rosy
rotten
round
rubber
rude
ruffled
rural

rusty
rye

S

sad
safe
safety
salad
salmon
salt
salty
same
sand
sandy
satin
scarlet
scary
school
scrambled
scrap
scrub
sea
secret
selfish

Words That Tell What Kind or Color

separate	sister	sour
serious	slant	space
shadow	sleepy	spare
shadowy	sliced	special
shady	slick	spelling
shaggy	slim	splendid
shaky	slow	split
sharp	slower	spoken
sheepish	slowest	sport
shiny	sly	spotted
shopping	small	sprained
short	smart	spring
shrill	smoke	spruce
shrimp	smoked	square
shut	smoky	stamp
shy	smooth	state
sick	snug	steady
signal	social	steam
silent	soft	steel
silk	soiled	steep
silly	soothing	stewed
silver	sore	stick
simple	sorry	stiff
single	sound	still

Words That Tell What Kind or Color

stone

stout

straight

strange

straw

strawberry

stray

striped

strong

stubborn

stuffed

stupid

sturdy

sudden

sugar

summer

sun

sunny

sure

surprise

swampy

sweet

swift

switch

table

tack

tall

tame

tan

tape

tar

tardy

tea

team

telephone

tender

terrible

terrified

test

thatched

these

thick

thin

thirsty

thoughtful

tidy

tight

timid

tin

tiny

tired

tiresome

toasted

tomato

torn

town

toy

train

trap

trash

treasure

trick

true

tulip

turquoise

twisted

U

ugly

unable

uncertain

Words That Tell What Kind or Color

uneasy
unfair
unfriendly
unhappy
unhealthy
uniform
unjust
unkind
unknown
unlucky
unpleasant
unsafe
unseen
unsteady
unusual
unwilling
unwise
used
useful

V

vacation
vegetable
velvet

village
violet

W

walnut
warm
waste
water
wax
weak
weather
wedding
wee
weekly
wet
wheat
white
whole
wholesale
wicked
wide
wild
willing
willow

window
windy
winter
wise
wonderful
wood
wool
worn
worse
worst
wrinkled
written
wrong

Y

yearly
yellow
yellowish
yew
young

Z

zigzag
zoo

Words That Help Tell How Much, How Many, or Which One

A

a an
all
almost
another
any
apiece

B

back
bit
both
bottom
bushel

C

cent
certain
couple

D

deal
dollar

double
dozen
drop

E

each
east
eastern

eight | 8
  eighth

eighteen | 18
  eighteenth

eighty | 80
  eightieth
either

eleven | 11
  eleventh
else
enough

equal
even
every
except
extra

F

far
farther
farthest
feet
few

fifteen | 15
  fifteenth

fifty | 50
  fiftieth
final
first

five | 5
  fifth

Words That Help Tell How Much, How Many, or Which One

foot

forty | 40
fortieth

four | 4
fourth

fourteen | 14
fourteenth
front
full

G

gallon
group

H

half
handful
hardly
her
hers

his
hour

hundred | 100
hundredth

I

inch
inside
its

J

just

L

last
late
least
left
length
less
little
load

long
lot
lots

M

main
many
middle
mile
million
mine
minute
moment
month
more
most
much
my

N

near
nearly
neither

Words That Help Tell How Much, How Many, or Which One

next

nine   `9`

  ninth

nineteen   `19`

  nineteenth

ninety   `90`

  ninetieth

north

northeast

northern

northwest

nothing

number

O

once

one   `1`

  first

only

other

ounce

our

ours

outside

P

pair

part

partly

past

pint

plenty

pound

present

primary

principal

Q

quart

quarter

quite

R

rear

remainder

rest

right

row

S

same

second

seven   `7`

  seventh

seventeen   `17`

  seventeenth

seventy   `70`

  seventieth

several

short

single

sip

Words That Help Tell How Much, How Many, or Which One

six **6**
  sixth

sixteen **16**
  sixteenth

sixty **60**
  sixtieth
size
slice
some
south
southeast
southern
southwest
spare

T

temperature

ten **10**
  tenth
that

the
their
these

thirteen **13**
  thirteenth

thirty **30**
  thirtieth

31
thirty-one
  thirty-first
this
those

1000
thousand
  thousandth

three **3**
  third
too

top

twelve **12**
  twelfth

twenty **20**
  twentieth

28
twenty-eight
  twenty-eighth

25
twenty-five
  twenty-fifth

24
twenty-four
  twenty-fourth

29
twenty-nine
  twenty-ninth

Words That Help Tell How Much, How Many, or Which One

21

twenty-one
twenty-first

27

twenty-seven
twenty-seventh

26

twenty-six
twenty-sixth

23

twenty-three
twenty-third

22

twenty-two
twenty-second
twice

2

two
second

V

value
very

W

week
west
western

which
whole
whose
width
worse
worst
worth
wrong

Y

yard
your
yours

Z

zero

Words That Help Tell Where

A

above
across
after
against
ahead
along
anywhere
apart
around
at
away

B

back
before
behind
below
beneath
beside
between
beyond
bottom
by

C

center
close

D

deep
direction
distance
distant
down
downstairs

E

east E
eastern
eastward
edge
end
everywhere

F

far
faraway
farther

farthest
first
forth
forward
from
front

H

halfway
here
high
higher
highest

I

in
indoors
inside
into

L

last
left
locally

Words That Help Tell Where

low
lower
lowest

M

middle

N

near
next
north N
northeast NE
northern
North Pole
northward
northwest NW
nowhere

O

off
on
opposite
out
outdoors

outside
over

P

past
place
point
position
present

R

rear
right
round

S

side
south S
southeast SE
southern
South Pole
southward
southwest SW
surface

T

there
through
to
top
toward

U

under
underneath
up
upon
upstairs
upward

W

way
west W
western
westward
where
wherever
within
without

Words That Help Tell When

A

about
after
afternoon
again
ago
already
always
April   Apr.

Arbor Day
around
at
August   Aug.
autumn

B

bedtime
before

beginning
between
birthday
breakfast time
by

C

Christmas

Columbus Day

D

daily
date

dawn
day
daybreak
daytime
December   Dec.
dinnertime
during

E

early
Easter

eight   8
  eighth

eighteen   18
  eighteenth

eleven   11
  eleventh
end
eve
evening
ever

Words That Help Tell When

F

fall

February   Feb.

fifteen   15
   fifteenth

fifty   50
   fiftieth
final
finally
finish
first

five   5
   fifth

Flag Day
forenoon
forever

four   4
   fourth

fourteen   14
   fourteenth

Fourth of July
Friday   Fri.
from
future

H

half

Halloween

Hanukkah
hour
hourly

I

immediately
in
instant
instantly

J

January   Jan.
July
June

L

Labor Day
last
late

165

Words That Help Tell When

lately

Lincoln's
  Birthday
long
lunchtime

M

March Mar.
May
meanwhile
Memorial Day
midnight
minute
moment
Monday Mon.
month
monthly
morning

N

near
nearly
never
newly

JANUARY 1

New Year's Day
next
night
nighttime

nine 9
  ninth

nineteen 19
  nineteenth
noon
November Nov.
now

O

occasionally
o'clock
October Oct.
often
on
once

one 1
  first

P

Passover
past
period
present

Q

quarter

R

rarely
ready
recess time

Words That Help Tell When

S

Sabbath
Saturday   Sat.
season
second
September   Sept.

seven   **7**
  seventh

seventeen   **17**
  seventeenth
since

six   **6**
  sixth

sixteen   **16**
  sixteenth
soon
spring
springtime
start
still

suddenly
summer
summertime
Sunday   Sun.
sunrise
sunset
suppertime

T

ten   **10**
  tenth

Thanksgiving
then

thirteen   **13**
  thirteenth

thirty   **30**
  thirtieth

31
thirty-one
  thirty-first

three   **3**
  third
through
Thursday Thurs.
till
time
today
tomorrow
tonight
Tuesday   Tues.

twelve   **12**
  twelfth

twenty   **20**
  twentieth

28
twenty-eight
  twenty-eighth

Words That Help Tell When

25
twenty-five
twenty-fifth

24
twenty-four
twenty-fourth

29
twenty-nine
twenty-ninth

21
twenty-one
twenty-first

27
twenty-seven
twenty-seventh

26
twenty-six
twenty-sixth

23
twenty-three
twenty-third

22
twenty-two
twenty-second
twice

2
two
second

U
until
usually

V
vacation

Valentine's Day

W

Washington's
Birthday
Wednesday Wed.
week
weekday
weekend
weekly
when
whenever
while
winter
wintertime

Y

year
yearly
yesterday
yet

Words That Tell How

A

alone
aloud
alphabetically
altogether
angrily
apart
awfully

B

backward
badly
beautifully
best
better
boldly
bravely
brightly

C

calmly
carefully
carelessly
cheerfully

clearly
closely
completely
correctly
crossly
cruelly

D

dangerously
dearly
deeply
differently

E

eagerly
easily
equally
evenly
exactly
excellently
excitedly

F

faintly

fairly
fast
faster
fastest
feebly
fiercely
firmly
flat
fondly
foolishly
freely
freshly
fully

G

gently
gladly
gruffly

H

happily
hard
hastily
heavily

Words That Tell How

helpfully
high
higher
highest
highly
hopefully
hungrily

I

impatiently

J

joyfully

K

kindly

L

laughingly
lightly
loosely
loudly
low
lower

lowest
luckily

M

magnificently

N

narrowly
neatly
nicely
noisily

O

oddly
openly

P

partly
patiently
perfectly
pleasantly
politely
poorly
proudly

Q

quickly
quietly

R

rapidly
right
rudely

S

sadly
safely
same
secretly
selfishly
separately
sharply
silently
sleepily
slow
slower
slowest
slowly
slyly

Words That Tell How

smoothly
snugly
softly
soundly
specially
steadily
stiffly
straight
strangely
strongly
stubbornly
stupidly
suddenly
surely

sweetly
swiftly

T

terribly
thickly
thinly
thoughtfully
tightly
timidly
together

U

unfairly
unhappily

unjustly
unsteadily
unwisely

W

warmly
wastefully
watchfully
well
widely
wildly
wisely
wonderfully
worse
worst

Words That Help in Different Ways

A

a
about
after
against
ago
ah
ahead
along
also
although
am
among
an
and
any
apart
are
around
as
at

B

be

because
been
before
behind
below
beneath
beside
besides
between
beyond
both
but
by

C

can
certainly
could

D

dear
did
do
does

down
during

E

each
except

F

for
fore
from

G

good
good-by
goodness

H

had
has
have
hello
hi
how

Words That Help in Different Ways

hurrah
 hurray

I

if
in
indeed
inside
instead
into
is

J

just

L

let
like

M

matter
may
maybe
might

minus
more
most
much
must

N

no
nonsense
nor
not
nothing
now

O

of
off
oh
on
only
or
ouch
ought
out

over
own

P

pardon
perhaps
please
plus
possibly
probably

Q

quite

R

rather
really
round

S

seem
seemed
shall
shame

Words That Help in Different Ways

should
since
sincerely
so
still
such
sure

T

than
that
the
then
there
this
though
through
till

to
too
toward
truly

U

unless
until
up
upon

V

very

W

was
welcome
were

what
when
where
whether
which
while
who
why
will
with
within
without
would

Y

yes
yet
yonder

Words That Help in Different Ways

Contractions

aren't	it'll	we'd
can't	it's	we'll
couldn't	I've	we're
didn't	let's	weren't
doesn't	shan't	we've
don't	she'd	what's
hadn't	she'll	who'd
hasn't	she's	who'll
haven't	shouldn't	who're
he'd	that's	who's
he'll	there's	who've
he's	they'd	won't
I'd	they'll	wouldn't
I'll	they're	you'd
I'm	they've	you'll
isn't	wasn't	you're
		you've

Words and
Meanings

ABCDEFGHIJKLMNOPQRSTUVWXYZABCDEFGHIJKL

A

A or **a**   the first letter of the alphabet.

a   **1.** any: *Is there a book for me?*   **2.** one: *Here is a pen for you.*   **3.** each: *Christmas comes once a year.*

ab bre vi a tion   a short form, such as *St.* for *Street* or *Ave.* for *Avenue.*

able   having power: *A cat is able to see very well in the dark.*   **abler, ablest.**

about   **1.** of; having something to do with: *This book is about trains.*   **2.** nearly; almost: *It is about ten o'clock.*   **3.** around: *He splashed about in the water.*   **4. About to** means on the point of; going to; ready to: *The train is about to leave.*

above   **1.** in a higher place: *She lives on the first floor, and I live on the floor above.*   **2.** higher than; over: *The sky is above us.*

ab sent   away; not present: *Three boys were absent from class.*

ac cent   **1.** the greater force or stronger tone of voice given to certain syllables or words.   **2.** a mark (′) written or printed to show the spoken force of a syllable, as in *yes′ter day, to day′, to mor′row.*   **3.** pronounce or write with an accent: *Is "rabbit" accented on the first syllable?*   **ac cent ed, ac cent ing.**

ac ci dent   something harmful or unlucky that happens: *She was hurt in an automobile accident.*

ac count   **1.** a story about what happened: *The boy gave his father an account of the ball game.*   **2. On account of** means because of; for the reason of: *The game was called off on account of rain.*

ac cuse   **1.** charge with being or doing something bad: *The driver was accused of speeding.*   **2.** find fault with; blame.   **ac cused, ac cus ing.**

ache   **1.** continuing pain, such as a stomach ache, headache, or toothache.   **2.** suffer continuing pain; be in pain: *My back aches.*   **ached, ach ing.**

acorn   the nut of an oak tree.

ac ro bat   a person who turns somersaults, dances on a tightrope, or swings high in the air.

across   **1.** from one side to the other of; over: *We ran across the yard.*   **2.** on the other side of; beyond: *She called to a friend who lived across the street.*

act   **1.** *The farmer caught the boys in the act of stealing his apples.*   **2.** *The dog's act was the best in the show.*   **3.** *The firemen acted quickly to save the burning house.*   **4.** *The cat did not act at all interested in the food.*   **5.** *He acts very well.*   **act ed, act ing.**

add   **1.** put together: *When you add three and four, you have seven.*   **2. Add to** means put with: *She added more sugar to her tea.*   **add ed, add ing.**

ad dress   **1.** the place to which mail is directed: *Write the name and address on the letter.*   **2.** write on an envelope or package the place to which it is being sent.   **ad dress es; ad dressed, ad dress ing.**

ad mire   look at with wonder and pleasure: *We all admire a brave boy.*   *He was admiring the beautiful picture.*   **ad mired, ad mir ing.**

ad mit   **1.** say something is real or true: *He has admitted that he was wrong.*   **2.** allow to enter: *He was admitted to school this year.*   **ad mit ted, ad mit ting.**

ad ven ture   a bold undertaking, usually exciting and somewhat dangerous.

ad ver tise   **1.** give public notice of; announce: *Stores advertise things they wish to sell.*   **2. Advertise for** means ask for by a public notice: *He advertised for a job.*   **ad ver tised, ad ver tis ing.**

ad vice   something suggested about what should be done: *To keep well, follow the doctor's advice.*

aer i al   a radio or television antenna.

afraid   **1.** frightened; feeling fear: *She is afraid of snakes.*   **2.** sorry: *I'm afraid I must ask you to go.*

Af ri ca   one of the large masses of land on the earth.

af ter   **1.** later than: *After dinner we can go.*   **2.** behind: *All the children ran after him.*   **3.** because of: *After the way she acted, how can you like her?*

af ter noon   **1.** part of a day.   **2.** the time from noon to evening.

again   another time; once more: *Say that again.*

against 1. *The two teams played against each other.*
2. *Rain beats against the window.*

age *The boy is ten years of age.*

agent a person or company that acts for another:
My father is an agent for an insurance company.

ago gone by; past: *I met her a long time ago.*
Long ago men lived in caves.

agree 1. have the same idea about something: *We
all agree that it is a good story.* 2. *He has agreed to go
with us.* **agreed, agree ing.**

ah an exclamation that shows pain, surprise, or joy,
depending on how it is said.

ahead 1. in front; before: *Walk ahead of me.*
2. forward: *Go ahead with your work.* 3. *He was
ahead of his class in reading.*

aim 1. *His aim was so poor that he missed the lion.*
2. *If you aim the gun carefully, you will hit the lion.*
3. *She aimed to please her teachers.* **aimed, aim ing.**

air 1. what we breathe. 2. space overhead; sky.

air craft 1. any airplane, airship, helicopter, or
balloon. 2. *We saw twelve aircraft.* **air craft.**

air craft car ri er a warship designed as a base
for airplanes. See the picture.

Air Force one part of the armed forces of the
United States.

air man 1. a member of the Air Force. 2. a pilot of
an airplane, airship, helicopter, or balloon. **air men.**

air plane a flying machine driven by a propeller
or jet engine. See the picture.

air port a place for airplanes to land and start
from, with buildings for keeping, checking, and
repairing airplanes. See the picture.

aisle a space between rows of seats: *The bride
walked down the aisle.*

Al a bama one of the fifty states of the
United States.

alarm 1. sudden fear: *The deer ran off in alarm.*
2. a bell or other signal that warns people. 3. make
uneasy; frighten. **alarmed, alarm ing.**

Alas ka the largest state of the United States.

aircraft carrier

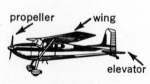
propeller / wing / elevator
airplane

airport

al fal fa   a plant used as a food for animals.

alike   like one another: *These twins look and act very much alike.*

alive   living: *Is the snake alive or dead?*

all   **1.** the whole of: *The mice ate all the cheese.*
2. every one of: *All these books are funny.*
3. completely: *I'm all ready.*   **4.** *All right, I'll go.*
5. All at once means suddenly.

al li ga tor   a large, crawling animal that lives in rivers and swamps.

al low   **1.** let: *Dogs are not allowed in this store.*
2. give; let have: *Our mothers have allowed us fifty cents for lunch.*   **al lowed, al low ing.**

al low ance   a share set apart; an amount given out: *She has an allowance of fifty cents a week.*

al most   nearly: *I have saved almost a dollar.*

alone   **1.** apart from others: *One tree stood alone on the hill.*   **2.** without anyone or anything else: *This play alone could win the game.*

along   **1.** *Trees are planted along the street.*
2. *As she walked along, she sang.*

aloud   loud enough to be heard: *She read the story aloud to the others.*

al pha bet   all of the letters used to write a language, such as the English alphabet with twenty-six letters arranged a b c d e f g h i j k l m n o p q r s t u v w x y z.

al pha bet i cal   arranged by letters in the order of the alphabet.

al pha bet i cal ly   *The names of the children were arranged alphabetically.*

al ready   before this time; by this time; even now: *He has already read this book.*

al so   too: *He has a brother and a sister also.*

al though   even though: *Although it was true, they did not believe it.*

al to geth er   **1.** completely: *The house was altogether destroyed by fire.*   **2.** all included: *Altogether there were fourteen blocks.*

al ways   at all times; all the time.

181

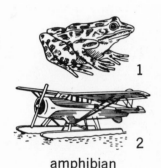

amphibian

am   *I am six years old.   I am going to school.
I am a boy.   I am happy.   I am running.*

am a teur   **1.** one who does something for fun,
not money.   **2.** one who does something rather
poorly.   **3.** *He is an amateur musician.*

Amer i ca   **1.** the United States.   **2.** North
America.   **3.** North America and South America.

Amer i can   **1.** a citizen of the United States:
Many Americans travel in other countries.   **2.** a citizen
of North or South America.   **3.** *The American flag
is red, white, and blue.*

ami able   friendly; pleasant and agreeable.

among   **1.** surrounded by: *Our house is among the
trees.*   **2.** to each of: *Divide the fruit among the boys.*

amount   **1.** *No amount of coaxing would make the
dog go.*   **2.** *What is the amount of the bill for the toys?*

am phib i an   **1.** an animal that lives both on land
and in water.   **2.** a plane that lands on water or land.
See the pictures.

amuse   cause to laugh or smile: *The puppy amused
the baby.*   **amused, amus ing.**

amuse ment   anything that amuses: *Baseball is a
healthy amusement.*

an   **1.** any: *Is there an apple for me?*   **2.** one:
He is an inch taller than I am.   **3.** each: *She
earns twenty-five cents an hour for babysitting.*

and   as well as: *My little brother and I were
invited to the party.*

an gri ly   *"Stop that," he said angrily.*

an gry   *I was angry when he kicked my dog.   Her
angry words hurt my feelings.*   **an gri er,   an gri est.**

an i mal   **1.** any living thing that can feel and
move.   **2.** *At the circus I saw many animal acts.*

an kle   the part of the leg between the foot and the
calf.   See the picture under **leg.**

an nounce   give notice of; make known: *Tomorrow
they will announce the names of those
who won prizes.*   **an nounced, an nounc ing.**

an nounc er   **1.** a person who announces.   **2.** one
who makes announcements over the radio or TV.

an noy   tease; make angry: *The baby annoys his sister by pulling her hair.*   **an noyed, an noy ing.**

an oth er   **1.** one more: *He will get another ride after this one.*   **2.** a different: *She went to another store to find what she wanted.*   **3. One another** means each other: *Friends should help one another.*

an swer   **1.** words spoken or written in return to a question: *What is the correct answer to this arithmetic problem?*   **2.** speak or write words in return to a question: *I asked him a question, but he would not answer.*   **an swered, an swer ing.**

ant   a small insect that lives in tunnels in the ground or in wood.

Ant arc ti ca   one of the large masses of land on the earth.

an te lope   any one of certain animals somewhat like deer.   **an te lope.**

an ten na   **1.** a feeler on the head of an insect, lobster, or other such animal.   **2.** the part of a radio or television set that receives or brings in the sounds.   **an ten nae** for **1, an ten nas** for **2.**

ant ler   the horn of a deer.

anx ious   uneasy because of what may happen; troubled; worried.

any   **1.** one out of many: *Choose any book you like.* **2.** some: *Have you any fresh fruit?*   **3.** every: *Any child knows that.*

apart   **1.** to pieces; in pieces; in separate parts: *When I dropped the chair, it fell apart.*   **2.** away from each other: *Keep the dogs apart.*   **3.** to one side: *He stood apart from the others.*

apart ment   a group of rooms to live in.

apiece   each; for each one: *These apples are five cents apiece.*

apos tro phe   a sign (') used to show that one or more letters have been left out or to show who owns something: *Can't you come?   It is the boy's book.*

ap pear   **1.** be seen; come in sight: *One by one the stars appear.*   **2.** seem; look: *The apple appeared good, but it was rotten inside.*   **ap peared, ap pear ing.**

ap ple   1. the fruit of a tree that grows in many parts of the world.   2. *We have an apple tree in our yard. Mother makes good apple pie.*

ap ple blos som   the flower of an apple tree: *The Apple Blossom is the State Flower of Arkansas and of Michigan.*

ap proach   come near or nearer to: *Slow down as you approach the river. Winter is approaching.*   **ap proached, ap proach ing.**

apri cot   1. a fruit somewhat like a peach but smaller.   2. *We have an apricot tree in our yard.*

April   the fourth month of the year.

apron   something worn over the front of the body to protect clothes: *Wear an apron when you cook.*

aquar i um   1. a tank or glass bowl in which living fish are kept.   2. a building where you can see living fish and water animals.

ar bor   a shaded place formed by vines and plants growing on frames.

Ar bor Day   a day when many people plant trees.

ar chae ol o gist   a scientist who finds and studies old bones and objects of long ago.

are   *We are ready.   You are next.   They are waiting.*

aren't   are not.

arith me tic   the science and art of numbers, in which you add, subtract, multiply, and divide.

Ar i zo na   one of the fifty states of the United States.

Ar kan sas   one of the fifty states of the United States.

arm   1. the part of a person's body between the shoulder and the hand.   See the picture under **body**.   2. something shaped or used like an arm: *Sit down on the arm of the chair.*

ar ma dil lo   a small, burrowing animal, with a very hard shell.

armed   having guns and other materials for defense.

Ar my   one of the armed forces of the United States.   **ar mies.**

around   1. *He has traveled around the world.*   2. *He spun around like a top.*   3. *The sun shines all around us.*   4. *They went around noon.*

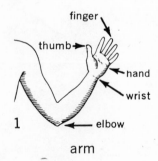

finger

thumb

hand

wrist

1

elbow

arm

ar range 1. put in the proper order: *The table is arranged for dinner.* 2. plan; form plans: *Can you arrange to go by six o'clock?* **ar ranged, ar rang ing.**

ar rive come to a place: *We arrived in the city a week ago.* **ar rived, ar riv ing.**

ar row 1. a slender, pointed stick, which is shot from a bow. 2. a sign (→) used to show direction or position in maps, on road signs, and in writing.

art drawing and painting.

ar ti choke 1. a plant the head of which is cooked and eaten. 2. *Did you eat any artichoke hearts?*

art ist a person who draws or paints pictures.

as 1. equally: *He is as tall as I am.* 2. doing the work of: *She will act as teacher today.* 3. while: *As they were walking, the rain began.* 4. in the same way that: *Treat others as you wish them to treat you.*

ash what remains after a thing has been burned: *When the ashes are cold, they should be removed from the stove.* **ash es.**

ashamed feeling shame because one has done something wrong or silly: *I was ashamed when I cried.*

Asia part of the largest mass of land on the earth.

ask 1. try to find out by words: *Why don't you ask the way?* 2. seek the answer to: *Ask any questions you wish.* 3. invite: *She asked ten guests to her birthday party.* **asked, ask ing.**

asleep sleeping: *The cat is asleep on the bed.*

as par a gus 1. a plant the tender shoots of which are used for food. 2. *Asparagus soup is delicious.*

as tro naut a pilot or member of the crew of a space ship.

at 1. *Mother is at home.* 2. *The boy goes to bed at eight o'clock.* 3. *We have nothing at all.*

ate See **eat**. *The boy ate his dinner an hour ago.*

ath lete a person such as a baseball player or a boxer who is trained by exercise to be strong and fast.

At lan tic the ocean east of North and South America.

at tack set upon to hurt; go against as an enemy: *The dog attacked the cat.* **at tacked, at tack ing.**

attic

at ten tion *The teacher asked the children to pay attention. He called my attention to the cat in the tree. The boy shows his mother much attention.*

at tic the space just below the roof and above the other rooms in a house. See the picture.

at tract **1.** *A magnet attracts iron.* **2.** *Bright colors attract children.* **at tract ed, at tract ing.**

au di ence **1.** people gathered in a place to hear or see something: *The audience liked the circus acts.* **2.** *The man spoke to the television audience.*

au di om e ter a machine that helps find out how many different sounds a person can hear.

au di to ri um a large room for an audience.

Au gust the eighth month of the year.

aunt your father's sister or your mother's sister or your uncle's wife.

Aus tral ia one of the large masses of land on the earth.

au thor a person who writes books or stories.

au to an automobile.

au to graph **1.** a person's name written by himself. **2.** write one's name on or in: *The author autographed her book for me.* **au to graphed, au to graph ing.**

au to mo bile a vehicle with an engine that makes it run: *People ride in automobiles.*

au tumn **1.** the season of the year between summer and winter. **2.** *Autumn flowers are bright.*

av e nue a wide street: *The parade went up the avenue.*

awake not asleep: *He was still awake at midnight.*

away **1.** from a place: *Stay away from the fire.* **2.** at a distance: *The sailor was far away from home.* **3.** not present; gone: *My mother is away today.*

aw ful causing fear: *There was an awful storm with thunder and lightning.*

aw ful ly *I'm awfully sorry you can't come.*

ax or **axe** a tool for chopping wood. **ax es.**

ax le **1.** a bar on which or with which a wheel turns. **2.** a crossbar on the two ends of which wheels turn. See the picture.

azal ea a bush bearing many flowers.

axle

B

ba by   1. a very young child: *Some babies cry a good deal.*   2. *The baby chickens are yellow.*   **ba bies.**

back   1. the part opposite to the front: *The back of my head hurts.*   2. the part of a chair that a person leans against when he sits down.   3. move backward: *He backed his car slowly.*   4. *Get in the back seat.*   5. *It happened back in the spring.*   6. *Go back to your seat.*   **backed, back ing.**

back ward   1. toward the back: *She went without a backward look.*   2. *Walk backward.*

ba con   salted and smoked meat from the back and sides of a hog.

bad   1. not good; not as it ought to be: *Teasing animals is a bad habit.*   2. rotten; spoiled: *This is a bad egg.*   3. sorry: *I feel bad about missing the game.*   4. sick: *I feel bad today.*   **worse, worst.**

badg er   an animal that digs holes in the ground: *The Badger is the State Animal of Wisconsin.*

bad ly   *She sings badly.*

bag   a container made of paper, cloth, or leather, that can be closed at the top.   See the pictures.

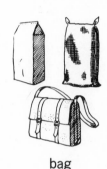

bag

bag gage   the trunks, bags, and suitcases that a person takes with him when he travels.

bait   1. anything used to attract fish or other animals so they may be caught: *Worms are good fishing bait.*   2. put bait on a hook or in a trap to catch something.   **bait ed, bait ing.**

bake   cook food in an oven.   **baked, bak ing.**

bak er   a person whose business is making or selling bread, pies, cakes, and cookies.

1

bak ery   a baker's shop; a place where bread and cakes are made or sold.   **bak er ies.**

bal ance   1. being steady; not falling over: *He lost his balance and fell off the ladder.*   2. keep or put in a steady position.   **bal anced, bal anc ing.**

bal co ny   1. a platform that sticks out from a floor of a building.   2. a floor above the first floor in a theater or hall.   See the pictures.   **bal co nies.**

2

balcony

bale

1

3

bar

bale   **1.** a large bundle of material such as cotton or hay wrapped and tied.   See the pictures.   **2.** make into bales; tie in large bundles.   **baled, bal ing.**

ball¹   **1.** anything round: *Here is a ball of string.*   **2.** a round body thrown, kicked, knocked, or batted about in games.   **3.** *Dad took us to the ball game.*

ball²   a large party for dancing.

bal le ri na   a woman dancer who dances on her toes.

bal loon   **1.** a brightly colored rubber bag filled with air.   **2.** an airtight bag filled with some gas that makes it rise and float in the air.

ba na na   a fruit that grows in bunches.

band   **1.** a group of musicians playing instruments.   **2.** *A band of bad men stopped the train.*   **3.** a flat strip: *Put rubber bands around that box.*

band age   **1.** a strip of cloth or other material used in covering or wrapping up a wound.   **2.** wrap or tie up a wound.   **band aged, band ag ing.**

bang   **1.** a sudden, loud noise.   **2.** make a sudden, loud noise.   **banged, bang ing.**

bangs   a fringe of hair across the forehead.

ban jo   a musical instrument.

bank¹   a place for keeping money.

bank²   **1.** a long pile or heap: *There was a bank of snow over ten feet deep.*   **2.** ground along a river or lake.   **3.** slant to one side when making a turn: *The airplane banked sharply and headed north toward the airport.*   **banked, bank ing.**

bank er   a person that helps run a bank.

bar   **1.** a piece of something such as iron, soap, or chocolate, longer than it is wide or thick.   **2.** a pole or rod across a door or gate to fasten or shut off something.   **3.** the dividing line between two measures of music.   See the pictures.

bar be cue   **1.** an open pit or pan on which meat is roasted.   **2.** meat roasted before an open fire.   **3.** a feast at which meat is roasted.   **4.** meat cooked in barbecue sauce.   **5.** roast meat before or over an open fire.   **6.** roast an animal whole.   **7.** kind of sauce.   **bar be cued, bar be cu ing.**

bar be cued **1.** See **barbecue.** **2.** *Barbecued chicken is easy to make.*

bar ber a person whose business is cutting people's hair and shaving men's faces.

bare *His bare hands were cold.* **bar er, bar est.**

bar gain an agreeing to trade: *We made a bargain with Father to wash the car for fifty cents.*

barge a large, flat-bottomed boat, usually pushed by a small boat, for carrying sand, coal, and so on.

bark[1] the outside covering of the trunk, branches, and roots of a tree. See the picture under **tree.**

bark[2] **1.** a sharp sound such as that made by a dog. **2.** make this sound. **barked, bark ing.**

bar ley **1.** a grasslike plant or its grain. See the picture under **grain.** **2.** *She likes barley soup.*

barn a building for storing hay and grain and for sheltering cows and horses. See the picture.

bar rel a large container with a round, flat top and bottom and with curved sides.

base **1.** the part of a thing on which it rests. **2.** *He stopped on third base.*

base ball **1.** a game played with bat and ball by two teams of nine players each, on a field with four bases. See the picture. **2.** the ball used in this game.

base ment the bottom story of a building, sometimes below ground.

bas ket **1.** a container made of grasses or strips of wood woven together. **2.** anything that looks like a basket: *Please use the wastepaper basket.* **3.** a ring and net through which a basketball drops.

bas ket ball **1.** a game played with a large, round leather ball between two teams of five players each. **2.** the ball used.

bass[1] a fish used for food. **bass es** or **bass.**

bass[2] *The man has a bass voice.*

bat[1] a flying animal that looks like a mouse.

bat[2] **1.** a thick stick or club, used to hit the ball in baseball. **2.** hit with a bat. **bat ted, bat ting.**

bath **1.** a washing of the body: *I took a bath last night.* **2.** a room for bathing: *The bath is upstairs.*

barn

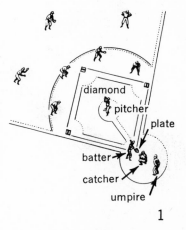

diamond

pitcher

plate

batter

catcher

umpire

1

baseball

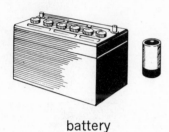

battery

bathe 1. take a bath. 2. give a bath to. 3. go in swimming. **bathed, bath ing.**

bath ing 1. See **bathe.** 2. *I wore my bathing cap.*

ba ton 1. the stick used by the leader of an orchestra or band for beating time to the music. 2. a long metal rod with a ball at one end.

bat ter[1] a player whose turn it is to bat. See the picture under **baseball.**

bat ter[2] flour, milk, eggs, or the like, mixed together to make cake, pancakes, and so on.

bat tery a set of electric cells that produce electric current. See the pictures. **bat ter ies.**

be *Can you be here all year? She tries to be good. They will be punished.*

beach an almost flat place at the edge of a lake or ocean, covered with sand or stones. **beach es.**

bead a small bit of glass or other material, with a hole, that can be strung on a thread or chain.

bea gle a small hunting dog.

beam 1. a large, long piece of timber or metal, ready for use in building. 2. a ray of light.

bean 1. a smooth, somewhat flat seed used as a vegetable. 2. the shell containing such seeds and also used as a vegetable. 3. *Have a bowl of bean soup.*

bear[1] a large animal with coarse hair and a very short tail: *The Black Bear is the State Animal of West Virginia. The California Grizzly is the State Animal of California.*

bear[2] 1. carry: *It will take two men to bear that heavy load.* 2. hold up: *The ice is too thin to bear your weight.* 3. suffer: *He cannot bear any more pain.* 4. bring forth: *That grapefruit tree bears good fruit.* **bore, borne** or **born, bear ing.**

beard the hair growing on a man's face.

beast any animal except man; a four-footed animal.

beat 1. *The cruel man beats his horse.* 2. *Beat three eggs for the cake.* 3. *The bird beat its wings.* 4. *Our team beat yours.* **beat, beat en, beat ing.**

beat en 1. See **beat.** *We have beaten your team twice.* 2. *The beaten dog crawled away.*

beau ti ful   very pleasing to see or hear.
beau ti ful ly   *She plays the piano beautifully.*
beau ty   **1.** being good to look at: *We were thrilled by the beauty of the sunset.*   **2.** that which pleases: *There is beauty in a fine thought or act.*   **beau ties.**
bea ver   a mammal that lives both in water and on land and builds dams across streams.
be came   See **become.**   *The seed became a plant.*
be cause   for the reason that; since: *Boys play ball because it's fun.*
be come   **1.** come to be; grow to be: *It is becoming colder.*   **2.** *He has become wiser as he has grown older.*
3. Become of means happen to: *What has become of the box of candy?*   **be came, be come, be com ing.**
bed   **1.** anything to sleep or rest on.   **2.** a piece of ground in which plants are grown.   See the pictures.
bee   an insect that makes honey and wax.
beef   **1.** the meat from a steer or cow, used for food.
2. *I like to eat beef stew.*
been   *I have been asleep.   He has been here before. What have you been doing?   The books have been read.   The boys have been friends for many years.*
beet   a plant with a thick root that is used as a vegetable or from which sugar is made.
bee tle   an insect that has two hard, shiny cases to cover its wings when folded.
be fore   **1.** *Before the bell rings, you may play games.*
2. *You come before us in line.*   **3.** *You were never late before.*
beg   **1.** ask for something, such as food, clothes, or money: *The dog was begging for some meat.*
2. *I beg your pardon.*   **begged, beg ging.**
be gan   See **begin.**   *Snow began to fall early.*
be gin   do the first part; start: *We will begin work soon.*   **be gan, be gun, be gin ning.**
be gin ning   **1.** the first part of something such as a book.   **2.** the time when anything starts.
be gun   See **begin.**   *It has begun to rain.*
be have   act well; do what is right: *The little boy behaves in school.*   **be haved, be hav ing.**

bed

bell

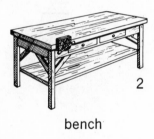

bench

be hind   **1.** at the back of: *Stand behind me.*
2. not on time; late: *The class is behind in its work.*
3. *He is behind the other boys in his class.*

be lieve   **1.** think something is true: *We believe the earth is round.*   **2.** think someone tells the truth: *His friends believe him.*   **be lieved, be liev ing.**

bell   a hollow metal object shaped like a cup that makes a ringing sound when struck by another piece of metal inside it or by a hammer.   See the picture.

be long   **1.** *Does this cap belong to you?*   **2.** *She belongs to the Girl Scouts.*   **3.** *That book belongs on this shelf.*   **be longed, be long ing.**

be low   **1.** *From the airplane we could see the fields below.*   **2.** less than: *It is below zero tonight.*

belt   **1.** a strip of leather or cloth worn around the body to hold in or hold up clothes.   **2.** a band having no end that moves the wheels it passes over: *A belt moves the fan in our automobile.*

bench   **1.** a long seat.   **2.** a strong, heavy table on which one works with tools: *A carpenter works at a bench.*   See the picture.   **bench es.**

bend   **1.** a part that is not straight: *There is a sharp bend in the road here.*   **2.** curve; be crooked: *The branch began to bend as I climbed along it.*
3. *Bend over and touch your toes fifteen times every morning.*   **bent** or **bend ed, bend ing.**

be neath   below; under; in a lower place: *The leaves fell to the ground beneath the tree.*

bent   **1.** See **bend.**   **2.** *I used a bent pin for a hook.*

ber ry   a small fruit, such as a strawberry or raspberry, having many seeds.   **ber ries.**

be side   **1.** *Grass grows beside the brook.*
2. *He looks tall beside his brother.*

be sides   **1.** *He didn't want to hurry home; besides he was having fun.*   **2.** *Others came to the picnic besides our own family.*

best   **1.** See **good.**   *Who does the best work?*
2. See **well.**   *Who reads best?*

bet   say you will give something to another if he is right and you are wrong.   **bet** or **bet ted, bet ting.**

bet ter 1. See **good**. *Which of these two dresses is better?* 2. See **well**. *He did better today.*

be tween 1. *There is a rock between the two trees.* 2. *Come between three and four o'clock.* 3. *The boys had ten cents between them.*

be yond 1. farther away: *Look beyond the fence for your ball.* 2. farther on than: *Don't go beyond the corner.* 3. *What the speaker meant is beyond me.*

bib 1. a cloth worn under the chin. 2. the top part of an apron.

Bi ble *Do you read the Bible in Sunday school?*

bi cy cle a vehicle with two wheels, one behind the other, and moved by pushing two pedals.

big 1. great in amount or size; large. 2. grown-up. 3. important. **big ger, big gest.**

bike a bicycle.

bill[1] 1. an account of how much money a person owes someone. 2. a piece of paper money.

bill[2] the mouth of a bird. See the picture under **bird**.

bin a box or place shut in on all sides, for holding such things as grain and coal.

bind 1. tie together; hold together; fasten: *Bind the packages with string.* 2. wrap, tie up, or dress a wound: *Bind up their wounds.* **bound, bind ing.**

bi og ra phy the story of a person's life written by someone else. **bi og ra phies.**

birch 1. a tree with smooth bark and hard wood: *The White Birch is the State Tree of New Hampshire.* 2. *Birch wood is used in furniture.* **birch es.**

bird an animal that has wings and feathers. See the picture.

birth being born: *We heard about the birth of the baby.*

birth day 1. the day on which a person was born. 2. *There were nine candles on her birthday cake.*

bis cuit soft bread baked in small pieces.

bit[1] 1. a piece of metal put in a horse's mouth so its rider or driver can control it. 2. a tool for boring or drilling. See the pictures.

bit[2] a small piece; a small amount.

bird

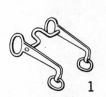

1

bit[1]

bit[3] See **bite**.   *He bit off more than he could chew.*

bite   **1.** the amount one bites off: *Take a bite.*
2. cut off with the teeth.   **3.** wound with teeth; sting:
A mosquito bit me.   **bit, bit ten** or **bit, bit ing.**

bit ten See **bite**.   *The dog has bitten the boy.*

bit ter root   a small plant with thick roots and pink
flowers: *The Bitterroot is the State Flower of Montana.*

black   opposite of white: *I want to ride the black pony.*

black ber ry   **1.** a small black or purple fruit.
2. *We have a blackberry bush.*   **black ber ries.**

black-eyed   Su san   a yellow daisy: *The
Black-Eyed Susan is the State Flower of Maryland.*

black smith   a man who works with iron, mending
tools and putting shoes on horses.

blade   **1.** the cutting part of anything like a knife or
scissors: *My father's hunting knife has a very sharp
blade.*   **2.** a leaf of grass.   **3.** part of a propeller.

blame   **1.** *We blamed the fog for our accident.*
2. *He will not blame us if we always try
to do our best.*   **blamed, blam ing.**

blank   **1.** *Write the correct word in each blank.*
2. *Fill out this blank and return it to your teacher.*
3. *This is a piece of blank paper.*

blan ket   **1.** a soft, heavy covering.   **2.** *A blanket
of snow covered the ground.*

blaze   **1.** a bright flame or fire.   **2.** burn with a
bright flame.   **blazed, blaz ing.**

bleat   **1.** the cry made by a sheep, goat, or calf, or a
sound like it.   **2.** make the cry of a sheep, goat, or
calf, or a sound like it.   **bleat ed, bleat ing.**

bled See **bleed**.   *The cut has bled for ten minutes.*

bleed   lose blood.   **bled, bleed ing.**

bless   ask God's care for: *Bless these little
children.*   **blessed** or **blest, bless ing.**

blew See **blow**.   *All night long the wind blew.*

blind   **1.** something that keeps out light.
See the picture.   **2.** not able to see.

blink   **1.** look with the eyes opening and shutting.
2. move the eyelids; wink.   **blinked, blink ing.**

bliz zard   a bad snowstorm.

blind

block **1.** a thick piece of wood, stone, or metal.
2. a square piece of land with a street along each side.
3. fill up so as to keep something from passing:
The car was blocking traffic. **blocked, block ing.**
blood the red liquid that flows from a cut.
bloom **1.** a flower; a blossom. **2.** have flowers:
Many plants bloom in spring. **bloomed, bloom ing.**
blos som a flower, usually of a plant
that produces fruit.
blouse a loose-fitting piece of clothing for the top
part of the body.
blow[1] a hard hit; a knock: *He struck the man
a blow that sent him to the floor.*
blow[2] **1.** send forth a strong current of air: *Blow
out the match.* **2.** *The wind is blowing hard.*
3. make a sound by a current of air: *The whistle
blows at noon.* **blew, blown, blow ing.**
blown See **blow**[2]. *The wind has blown the leaves.*
blue **1.** the color of the clear sky in daylight.
2. *Your blue dress is pretty.* **blu er, blu est.**
blue ber ry **1.** a small, blue berry that is good to eat.
2. *A blueberry bush is not very big.* **blue ber ries.**
Blue Bird a member of a group for girls:
*Most Blue Birds become Camp Fire Girls when they
grow older.*
blue bird a small songbird: *The Bluebird is the
State Bird of Missouri. The Mountain Bluebird is the
State Bird of Nevada and of Idaho.*
blue bon net a plant with blue flowers:
The Bluebonnet is the State Flower of Texas.
blue jay a noisy, chattering North American bird.
board **1.** a group of persons managing something:
The school board meets tonight. **2.** a broad, thin piece
of wood. **3.** cover with boards. **4.** get on a ship,
train, or plane. **board ed, board ing.**
boast speak too well of yourself or what you own:
He boasts about his new car. **boast ed, boast ing.**
boat a vehicle that floats on water and can be
moved by a motor or by oars.
bob o link a common American songbird.

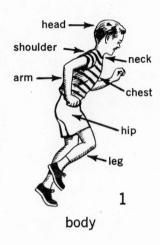

head

shoulder

arm

neck

chest

hip

leg

1

body

body   **1.** *This boy has a strong, healthy body.*
See the picture.   **2.** the main part of anything.
3. the outside part of an automobile.   **bod ies.**
boil[1]   a red, painful sore on the skin.
boil[2]   **1.** bubble up and give off steam: *Water boils*
when heated.   **2.** cook by boiling.   **boiled, boil ing.**
boiled   **1.** See **boil**[2].   **2.** *I like boiled eggs.*
boil er   **1.** a container for heating liquids.
2. a tank for making steam or holding hot water.
bold   without fear; showing courage: *The bold boy*
stood ready to protect his mother.   **bold er, bold est.**
bold ly   *The fireman ran boldly into the burning shed.*
bone   one of the pieces of the skeleton of an animal
with a backbone: *He broke a bone in his hand.*
book   written or printed sheets of paper bound
together: *She read the first ten pages in her book.*
book case   a piece of furniture with shelves
for holding books.
boom   **1.** a deep, hollow sound like the roar of big
waves.   **2.** make a deep, hollow sound: *The man's*
voice boomed out above the rest.   **boomed, boom ing.**
boot   a heavy covering for the foot and leg.
bore[1]   make a hole: *Bore through the handle of that*
brush so we can hang it up.   **bored, bor ing.**
bore[2]   See **bear**[2].   *She bore the pain bravely.*
born   See **bear**[2].   *A baby was born today.*
borne   See **bear**[2].   *He has borne heavy loads.*
bor row   get from another person something you
will give back.   **bor rowed, bor row ing.**
boss   **1.** a person who hires people to work or who
watches over and directs them.   **2.** be the boss of;
direct; control.   **boss es; bossed, boss ing.**
both   **1.** *Both houses are white.*   **2.** *Why don't we*
both go?
both er   **1.** worry; trouble: *What a lot of bother about*
nothing.   **2.** take trouble; concern oneself: *Don't*
bother about getting breakfast.   **3.** annoy: *Do not*
bother me while I work.   **both ered, both er ing.**
bot tle   a container, usually made of glass and
without handles, used for liquids.

bot tom **1.** *The bottom of your cup is wet.* **2.** *Don't take the bottom piece of meat on the plate.* **3.** *It's at the bottom of the box.*

bought See **buy.** *We bought apples from the farmer.*

bounce spring back after hitting something: *The ball bounced five times.* **bounced, bounc ing.**

bound¹ See **bind.** *The doctor bound up the cut.*

bound² **1.** bounce. **2.** spring lightly: *Mountain goats can bound from rock to rock.* **bound ed, bound ing.**

bou quet a bunch of flowers.

bow¹ **1.** a strip of wood bent by a string, and used to shoot arrows. **2.** a thin rod with hairs from a horse's tail stretched on it for playing the violin. **3.** a loop or knot. See the pictures.

bow² the front part of a ship, boat, or airplane. See the picture.

bow³ **1.** a bending of head or body in greeting: *He made a low bow to them.* **2.** bend the head or body in greeting. **bowed, bow ing.**

bowl¹ **1.** a hollow, round dish. **2.** *The bowl of a pipe is usually made of wood.*

bowl² play a game by rolling a heavy ball at wood pins to knock them down. **bowled, bowl ing.**

box¹ a container made of wood, metal, or paper to put things in. **box es.**

box² fight another person with the fists, following special rules. **boxed, box ing.**

box er a man who boxes, wearing padded gloves.

boy a male child.

Boy Scout a member of the Boy Scouts of America.

brace let a band or chain worn on the arm.

braid **1.** *She liked to wear her hair in braids.* **2.** *Every morning the little girl's mother braided her hair neatly.* **braid ed, braid ing.**

braid ed **1.** See **braid.** **2.** *She carried a braided straw purse.*

brain the part of the body used to feel and think.

brake anything used to stop or slow down: *The brakes on a railroad train press against the wheels.*

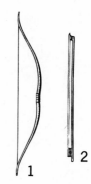

bow ¹

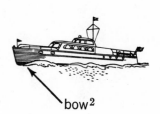

bow ²

brake man   a man who works brakes or helps the conductor of a railroad train.   **brake men.**

branch   1. part of a tree that grows out from the trunk.   See the picture under **tree.**   2. *The river divides into two branches.*   **branch es.**

brand   1. *Do you like this brand of groceries?* 2. a mark made on cattle and horses to show who owns them.   3. mark with a hot iron: *Cowboys brand cattle.*   **brand ed, brand ing.**

brass   1. a yellow metal.   2. *Clean the brass bowl.*

brave   without fear.   **brav er, brav est.**

brave ly   *The soldiers fought bravely.*

bread   food made of flour or meal mixed with milk or water and baked: *We eat bread and butter.*

break   1. *A break in the water pipe caused the leak.* 2. make come to pieces by a blow or pull.   3. come apart; crack; burst.   4. *People who break the law are punished.*   **broke, bro ken, break ing.**

break fast   the first meal of the day.

breath   air drawn into and forced out of the lungs.

breathe   draw air into the lungs and then force it out.   **breathed, breath ing.**

breeze   a stirring of air; a light wind.

brick   1. a block of clay baked by sun or fire. See the picture.   2. *The boy climbed a brick wall.*

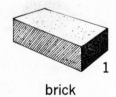

brick

bride   a woman just married or about to be.

bride groom   a man just married or about to be.

bridge   something built above water or land so that people can cross over.

bright   1. *Sunshine is bright.*   2. *A bright child learns quickly.*   **bright er, bright est.**

bright ly   *The fire burned brightly.*

bring   1. come with something from another place: *Please bring me a clean plate.*   2. **Bring up** means care for as a child.   **brought, bring ing.**

broad   wide; large across: *The wagons crossed a broad river.*   **broad er, broad est.**

broad cast   1. a radio or television program. 2. send out a signal or program by radio or television.   **broad cast or broad cast ed, broad cast ing.**

broke   See **break**.   *She broke her doll.*
bro ken   **1.** See **break**.   *The boy's ball has broken a window.*   **2.** *Pick up the broken cup.*
brook   a small stream.
broom   a brush with a long handle for sweeping.
broth er   a boy who has the same parents as you.
brought   See **bring**.   *He brought his lunch yesterday.*
brown   **1.** a dark color like that of toast, potato skins, or coffee.   **2.** *Many boys and girls have brown hair.*   **brown er, brown est.**
Brown ie[1]   a member of a group for girls: *Most Brownies become Girl Scouts when they grow older.*
brown ie[2]   in stories, a helpful elf.   See the picture.
brown ie[3]   a flat chocolate cake with nuts.
brush[1]   **1.** a tool made of animal hair or wire, set in a stiff back or fastened to a handle.   **2.** clean, rub, or paint with a brush; use a brush on: *Brush your teeth.*   **brush es; brushed, brush ing.**
brush[2]   bushes and small trees growing in the woods.
bub ble   a round drop of water that is full of air.
buck et   a container usually made of wood or metal and having a handle.
buck eye   **1.** a tree with large brown seeds: *The Buckeye is the State Tree of Ohio.*   **2.** *Ohio is known as "The Buckeye State."*
buck le   **1.** an object to hold together two loose ends of a belt, strap, or ribbon.   **2.** fasten together with a buckle.   **buck led, buck ling.**
buck skin   **1.** strong, soft leather, made from the skins of deer or sheep.   **2.** *I have a buckskin jacket.*
bud   the beginning of a flower, leaf, or branch.
buf fa lo   a large animal with a great, shaggy head: *The American Buffalo is the State Animal of Kansas.*
bug   a crawling or a flying insect.
bug gy   **1.** a vehicle to ride in: *We rode in a buggy pulled by horses.*   See the picture.   **2.** a vehicle to carry a baby or doll.   **bug gies.**
bu gle   a musical instrument.
build   make by putting materials together: *Men build houses and ships.*   **built, build ing.**

brownie[2]

buggy

bulb

build ing a thing built, such as a barn or house.

built See **build**. *The birds have built a nest.*

bulb 1. a round, underground bud or stem from which plants such as onions, tulips, and lilies grow. 2. any rounded, swelling object. See the pictures.

bull dog a heavily built dog with a large head.

bul le tin board a board for posting notices.

bum ble bee a large bee with a thick body.

bump 1. *The baby got a bump on his head.* 2. *The children all bumped against one another.* 3. *Our car bumped along the rocky road for miles and miles.* **bumped, bump ing.**

bun bread or cake, sometimes sweet, baked in a small piece.

bunch a group of things of the same kind growing or fastened together, placed together, or thought of together. **bunch es.**

bun dle 1. a number of things tied together or wrapped together. 2. a parcel; a package.

bun ny a pet name for a rabbit. **bun nies.**

bun ting a small bird something like a sparrow: *The Lark Bunting is the State Bird of Colorado.*

bur ied 1. See **bury**. 2. *We found buried treasure.*

burn 1. *She got a burn on her arm from the iron.* 2. be on fire; be very hot. 3. set on fire: *Please burn the trash.* **burned** or **burnt, burn ing.**

bur ro a kind of small donkey.

bur row *Rabbits live in burrows.*

burst *The team will burst out the door. When it got too full of air, the balloon burst. Have you ever burst a bag?* **burst, burst ing.**

bury 1. *The children wanted to bury their dead pet.* 2. *Squirrels bury nuts.* **bur ied, bur y ing.**

bus a large automobile, used to carry passengers along certain streets or roads. **bus es** or **buss es.**

bush a plant like a tree but smaller, with branches starting from near the ground. **bush es.**

bush el a measure for grain, fruit, and vegetables.

bushy spread out like a bush; growing thickly: *Squirrels have bushy tails.* **bush i er, bush i est.**

bus i ness   the thing one is busy at; work: *A carpenter's business is building.*   **bus i ness es.**

busy   1. working; having plenty to do.   2. *We live on a busy street.*   **bus i er, bus i est.**

but   1. *You may go, but you must come home soon.*   2. *Father works every day but Sunday.*

butch er   a man whose work is killing animals for food or who sells meat.

butt   strike by pushing or knocking hard with the head: *A goat butts.*   **butt ed, butt ing.**

but ter   the yellow fat formed by churning cream.

but ter fly   an insect with a small, thin body and four large, bright-colored wings.   **but ter flies.**

but ton   1. a knob or object on clothing to hold it closed.   2. a knob to take hold of, push, or turn: *When I pushed the button, the bell rang.*   3. fasten the buttons of.   **but toned, but ton ing.**

buy   get by paying some money: *You can buy a pencil for five cents.*   **bought, buy ing.**

buzz   1. the humming sound made by flies, mosquitoes, or bees.   2. make a steady humming sound.   **buzz es; buzzed, buzz ing.**

by   1. *He lives in the house by the railroad tracks.*   2. *They went by the shortest road.*   3. *He travels by train.   We buy eggs by the dozen.*   4. *Come by six o'clock.*   5. *It happened in days gone by.*   6. **By and by** means after a while.

C

cab   an automobile that can be hired; a taxi.

cab bage   a vegetable with a round head.

cab in   a small house or hut.   See the picture.

ca ble   a strong, thick rope, often made of wires twisted together.   See the picture.

ca boose   a small car, usually the last one, on a freight train, in which the train crew can rest.

cac tus   1. a plant with thorns: *The Saguaro Cactus is the State Flower of Arizona.*   2. *Don't touch a cactus plant.*   **cac tus es** or **cac ti.**

cabin

cable

cage

caf e te ria   an eating place where people wait on themselves.

cage   a frame or place closed in with wires or bars, used to keep birds and different kinds of animals. See the pictures.

cake   1. food baked from flour, sugar, and eggs. 2. food or other material pressed into the shape of a cake: *Please hand me a cake of soap.*

cal en dar   a table or chart showing the months, weeks, and days of the year.

calf[1]   1. a young cow, elephant, or whale. 2. leather made of the skin of a calf.   **calves.**

calf[2]   the thick part of the back of the leg below the knee.   See the picture under **leg.   calves.**

Cal i for nia   one of the fifty states of the United States.

call   1. a shout.   2. the cry an animal or bird makes.   3. a short visit.   4. speak loudly; cry; shout: *He called from across the street.*   5. *That boy is called John.*   6. telephone to.   **called, call ing.**

calm   quiet; still; not windy; not stirred up; not excited.   **calm er, calm est.**

calm ly   *She faced him calmly and without fear.*

came   See **come.**   *He came to school late today.*

cam el   a large animal used in the desert.

ca mel lia   a plant with shiny leaves: *The Camellia is the State Flower of Alabama.*

cam era   a machine for taking photographs.

camp   1. a group of tents or huts where people live for a time.   2. live in a tent or a hut or outdoors: *We camped out for a week.*   **camped, camp ing.**

Camp Fire Girl   a member of a group for girls.

can[1]   1. a container of metal or glass.   2. keep by sealing tightly: *Do you can fruit?*   **canned, can ning.**

can[2]   1. be able to.   2. know how to.   3. have the right to: *Anyone can cross the street here.*   **could.**

Can a da   the country north of the United States.

Ca na di an   1. a person born or living in Canada. 2. *Here is a Canadian flag.*

ca nary   a small songbird.   **ca nar ies.**

can dle   a stick of tallow or wax with a wick in it, burned to give light.   See the picture.

can dy   sugar boiled with water or milk and cooled, made into pieces for eating.   **can dies.**

cane   a stick used as a help in walking.

canned   **1.** See **can**[1].   **2.** *We ate canned peaches.*

ca noe   a light boat moved with paddles.

can't   cannot.

can ta loupe or **can ta loup**   a kind of sweet melon, having lots of juice.

can vas   **1.** a strong, coarse cloth.   **2.** *I am wearing canvas shoes.*   **can vas es.**

can yon   a narrow valley with high, steep sides.

cap   **1.** a soft covering for the head.   **2.** anything like a cap: *Milk bottles have caps.*

cape[1]   a piece of clothing, without sleeves.

cape[2]   a point of land with water almost all around it.

cap i tal   **1.** the city where the government of a nation or state is located: *Washington is the capital of the United States.   Each State has a capital.*   **2.** A, B, C, D, or any large letter.   **3.** *A capital letter is used to begin a sentence.*

Cap i tol   the building in a capital city in which laws are made.

cap sule   **1.** a small case or covering.   **2.** the part of a rocket that goes into orbit.

cap tain   **1.** the one who leads: *He is captain of the team.*   **2.** an officer in the armed forces.

car   **1.** a vehicle, such as an automobile, that can carry people and baggage.   **2.** *Where can we get a car wash?*

card   a flat piece of stiff paper: *We sent post cards.*

car di nal   an American songbird: *The Cardinal is the State Bird of Illinois, of Indiana, of North Carolina, of Ohio, of Virginia, and of West Virginia. The Kentucky Cardinal is the State Bird of Kentucky.*

care   **1.** *A good cook does her work with care.* **2.** *The baby was left in her sister's care.* **3.** *He cares about music.*   **4.** *A cat does not care to be washed.*   **cared, car ing.**

wick→

candle

care ful 1. full of care for something; watching for or over. 2. done with care.

care ful ly *He opened the box carefully.*

care less not thinking or watching what you do.

care less ly *She copied the words carelessly.*

car na tion a red, white, or pink flower: *The Scarlet Carnation is the State Flower of Ohio.*

car ol ers people who sing Christmas songs together, usually outside of houses at Christmas time.

car pen ter a person who builds with wood.

car pet 1. heavy woven material used for covering floors. 2. a patch of something such as grass or snow. 3. cover with a carpet. **car pet ed, car pet ing.**

car ri er a person or thing that takes packages and messages from one place to another.

car rot a vegetable with an orange-colored root.

car ry take from one place to another: *The man carried the child home.* **car ried, car ry ing.**

cart 1. a strong wagon with two wheels. 2. a small box or frame on wheels, pushed by hand.

car ton a container made of paper.

car toon a picture showing events which interest people: *The cartoon was very amusing.*

carve 1. cut into slices or pieces: *Father carves the meat at the table.* 2. *The boy carves animals out of soap.* carved, **carv ing.**

case[1] 1. *A case of measles kept me away from school.* 2. *In case of fire, walk to the door.*

case[2] 1. a holder or covering: *Put the knife back in its case.* 2. a box: *That is a case full of books.*

cash 1. money. 2. give money for: *The bank will cash your check.* **cashed, cash ing.**

cash ier a person in charge of money.

cast throw: *He cast his fishing line into the pool and waited.* **cast, cast ing.**

cas tle a large building or group of buildings with thick walls and towers.

cat a small animal often kept as a pet.

catch take and hold something that is moving: *Catch the ball with both hands.* caught, **catch ing.**

204

catch er a baseball player who stands behind the batter. See the picture under **baseball.**

cat er pil lar the wormlike form in which insects such as the butterfly and the moth hatch from the egg.

ca the dral a large or important church. See the picture.

cat sup a tomato sauce.

cat tle farm animals such as cows, steers, oxen.

caught See **catch.** *He caught the ball.*

cau li flow er a vegetable having a hard, white head that is good to eat.

cause **1.** something that makes something else happen: *What was the cause of the fire?* **2.** make happen: *A noise causes me to jump.* **caused, caus ing.**

cave a hollow space underground.

cav i ty a hole; a hollow place: *Cavities in teeth should be filled by a dentist.* **cav i ties.**

ce dar **1.** an evergreen tree with good-smelling wood. **2.** *We have a cedar closet.*

ceil ing the inside top covering of a room.

cel e brate do special things on a birthday or holiday. **cele brat ed, cel e brat ing.**

cel e bra tion special things to do to celebrate something.

cel ery a vegetable with long green or white stalks.

cell **1.** a small room. **2.** a small piece of living matter, from which animals and plants are made. **3.** a container for materials that produce electricity.

cel lar an underground room or space, usually under a building and often used for storing food.

cel lo a musical instrument.

ce ment **1.** a powder that becomes hard when it is mixed with water. **2.** *We have a cement walk.*

cent **1.** a copper coin of the United States and Canada. **2.** *A dime is worth ten cents.*

cen ter **1.** a person on a football or a basketball team. **2.** a point in a circle that is equally far from all points on the edge. **3.** the middle point or part.

ce re al **1.** any grain used as food. **2.** food usually eaten for breakfast.

cathedral

chain   1

cer tain **1.** sure. **2.** some but not all.

cer tain ly *Hurry or you will certainly be late.*

chain **1.** metal rings joined together. See the picture. **2.** fasten with a chain. **chained, chain ing.**

chair a single seat with a back and often with arms.

chair man the person who is in charge of a meeting or of a committee. **chair men.**

chalk a soft, white or gray limestone used for writing and drawing.

chance something that may happen: *He had a chance to make some money.* *There is a chance of snow.*

change **1.** *There has been a change in the weather.* **2.** *When I paid for the bread, I got five cents change.* **3.** *The wind changed from east to south.* **4.** *You change your clothes after school.* **changed, chang ing.**

chap ter a part of a book.

char ac ter a person in a play or book.

charge **1.** load; fill: *The battery in our car needs to be charged.* **2.** *The grocer charged seventy cents a dozen for eggs.* **3.** buy now and pay for later: *Mother charged the things we bought.* **4. In charge of** means be at the head of. **charged, charg ing.**

charm **1.** something special about a person or thing which delights or pleases. **2.** a small object worn on a bracelet. **3.** please greatly; delight: *The boys were charmed by the sailor's tales.* **charmed, charm ing.**

charm ing very pleasant; able to charm.

chart **1.** a map of the sea. **2.** a picture or drawing that tells facts: *The chart tells which team won the most games.*

chase run after to catch. **chased, chas ing.**

chat an easy, friendly talk.

chat ter **1.** talk a lot in a quick, foolish way. **2.** make a rattling sound. **chat tered, chat ter ing.**

chauf feur a man whose work is driving a car.

check **1.** a mark (√). **2.** a written order for money from a bank account. **3.** prove true or right by comparing: *Check your answers with mine.* **4.** mark to show that something has been checked and found true or right. **checked, check ing.**

check er a person who checks things bought at a supermarket.

cheek the side of the face below either eye. See the picture under **face.**

cheer **1.** good feeling; hope; joy. **2.** give joy to: *Our visit cheered the old woman.* **cheered, cheer ing.**

cheer ful **1.** *She is a smiling, cheerful girl.* **2.** *This is a cheerful, sunny room.*

cheer ful ly *He did the work cheerfully.*

cheese **1.** food made from the thick part of milk. **2.** *I'd like a cheese sandwich.*

cher ry **1.** a small, red, round fruit with a pit in it. **2.** *She took cherries from the cherry tree to make cherry pie.* **cher ries.**

chest **1.** the top, front part of a person's body between the shoulders. See the picture under **body.** **2.** a large box with a lid. See the picture.

chest nut **1.** a sweet nut, good to eat, having a hard shell. **2.** a tree bearing this nut. **3.** *We had chestnut dressing in the turkey.*

chew *We chew our food.* **chewed, chew ing.**

chick a dee a small bird having a cry that sounds like its name: *The Chickadee is the State Bird of Maine and of Massachusetts.*

chick en **1.** a young hen or rooster: *The Blue Hen Chicken is the State Bird of Delaware. The Rhode Island Red is the State Bird of Rhode Island.* **2.** *We went to the chicken house to get the eggs.*

chief **1.** the head of a group; the one who leads. **2.** *The oldest man was the chief engineer.*

Chi hua hua a very small dog.

child **1.** a baby. **2.** a young boy or girl. **3.** a son or daughter. **chil dren.**

chill **1.** unpleasant cold: *Make a fire in the stove to take the chill off the room.* **2.** make or become cold: *We were chilled by the sudden storm.* **chilled, chill ing.**

chilled **1.** See **chill.** **2.** *The chilled juice was good.*

chim ney a brick-covered pipe built to carry away smoke: *Our house has two chimneys.*

chim pan zee an animal like a large monkey.

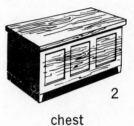

chest

chin **1.** the front of the lower jaw below the mouth. See the picture under **face.** **2.** hang by the hands on a bar and pull the body up. chinned, **chin ning.**

chip **1.** a small, thin piece cut or broken from something. **2.** cut or break small pieces from: *He chipped off the old paint.* **chipped, chip ping.**

chip munk a small, striped animal like a squirrel.

chipped **1.** See **chip.** **2.** *Don't use a chipped cup.*

choc o late **1.** a good-tasting powder made from the seeds of a certain tree. **2.** a drink made of this powder. **3.** *I like chocolate ice cream.*

choir the group of singers in a church.

choke stop the breath by squeezing the throat or by blocking it with food. **choked, chok ing.**

choose pick out from a number: *Choose the cake you like best.* **chose, cho sen, choos ing.**

chop **1.** a slice of meat with a piece of bone in it. **2.** cut by hitting with something sharp. **3.** cut into small pieces. chopped, **chop ping.**

chopped **1.** See chop. **2.** *Dogs like chopped meat.*

chose See **choose.** *She chose the red dress.*

cho sen See **choose.** *Have you chosen a book?*

Christ mas **1.** December 25, on which day many people go to church and give gifts. **2.** *Some Christmas trees have lights all over them.* **Christ mas es.**

chuck le **1.** a soft laugh; quiet laughter. **2.** laugh to oneself. **chuck led, chuck ling.**

church a building in which to worship. **church es.**

churn **1.** a machine that beats cream into butter. **2.** beat cream into butter. churned, **churn ing.**

cir cle **1.** a line on which every point is equally far from a point in the center. **2.** something flat and round or nearly so. **3.** move in a circle: *The airplane circled before it landed.* **cir cled, cir cling.**

cir cuit **1.** a going around; a moving around: *It takes a year for the earth to make its circuit of the sun.* **2.** the complete path or part of it over which an electric current flows.

cir cus **1.** a show that travels from place to place. **2.** *We liked to watch the circus clowns.* **cir cus es.**

cit i zen   **1.** a person who was born in or has become a member of a nation.   **2.** a person living in a city, town, county, or state.

city   **1.** a large, important town with many people living in it.   **2.** *The city streets are wide.*   **cit ies.**

clam   an animal with a soft body and a hard shell.

clap   **1.** a sudden noise, such as a single burst of thunder, the sound of the hands struck together, or the sound of a loud slap.   **2.** make such a noise with the hands.   **clapped, clap ping.**

clar i net   a musical instrument.

class   **1.** a group of persons or things of the same kind.   **2.** a group of pupils taught together.   **class es.**

class mate   a member of the same class in school.

claw   a sharp, hooked nail on the foot of a bird or an animal.   See the picture under **bird.**

clay   **1.** a kind of earth that gets hard when it is baked.   **2.** *She made a clay dish in school.*

clean   **1.** take away dirt or something not wanted: *Please clean your room.*   **2.** *Put on your clean shirt.*   **cleaned, clean ing; clean er, clean est.**

clear   **1.** make clean and free from; get everything else away: *He will clear the land of trees.*
2. *There is a clear view of the sea from that little hill.*   **cleared, clear ing; clear er, clear est.**

clear ing   an open space in a forest. See the picture.

clear ly   *You cannot see clearly in a fog.*

clerk   **1.** a person who sells things in a store.
2. a person who files papers or does other work in an office.   **3.** work as a clerk: *She clerks in a dress shop every Saturday.*   **clerked, clerk ing.**

clev er   **1.** bright; having a good mind.   **2.** able to do something very well.   **clev er er, clev er est.**

cliff   a very steep slope of rock.

climb   go up something steep: *I climbed a tree. The vine climbs up the wall.*   **climbed, climb ing.**

cling   stick or hold fast: *His wet clothes were clinging to his body.*   **clung, cling ing.**

clip[1]   cut a person's hair or an animal's fur short: *The dog has been clipped.*   **clipped, clip ping.**

clearing

209

clock

clip² **1.** a thing used for holding papers together, often made of bent wire. **2.** hold tight: *The teacher clipped our papers together.* **clipped, clip ping.**

clip per **1.** an instrument for cutting short: *I can't find my nail clipper. The barber used clippers on my neck.* **2.** a fast sailing ship.

clock an instrument for measuring time. See the picture.

clog fill up or choke up with waste matter: *Garbage clogged the drain.* **clogged, clog ging.**

close¹ **1.** an end: *He spoke at the close of the meeting.* **2.** shut: *Close the door.* **closed, clos ing.**

close² **1.** *She sat close to her mother.* **2.** *The water came close to the house.* **3.** *It turned out to be a close contest.* **clos er, clos est.**

closed **1.** See **close¹**. **2.** *He pulled and pulled at the closed door to open it.*

close ly *He followed closely.*

clos et a small room used for storing clothes or such things as dishes, towels, or canned food.

cloth **1.** material woven from threads. **2.** *She wore a blue cloth coat.*

clothes coverings for the body.

cloth ing clothes.

cloud **1.** a white or gray mass in the sky, made up of tiny drops of water. **2.** a mass of dust or smoke.

cloudy covered with clouds. **cloud i er, cloud i est.**

clo ver **1.** a plant with sweet-smelling heads of red or white flowers: *Red Clover is the State Flower of Vermont.* **2.** *Most clover leaves have three parts.*

clown a person whose business is making people laugh by wearing funny clothes and doing tricks.

club **1.** a group of people joined together: *Mother belongs to the garden club.* **2.** a heavy stick of wood. **3.** a stick or bat used to hit a ball in some games.

clue something that helps solve a mystery.

clung See **cling**. *She has clung to her mother.*

coach **1.** a person who teaches or trains people. **2.** a large railroad car or bus used to carry passengers. **3.** train or teach. **coach es; coached, coach ing.**

coal   **1.** black material that burns and gives off heat.   **2.** a piece of burned wood or coal, still red-hot.

coarse   not fine; made up of fairly large parts: *Coarse sand hurts your feet.*   **coars er, coars est.**

coast   **1.** the land along the sea; the seashore. **2.** slide downhill on a sled.   **coast ed, coast ing.**

Coast Guard   a group of men who guard the coasts of our nation.

Coast Guards man   a member of the United States Coast Guard.   **Coast Guards men.**

coat   **1.** a piece of clothing worn over other clothes. **2.** any covering, such as a dog's hair.   **3.** a thin layer: *This house needs a coat of paint.*

coax   try by soft words and pleasant ways to make someone do something.   **coaxed, coax ing.**

cob bler   **1.** a man whose business is mending shoes. **2.** a fruit pie baked on a deep dish.

cock a too   a large, brightly colored bird.

cock er span iel   a small dog with long, silky hair.

co coa   **1.** a powder much like chocolate.   **2.** a drink made from this powder.

co co nut or **co coa nut**   **1.** the large, brown fruit of one kind of palm tree.   **2.** *Did you ever have a drink of coconut milk?*

co coon   the silky case spun by caterpillars to live in while they are turning into moths or butterflies.

cod   a large fish used for food.

code   **1.** the laws of a country or of a group. **2.** words or figures used to write a secret message. **3.** signals for sending messages.

cof fee   a drink made from the roasted and ground seeds of a certain kind of bush.

coin   a piece of metal used as money, such as a penny, a nickel, a dime, or a quarter.

cold   **1.** a sick feeling with a running nose and a sore throat.   **2. Catch cold** means become sick with a cold.   **3.** a low temperature: *Come in out of the cold.*   **4.** *This coffee is cold.*   **cold er, cold est.**

col lar   the part of a coat, a dress, or a shirt that makes a band around the neck.

col lect bring together; come together; gather together: *Do you collect stamps?   A crowd soon collected at the fire.* **col lect ed, col lect ing.**

col lec tion 1. a group of things gathered from many places and belonging together. 2. *The boy put his money in the collection at church.*

col lec tor a person who collects.

col lie a large, long-haired dog.

col or 1. red, yellow, blue, or any of them mixed together: *I have eight colors in my paint box.* 2. give color to; paint: *Color the sky blue and the grass green.* **col ored, col or ing.**

Col o ra do one of the fifty states of the United States.

col ored 1. See color. 2. *Her colored shoes matched her dress.*

colt a young horse or donkey.

col um bine a plant with flowers shaped like hollow spurs: *The Blue-and-White Rocky Mountain Columbine is the State Flower of Colorado.*

Co lum bus Day October 12, the day in 1492 that Columbus discovered America.

col umn 1. a thick, tall post or pole used to hold up a roof or part of a building. 2. anything like a column: *A column of smoke rose from the fire.* 3. a part of a newspaper: *I always read the baseball column.*

comb 1. an instrument with teeth, used to arrange the hair or to hold it in place. 2. the thick, red piece on the top of a chicken's head.   See the pictures. 3. *You should comb your hair every morning before you go to school.*   **combed, comb ing.**

comb

come 1. move toward: *Come over to me.* 2. get near; reach; arrive: *The girls will come home tomorrow.* 3. take place; happen: *Winter has not come yet.* **came, come, com ing.**

com ics a funny story told by pictures.

com ma a mark (,) of punctuation.

com mand 1. an order; a direction. 2. give an order to. **com mand ed, com mand ing.**

com mit tee   a group of persons chosen to do a special thing: *A committee planned the party.*

com mon   often seen or found: *Snow is common here.*   **com mon er, com mon est.**

com mu ni ca tion   **1.** giving facts or news by speaking or writing: *Communication by telephone saves time.*   **2.** a letter or message.

com mu ni ty   **1.** a group of people living together that make up a family, school, neighborhood, town, city, county, state, or nation.   **2.** a place where people live.   **3.** *The picnic was held in the community park.*   **com mu ni ties.**

com pa ny   **1.** a group of people joined together to run a business or put on a play.   **2.** a visitor or visitors: *Are you expecting company?*   **com pa nies.**

com pare   find out or point out how persons or things are alike.   **com pared, com par ing.**

com pass   **1.** an instrument that shows directions.   **2.** an instrument for drawing circles and for measuring distances.   **com pass es.**

com pete   try to win: *The boys were competing for the prize.*   **com pet ed, com pet ing.**

com plain   say that something is wrong; find fault: *She is always complaining that her health is poor.*   **com plained, com plain ing.**

com plete   **1.** *She completes her homework early in the evening.*   **2.** *He has bought a complete set of garden tools.   The party was a complete success.*   **3.** *My collection is complete.*   **com plet ed, com plet ing.**

com plete ly   *We are completely satisfied with her. The glass is completely empty.*

com pose   **1.** make up: *Our family is composed of four people.*   **2.** put together: *To compose a song you must think up a tune and then write down the notes.*   **com posed, com pos ing.**

com pute   count or figure up: *Mother computed the cost of our trip.*   **com put ed, com put ing.**

con cern   **1.** *The teacher showed concern over pupils being absent.*   **2.** *This letter concerns only me.*   **con cerned, con cern ing.**

213

con cert a performance in which musicians play or sing.

con crete **1.** cement, sand, and water that have been mixed and have dried into a hard mass. **2.** *There is a concrete sidewalk along the fence.*

con duct **1.** how someone behaves: *Her conduct was good.* **2.** manage; direct: *He conducts an orchestra.* **3.** guide or lead: *Metals conduct heat and electricity.* **con duct ed, con duct ing.**

con duc tor **1.** a guide or one who leads. **2.** a person in charge of passengers on a train or a bus. **3.** a thing through which heat, sound, or electricity moves: *Copper wire is used as a conductor of electricity.*

cone **1.** an object that has a flat, round base and that comes to a point at the top. **2.** the part that bears seeds on some trees. **3.** *I like ice-cream cones.*

con fess admit; own up: *He confessed that he ate all the cake.* **con fessed, con fess ing.**

con fuse **1.** mix up: *So many people talking to me at once confused me.* **2.** be unable to tell apart; mistake one thing for another: *People often confuse this girl with her twin sister.* **con fused, con fus ing.**

con fused **1.** See **confuse.** **2.** *There were several confused people asking directions.*

con nect join one thing to another; fasten together. **con nect ed, con nect ing.**

con nect ed **1.** See **connect.** **2.** *Two connected railroad cars rolled down the track.*

Con nect i cut one of the fifty states of the United States.

con ser va tion protecting from being lost or being used up or being wasted.

con so nant **1.** any letter of the alphabet that is not a vowel. **2.** the sound such a letter stands for: *There are two consonant sounds in the word "ship."*

con stel la tion a group of stars: *The Big Dipper is a constellation that is easy to find in the sky.*

con tain **1.** have within itself; hold inside: *My purse contains money.* **2.** be equal to: *A quart contains two pints.* **con tained, con tain ing.**

214

con tent ed satisfied: *A contented person is happy.*

con test 1. a test of skill to see who will win, such as a game or race. 2. a struggle; a fight.

con tin ue 1. keep on; not stop: *The rain continued all day.* 2. take up; carry on: *The story will be continued next month.* **con tin ued, con tin u ing.**

con trac tion a shortened form: *"Can't" is a contraction of "cannot."*

con trary 1. opposite; completely different. 2. against others: *The contrary boy refused to go along.*

con trol 1. power; something that holds down: *A car is under its driver's control.* 2. a button or switch that runs a machine. 3. have power over; direct: *A captain controls his ship.* 4. hold back; keep down. 5. *Turn the control switch all the way to the left.* **con trolled, con trol ling.**

cook 1. *Mother cooked oatmeal for me.* 2. *Let the meat cook slowly.* **cooked, cook ing.**

cooked 1. See **cook.** 2. *Cooked vegetables can be used in salad.*

cook ie or **cooky** a small, flat cake. **cook ies.**

cool 1. *Yesterday was a cool day.* 2. *She wore a cool dress.* 3. *He looked cool and calm.* **cool er, cool est.**

coop a small cage or pen for chickens or rabbits.

cop per 1. a metal. 2. *We have a copper kettle.*

copy 1. a thing made to be just like another. 2. one of a number of the same book, magazine, or picture. 3. make something like something else: *Copy this page.* **cop ies; cop ied, cop y ing.**

cor al 1. a hard red, pink, or white material, made up of the skeletons of tiny sea animals and often used for jewelry. See the picture. 2. *I have a coral necklace.*

cord 1. a thick, strong string; a very thin rope. 2. a pair of wires covered with rubber, used to connect an iron or lamp with the electric current.

cor du roy 1. a kind of thick cloth. 2. *Many boys wear corduroy slacks.*

cork 1. the bark of a certain tree used for bottle tops, floats for fishing lines, and so on. 2. *See if you can pull the cork out of this bottle.* See the picture.

coral

cork

215

corn[1]   **1.** a grain that grows in large ears.   See the picture under **grain.**   **2.** the plant that it grows on. **3.** *Have a piece of corn candy.*

corn[2]   a hard spot on the foot.

cor ner   **1.** the place where two lines or surfaces meet.   **2.** the place where two streets meet. **3.** *We have a corner cupboard.*

cor net   a musical instrument.

cor ral   a pen for horses, cattle, and so on.

cor rect   **1.** mark the mistakes in: *The teacher corrects the test papers.*   **2.** *She gave the correct answer.*   **cor rect ed, cor rect ing.**

cor rect ed   **1.** See **correct.**   **2.** *The teacher returned the corrected papers.*

cor rect ly   *He wrote all the words correctly.*

cor ri dor   a long hall; a long space in a building.

cost   **1.** the price paid: *The cost of this hat was ten dollars.*   **2.** to be bought at the price of; require: *This hat cost ten dollars.*   **cost, cost ing.**

cos tume   clothes; what a person is wearing: *In our play one character wore a king's costume.*

cot   a narrow bed, sometimes made to fold up. See the picture.

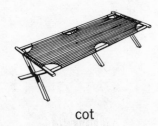

cot

cot tage   a small house, often used only in summer.

cot ton   **1.** the white part of a plant that can be spun into thread.   **2.** cloth made of this thread. **3.** *She bought two cotton dresses.*

cot ton wood   **1.** a kind of poplar tree: *The Cottonwood Tree is the State Tree of Kansas and of Wyoming.*   **2.** *Cottonwood seeds look like cotton balls.*

cough   **1.** *She has a bad cough.*   **2.** *He coughed hard all night.*   **coughed, cough ing.**

could   was able; was able to: *She would sing if she could.   He could eat.   They asked if I could see.*

couldn't   could not.

coun cil   a group of people chosen to settle questions or to manage a town or city.

count   **1.** name numbers in order: *The child can count up to ten.*   **2.** add up: *He counted fifty books.*   **3.** be of value: *Everything we do counts.*   **count ed, count ing.**

count er a long table in a store over which things are bought: *Put your money on the counter.*

coun try 1. the place a person lives in or comes from. 2. the land outside of a city. 3. *He likes country air.* **coun tries.**

coun ty 1. a place or government smaller than a country or state. 2. *Many people work in the county courthouse.* **coun ties.**

cou ple 1. a man and a woman who are married. 2. partners in a dance. 3. a pair.

cour age meeting danger without fear.

course 1. the direction taken: *Our course was straight north.* 2. way; path; track. 3. **Of course** means certainly; as should be expected.

court 1. a place where a king lives. 2. a place where a judge settles problems or decides how to punish people who have done wrong. 3. a place where games such as tennis and basketball are played.

court house a building in which judges work; a building used for the government of a county.

cous in the son or daughter of your uncle or aunt.

cov er 1. anything that protects or hides. 2. put something over. 3. spread over: *Dust covered his clothes.* **cov ered, cov er ing.**

cov ered 1. See **cover.** 2. *Men rode across the plains in covered wagons.*

cow a common dairy animal that gives milk.

cow ard a person who does not have courage.

cow boy a man who looks after cattle. See the picture.

coy o te a prairie wolf: *The Coyote is the State Animal of South Dakota.*

crab a water animal, used for food.

crack 1. a long, narrow break in something. 2. a sudden, sharp noise like that made by loud thunder. 3. break without separating into parts. 4. make or cause to make a sudden, sharp noise. 5. break with a sharp noise. **cracked, crack ing.**

cracked 1. See **crack.** 2. *Don't use the cracked cup.*

crack er a thin, crisp biscuit.

counter

cracker

cowboy

cra dle   a baby's little bed, usually one that rocks.

crane   **1.** a large bird that lives near water.
2. a machine for lifting and moving heavy things.

crash   **1.** a sudden, loud noise like many dishes falling and breaking.   **2.** make a loud, sudden noise: *The dishes crashed to the floor.*   **crashed, crash ing.**

crate   **1.** a large frame, box, or basket made of strips of wood, used to ship things that might break. **2.** pack in a crate for shipping.   **crat ed, crat ing.**

crawl   **1.** move slowly, pulling the body along the ground: *A worm or snake crawls.*   **2.** move slowly on hands and knees: *The boys crawled through a hole in the wall.*   crawled, **crawl ing.**

cray fish   a water animal that looks like a small lobster.   **cray fish es** or **cray fish.**

cray on   a stick or pencil of colored chalk or wax for drawing or writing.

cra zy   *That crazy man thought he was George Washington.*   **cra zi er, cra zi est.**

creak   squeak loudly: *Hinges on doors creak when they need oil.*   **creaked, creak ing.**

creak ing   *His creaking shoes disturbed the people in the library.*

cream   **1.** the oily, yellowish part of milk: *Butter is made from cream.*   **2.** *Please put some cream in the cream pitcher.*

crea ture   any living person or animal.

creek   a small stream or strip of water.

creep   move slowly with the body close to the ground or floor; crawl.   **crept, creep ing.**

crept   See **creep.**   *The baby has crept over to Mother.*

crew   **1** the men needed to do the work on a ship, or to row a boat: *We watched the crew win the race.* **2.** a group of people working together.

crib   **1.** a small bed with bars on the sides so that a baby cannot fall out.   **2.** a frame to hold food for animals.   **3.** a building or box for keeping grain or corn.

crick et   a black insect.

crisp   *Dry toast is crisp.   Fresh celery is crisp.*

croak **1.** the deep, scraping, hoarse sound made by a frog or a crow. **2.** make that deep, scraping, hoarse sound. **croaked, croak ing.**

cro cus a small plant that blooms early in spring and has white, yellow, or purple flowers. **cro cus es.**

crook ed **1.** not straight; bent; curved; twisted. **2.** not honest.

crop *Wheat, corn, and cotton are three of our main crops.* *The potato crop was very small this year.*

cross **1.** a stick with another across it like a T or an X. **2.** mark with an X or draw a line through: *He crossed out the wrong word.* **3.** move from one side to another: *We will cross a bridge.* **4.** make the sign of a cross: *The priest crossed himself.* **5.** *The baby was cross because he was sleepy, but we felt cross, too.* **cross es; crossed, cross ing; cross er, cross est.**

cross ly *He spoke crossly to me.*

crow[1] a large, shiny black bird with a loud cry.

crow[2] **1.** the loud cry of a rooster. **2.** make this cry. **crowed, crow ing.**

crowd **1.** a large number of people or things together: *A crowd gathered to hear the man speak.* **2.** collect or gather in large numbers: *Don't crowd around the swimming pool.* **crowd ed, crowd ing.**

crowd ed **1.** See **crowd.** **2.** *The crowded room was noisy.*

crown a head covering for a king or queen.

cru el ready to give pain to others or to delight in their pain: *The dog had a cruel master.* **cru el er, cru el est.**

cru el ly *She treated him cruelly.*

crumb a very small piece broken from a larger piece: *A crumb of bread fell on the floor.*

crunch **1.** crush noisily with the teeth: *He crunched the celery.* **2.** make such a sound: *The hard snow crunched under our feet.* **crunched, crunch ing.**

crush **1.** squeeze or be squeezed together very hard in order to break: *The box was crushed in the mail.* **2.** break into fine pieces by grinding, pounding, or pressing. **crushed, crush ing.**

crushed   **1.** See **crush.**   **2.** *Crushed ice is cold.*
crust   **1.** the hard outside part of bread.   **2.** the bottom part and top covering of pies.   **3.** any hard outside covering: *The crust of the snow was thick.*
cry   **1.** *We heard his cry for help.*   **2.** *He cried, "Help!"*   **3.** make a noise from pain, usually with tears.   **cries; cried, cry ing.**
cub   a young bear, fox, lion, or other large animal.
cube   a block with six square faces, or sides, all equal.
Cub Scout   a member of a group for boys: *Most Cub Scouts become Boy Scouts when they grow older.*
cun ning   **1.** smart or sly in getting what one wants, or in escaping one's enemies.   **2.** clever in doing: *With cunning hands he shaped the little pieces.*   **cun ning er, cun ning est.**
cup   **1.** a dish to drink from, usually with high sides and a handle.   **2.** something shaped like a cup.
cup board   a closet or piece of furniture with shelves for dishes or food.
curb   **1.** the raised edge along a street.   **2.** a chain or strap fastened to a horse's bit.   **3.** something that holds back.   **4.** hold back: *You must curb your laughing when you are in church.*   **curbed, curb ing.**
cure   **1.** bring back to health; make well: *The doctor cured the child of a cold.*   **2.** get rid of: *Try to cure yourself of this bad habit.*   **cured, cur ing.**
cu ri ous   **1.** eager to know: *Small children are very curious and ask many questions.*   **2.** strange; odd: *I found a curious old book.*
curl   **1.** *The girl wore her hair in curls.*   See the picture.   **2.** *Mother curls her hair.*   **3.** *You can curl up in a big chair and read.*   **curled, curl ing.**
curly   *The baby had curly hair.*   **curl i er, curl i est.**
cur rant   **1.** a small, sour, red, white, or black berry, used for jelly.   **2.** *We have two currant bushes.*
cur rent   **1.** a flow; a stream: *Running water makes a current.*   **2.** a flow of electricity through a wire.
cur tain   **1.** cloth hung at windows or doors.   **2.** a hanging screen that separates the stage of a theater from the place where the audience is.

curl
1

curve **1.** a line that has no straight part.
2. bend so as to form a line that has no straight part. **curved, curv ing.**
curved **1.** See **curve.** **2.** *We have a curved walk.*
cush ion **1.** a soft pillow or pad for a bed or chair, used to sit, lie, or kneel on. **2.** anything that makes a soft place: *Falling in a cushion of snow is fun.*
cus to di an a person whose business is taking care of a building or a collection of something.
cus tom er a person who buys.
cut **1.** an opening made by a knife or sharp-edged tool. **2.** separate, open, or take out or away with something sharp: *He has cut his hand. Who cut your hair?* **3.** *Her cut finger was very sore.* **cut, cut ting.**
cute **1.** pretty and dear: *He is a cute baby.*
2. clever; cunning. **cut er, cut est.**
cy clone **1.** a very strong windstorm. **2.** a storm moving around and toward a calm center.
cym bal one of a pair of brass plates that are struck together to make a ringing sound.

D

dachs hund a small dog with a long body.
dad father.
daf fo dil a yellow or white spring flower with long narrow leaves, grown from a bulb.
dai ly **1.** *He made a daily visit to the store.* **2.** *We go to school daily.* **3.** *Take the daily train.*
dairy **1.** a place where milk, cream, butter, and cheese are made or sold. **2.** *Her father owns a dairy farm.* **dair ies.**
dai sy a wild flower, usually white, pink, or yellow, with a yellow center. **dai sies.**
dam a wall built to hold back water.
damp a little wet: *Use a damp cloth to dust the furniture.* **damp er, damp est.**
dance **1.** *The girls were doing a new dance.*
2. *She can dance very well.* **danced, danc ing.**
danc er a person who dances.

dan de li on   a weed with bright-yellow flowers.

dan ger   **1.** a chance of harm; being near to harm: *A soldier's life is full of danger.*   **2.** a thing that may cause harm: *Hidden rocks are a danger to ships.*

dan ger ous   able to cause harm; not safe.

dan ger ous ly   *The car skidded dangerously.*

dare   **1.** *I took his dare to jump.*   **2.** *He does not dare jump from that wall.*   **3.** *I dare you to jump into the pool.*   **dared, dar ing.**

dark   **1.** darkness: *Come back after dark to see about it.*   **2.** without light: *A night without a moon is dark.*   **3.** nearly black in color: *She has dark-brown eyes and dark hair.*   **dark er, dark est.**

dark ness   being dark; having no light.

dart   **1.** a thin, pointed object thrown by the hand.   **2.** move suddenly and swiftly.   **dart ed, dart ing.**

dash   **1.** a small bit: *Put in a dash of pepper.*   **2.** rush: *They dashed by in a hurry to catch the bus.*   **dash es; dashed, dash ing.**

date[1]   **1.** time when something happens: *October 12, 1492, is the date Columbus discovered America.*   **2.** *What is the date today?*

date[2]   **1.** the sweet fruit of a kind of palm tree.   **2.** *Dates from a date palm are used in date cookies.*

daugh ter   a girl who is the child of her father and mother: *This couple has three daughters.*

dawn   **1.** the first part of day; the first light in the east: *Dawn came at last.*   **2.** *I've been here since dawn.*

day   **1.** the time of light between sunrise and sunset: *Days are longer in summer than in winter.*   **2.** the twenty-four hours of day and night.   **3.** *Take the day train.*

day break   dawn.

dead   with life gone from it: *The flowers in my garden are dead.*

deaf   **1.** not able to hear.   **2.** not willing to hear: *The king was deaf to all that the people asked.*   **deaf er, deaf est.**

deal   **1.** *We made a business deal.*   **2.** *A great deal of her money is spent for doctor's bills.*

dear　**1.** much loved: *His sister was very dear to him.*　**2.** *I visited a dear friend for a few days.*　**3.** *Oh, dear!*　**dear er, dear est.**
dear ly　*Mother loves the baby dearly.*
De cem ber　the twelfth month of the year.
de cide　**1.** settle or agree on something.　**2.** make up one's mind.　**de cid ed, de cid ing.**
deck　one of the floors of a ship. See the picture.
de clare　say; make known; say openly or strongly.　**de clared, de clar ing.**
deep　**1.** *The ocean is deep here.*　**2.** *The men dug deep before they found water.*　**3.** *She heard a deep voice.*　**deep er, deep est.**
deep ly　*The boys breathed deeply as they ran.*
deer　a swift animal that has antlers.　**deer.**
de fense　anything that guards or protects: *A wall around a city was a defense against enemies.*
def i ni tion　words that tell what something is or what a word means.
Del a ware　one of the fifty states of the United States.
de lay　**1.** putting off until a later time: *The delay upset our plans.*　**2.** put off: *We will delay the party for a week.*　**3.** make late: *The accident delayed the train for two hours.*　**de layed, de lay ing.**
del i cate　**1.** pleasing to taste; a light taste; soft.　**2.** of fine weave or make; thin; easily torn: *A spider spins a very delicate thread.*
de li cious　very pleasing or satisfying to taste or smell: *She baked a delicious cake.*
de light　**1.** great pleasure; joy.　**2.** please greatly: *The circus delights children.*　**de light ed, de light ing.**
de light ed　**1.** See **delight.**　**2.** *The delighted child laughed.*
de liv er　**1.** carry and give out: *The postman delivers letters.*　**2.** give up; hand over: *He delivered his mother's message.*　**de liv ered, de liv er ing.**
de mand　ask for in a firm manner: *The policeman demanded the truth.*　**de mand ed, de mand ing.**
den　**1.** a wild animal's home.　**2.** a small room.

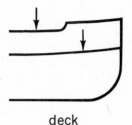
deck

dent   **1.** a hollow made by a blow or pressure: *A blow of the hammer made a dent in the steel helmet.* **2.** make a dent in: *That table has been dented in moving.*   **dent ed, dent ing.**

den tist   a doctor whose work is to care for teeth, filling them, cleaning them, making them straight, and sometimes pulling them.

de part ment   **1.** a separate part of some store, government, or business: *The fire department is a part of a city government.*   **2. Department store** means one store that sells many different kinds of things in separate parts of the store.

de pend   **1.** *You can depend on the alarm clock to ring.*   **2.** *Health depends on many things.*   **3.** *Children depend on their parents.*   **de pend ed, de pend ing.**

de pot   **1.** a railroad station.   **2.** a storehouse.

de scribe   tell in words how someone or something looks, feels, or acts.   **de scribed, de scrib ing.**

des ert   land without water and trees, usually sandy and hot in the daytime.

de sert ed   *They ran past the deserted house.*

de sire   **1.** wish: *His desire is to travel.*   **2.** wish for very much: *You may have whatever you desire.*   **de sired, de sir ing.**

desk   a piece of furniture with a slant or flat top on which to write.   See the picture.

des sert   a course of sweet food such as pie, cake, ice cream, or fruit served at the end of a meal.

de stroy   **1.** break to pieces; spoil; make no good: *Some children destroy all their toys.*   **2.** kill: *Fire destroys many trees.*   **de stroyed, de stroy ing.**

de tec tive   a policeman or person whose business is to get facts and news secretly.

de tour   **1.** a road that is used when the main road is closed.   **2.** a road going a longer way.   **3.** use a detour.   **de toured, de tour ing.**

de vel op   **1.** grow; bring or come into being: *Plants develop from seeds.*   **2.** treat film so that the picture shows: *We can see the pictures when the films are developed.*   **de vel oped, de vel op ing.**

desk

224

dew water that comes from the air and collects in small drops on cool surfaces during the night.

di al 1. an instrument that measures something, such as the amount of water in a tank or steam pressure in a boiler. 2. the knob on a radio or television for tuning in to a station. See the pictures. 3. the part of a telephone used in making telephone calls. 4. call by means of a telephone dial: *He dialed his father's office.* **di aled, di al ing.**

dia mond 1. a hard stone of great value. 2. a figure shaped like this ◇. 3. part of a baseball field. See the picture under **baseball.** 4. *Her mother has a diamond ring.*

dic tion ary a book in which words are listed alphabetically and that can be used to find out the meanings of words and how to say and spell them. **dic tion ar ies.**

did See **do.** *Did he go to school yesterday? Yes, he did. He said he did not do it.*

did n't did not.

die 1. stop living; become dead. 2. lose force; come to an end: *The music died away.* **died, dy ing.**

die sel *The truck has a diesel engine.*

dif fer not be like: *My answers differed from hers.* **dif fered, dif fer ing.**

dif fer ence 1. being different: *There is a great difference between night and day.* 2. what is left after subtracting one number from another: *The difference between 6 and 15 is 9.*

dif fer ent not alike; separate: *People have different names. We called three different times.*

dif fer ent ly *They both saw the same thing but described it differently.*

dig 1. make a hole in or turn over the ground. 2. make or get by digging. **dug, dig ging.**

dime 1. a silver coin of the United States and Canada. 2. *A dime is equal to ten cents.*

dine eat dinner. **dined, din ing.**

din ner the main meal of the day: *Some people have dinner at night, but many people have dinner at noon.*

dial

di no saur   a reptile that lived many years ago.

dip   **1.** put under water or any liquid and lift out
quickly.   **2.** go under water and come out
quickly.   **dipped, dip ping.**

di plo ma cy   skill in getting along with people:
He used diplomacy to get what he wanted. **di plo ma cies.**

dip per   **1.** a thing that dips.   **2.** a long-handled
cup or container for lifting water or other liquids.

di rect   **1.** manage; control; guide: *The conductor
directed the orchestra.*   **2.** command: *The captain
directed his men to move.*   **3.** show the way: *Can you
direct me to the airport?*   **di rect ed, di rect ing.**

di rec tion   **1.** guiding; managing; control: *The
school is under the direction of a good teacher.*
2. telling where to go or how to do: *Can you give me
directions to the lake?   Follow the directions on the
box.*   **3.** any way in which one may face or point:
North, south, east, and west are directions.

dirt   **1.** mud, dust, earth, or anything like them.
2. loose earth or soil.   **3.** *We got stuck on a dirt road.*

dirty   not clean; soiled by mud, dust, earth, or
anything like them.   **dirt i er, dirt i est.**

dis ap pear   **1.** pass from sight: *The ship
disappeared in the fog.*   **2.** be gone or lost: *Snow
disappears in the spring.*   **dis ap peared, dis ap pear ing.**

dis cov er   find out; see for the first time: *Columbus
discovered America.*   **dis cov ered, dis cov er ing.**

dish   **1.** a container for food: *We eat from dishes.*
2. food served: *My favorite dish is pie.*   **dish es.**

dis mount   get off a horse, bicycle,
and so on.   **dis mount ed, dis mount ing.**

dis tance   **1.** space in between: *The distance from
the farm to the town is five miles.*   **2.** being far away:
The farm is at a distance from any railroad.   **3.** a place
far away: *The sailors saw a light in the distance.*

dis tant   **1.** *The moon is distant from the earth.*
2. *I saw a distant light.*

Dis trict of Co lum bia   a piece of land owned
by the government and covered by Washington, the
capital of the United States.

dis turb 1. destroy the peace, quiet, or rest of. 2. break in upon with noise or change: *Do not disturb the baby; he is asleep.* **dis turbed, dis turb ing.**

ditch a long, narrow place along the edge of a road, used to carry off water. **ditch es.**

dive 1. a head-first plunge into water. 2. plunge head first into water. **dived** or **dove, dived, div ing.**

div er one who dives for fun or as a business.

di vide 1. give some of to each; share: *The children divided the candy.* 2. separate into parts: *When you divide 8 by 2, you get 4.* **di vid ed, di vid ing.**

di vid ed 1. See **divide.** 2. *He took his part of the divided cake.*

diz zy ready to fall, stumble, or spin around; not steady: *Do you feel dizzy?* **diz zi er, diz zi est.**

do 1. carry to an end an act or piece of work; carry out; perform: *Do your work well.* 2. act; behave: *He is doing very well today.* 3. *Do come, please. Do you like milk? We do not want to go, do we? My dog goes where I do.* 4. **Do up** means wrap up. **did, done, do ing.**

dock 1. a platform built out from the shore. 2. *The boys docked the sailboat.* **docked, dock ing.**

doc tor a person whose business is to cure the sick.

doe a female deer, antelope, rabbit, or hare.

does See **do.** *He does his work well. He does very well now. Does she like milk? She does not want to go, does she? Will you behave as he does?*

does n't does not.

dog 1. an animal used as a pet, for hunting, and for guarding property. 2. *Run and get some dog food.*

dog wood 1. a tree with white or pink flowers: *The American Dogwood is the State Tree of Virginia; the Flowering Dogwood is the State Tree of Missouri; Dogwood is the State Flower of North Carolina and of Virginia.* 2. *Dogwood trees have lovely blossoms.*

doll a toy that looks like a person.

dol lar 1. a large silver coin or a paper bill of United States money. 2. *A dollar is worth one hundred cents.*

disturb

dollar

227

dol phin 1. a small whale. 2. a large sea fish that changes color when it is taken out of the water.

done See **do.** *Have you done all your homework?*

don key a small animal like a horse.

don't do not.

door 1. a moving part that turns on hinges or slides open and shut to close an opening in a wall. 2. doorway: *Meet me at the door of the theater.*

dose the amount of medicine to be taken at once.

dot 1. a small spot or point; a tiny round mark: *There is a dot over each "i" in this line.* 2. mark with a dot or dots. 3. be here and there in: *Boats dotted the lake.* **dot ted, dot ting.**

dot ted 1. See **dot.** 2. *He wore a dotted tie.*

dou ble 1. two times as much, as large, or as strong. 2. twice. 3. become or make twice as much: *The number of people at the fire quickly doubled. He doubled his money.* 4. fold over: *The boy doubled his fists.* **dou bled, dou bling.**

doubt 1. not believe; not be sure; feel uncertain: *The captain doubted that the ship would sink.* 2. **No doubt** means certainly. **doubt ed, doubt ing.**

dough nut a small, sweet cake usually made in the shape of a ring.

dove a bird with a thick body; a pigeon.

down[1] 1. to a lower place; in a lower place: *They ran down from the top of the hill.* 2. down along: *You can ride down a hill or walk down a street.*

down[2] soft feathers; soft hair.

doz en twelve; a group of twelve things.

drag pull or move along the ground: *She dragged the old box.* **dragged, drag ging.**

drag on in stories, a creature like a huge winged snake that often breathes fire.

drag on fly a large, harmless insect with a long, thin body and two pairs of wings. **drag on flies.**

drain 1. a pipe for carrying off water or waste. 2. draw off; draw liquid from: *The baby drained his bottle.* 3. *Set the dishes here on the sink to drain.* **drained, drain ing.**

drank   See **drink**.   *She drank her milk an hour ago.*

draw   make a picture of anything with pen, pencil, or chalk.   **drew, drawn, draw ing.**

draw er   a box, with handles, built to slide in and out of a table or desk.

drawn   See **draw**.   *She has drawn a picture.*

dream   **1.** something thought, felt, or seen during sleep.   **2.** something not real: *The boy had dreams of being king.*   **3.** think, feel, hear, or see during sleep.   **4.** form fancies; imagine: *The girl dreamed of being in the movies.*   **dreamed** or **dreamt, dream ing.**

dreary   not cheerful; gloomy: *Cloudy days are often very dreary.*   **drear i er, drear i est.**

dress   **1.** a piece of clothing worn by women and girls: *Mother bought me a new dress for school.*   **2.** put clothes on.   **3.** make ready for use or to cook: *Mother dressed the turkey.*   **4.** clean and cover a wound. **5.** *Wear your dress shoes today.*   **dressed, dress ing.**

dressed   **1.** See **dress**.   **2.** *The dressed turkey was in the oven.*   *She was a well-dressed girl.*

dress er   a piece of furniture with drawers for clothes and usually a mirror.

dress ing   **1.** a sauce for salads, fish, meat. **2.** bread crumbs and other things used to stuff poultry.   **3.** medicine and a bandage put on a wound.

drew   See **draw**.   *He drew a picture of his mother.*

dried   **1.** See **dry**.   **2.** *Dried fruit is good in pie.*

drift   **1.** snow, sand, and so on, heaped up by the wind.   **2.** be carried along by currents of air or water: *A boat drifts.*   **3.** heap or be heaped up by the wind: *The wind drifts the snow.*   **drift ed, drift ing.**

drill[1]   **1.** a tool for boring holes.   **2.** doing a thing over and over for practice: *The class needs some drill in arithmetic.*   **3.** bore a hole.   **4.** teach by having something done over and over.   **drilled, drill ing.**

drill[2]   a machine for planting seeds in rows. See the picture.

drink   **1.** liquid swallowed to make one less thirsty: *The baby wants a drink.*   **2.** swallow anything liquid: *Drink water every day.*   **drank, drunk, drink ing.**

drill[2]

229

drip   fall or let fall in drops: *Rain drips from an umbrella.*   **dripped, drip ping.**

drive   **1.** going in a car: *We went for a drive in the country.*   **2.** a road: *He built a drive to his house.*   **3.** make go: *Drive the dog away.*   **4.** operate: *Can you drive a car?*   **drove, driv en, driv ing.**

driv en   See **drive.**   *Mother has just driven past.*

drop   **1.** a small amount of liquid in a round shape.   **2.** very small amount: *Drink a drop of this.*   **3.** a sudden fall: *There was a drop of thirty feet below the cliff.*   **4.** fall suddenly: *The cat dropped from the tree.*   **5.** let fall.   **dropped, drop ping.**

drove   See **drive.**   *We drove twenty miles yesterday.*

drown   **1.** die under water or other liquid because of having no air to breathe.   **2.** kill by holding under water or other liquid.   **drowned, drown ing.**

drug   something used as medicine or to put a person to sleep.

drug gist   a person who sells drugs and medicines.

drug store   a store where drugs are sold.

drum

drum   a hollow instrument, with animal skin stretched over the ends, that makes a sound when it is beaten with a stick. See the picture.

drum mer   a person who plays the drum.

drunk   See **drink.**   *The child has drunk his juice.*

dry   **1.** make dry: *She was drying dishes.*   **2.** not wet; not damp: *Dust is dry.*   **3.** having little or no rain: *This was a dry summer.*   **4.** not interesting: *I found the book dry and hard to read.*   **dried, dry ing; dri er, dri est.**

dry er   **1.** a thing that dries.   **2.** a machine that removes water: *Put the wet clothes in the dryer.*

duch ess   **1.** the wife of a duke.   **2.** a woman who is equal to a duke.   **duch ess es.**

duck[1]   a swimming bird with a flat bill.

duck[2]   **1.** dip the head or body under water and come up quickly, as a duck does; put under water for a short time.   **2.** bend the body quickly to keep off a blow.   **ducked, duck ing.**

dug   See **dig.**   *The dog dug a hole in the ground.*

duke   a man of very high birth or who has been given a high position by a king.

dumb   **1.** not able to speak: *Even smart animals are dumb.*   **2.** silent; not speaking.   **dumb er, dumb est.**

dump   **1.** a place for throwing garbage and waste. **2.** a heap of garbage and waste.   **3.** empty out; throw down.   **dumped, dump ing.**

dur ing   **1.** *The boys played during the afternoon.* **2.** *Come sometime during the day.*

dust   **1.** fine, dry dirt or earth; any fine powder: *Dust lay thick in the street.*   **2.** get dust off; brush or wipe the dust from: *Mother dusts the furniture every day.*   **3.** sprinkle with: *The nurse dusted powder over the baby.*   **dust ed, dust ing.**

dusty   **1.** covered with dust; filled with dust. **2.** dry and powdery.   **dust i er, dust i est.**

du ty   **1.** the thing that is right to do; what a person ought to do: *It is your duty to obey the laws.* **2.** the things a person has to do in doing his work: *The mailman's duties were to carry and deliver the mail.*   **3.** a tax on things you bring into or take out of the country.   **du ties.**

E

each   **1.** every one of: *Each boy has a name.* **2.** for each: *These pencils are five cents each.*

ea ger   wanting very much: *The child is eager to have the candy.   The eager boy tried to hit the ball.*

ea ger ly   *The puppy ran eagerly to the boy.*

ea gle   a large, strong bird that can see far.

ear[1]   the part of the body by which people and animals hear.   See the picture under **head.**

ear[2]   the part of certain plants that contains the grains.   See the picture.

ear ly   **1.** *In his early years he liked ships.* **2.** *She came to school early.*   **3.** *Take an early train.*   **ear li er, ear li est.**

earn   get a reward in return for doing something: *He earned his Boy Scout pin.*   **earned, earn ing.**

ear[2]

231

earth 1. the planet on which we live, a great ball that moves around the sun. 2. ground: *The earth in his garden is good, soft soil.* 3. *We are Earth men.*

ea sel a stand for holding a picture or chalkboard.

eas i ly *We can easily finish the work by tonight.*

east 1. the direction of the sunrise; opposite of west. 2. *Walk east to find the road.* 3. coming from the east: *An east wind is blowing.* 4. *Follow the east fork of the road.*

East er 1. a yearly holiday that comes on a Sunday in the spring. 2. *She wore her new Easter hat.*

east ern 1. toward the east: *Father took an eastern trip.* 2. from the east: *We have some eastern visitors.*

east ward toward the east.

easy 1. not hard to do or understand: *This was an easy lesson.* 2. free from pain or trouble: *Do it the easy way.* **eas i er, eas i est.**

eat chew and swallow food or have a meal. ate, **eat en, eat ing.**

eat en See eat. *Have you eaten your dinner?*

edge 1. the line or place where something ends; the part farthest from the middle; the side: *The edge of the paper is straight. He stood at the edge of the road.* 2. the thin side that cuts: *The knife had a very sharp edge.*

ed it 1. prepare writing to be printed: *The teacher edited our stories.* 2. be in charge of a newspaper and decide what shall be printed in it: *Two girls edit the class newspaper.* **ed it ed, ed it ing.**

ed i tor a person who edits.

ed u ca tion learning by going to school: *In the United States, education is free to all children.*

eel a long fish shaped like a snake.

egg *Birds and fish are hatched from eggs.*

eight 1. one more than seven. 2. *Come at eight o'clock in the morning.*

eight een 1. eight more than ten. 2. *She was born eighteen years ago.*

eight eenth 1. next after the seventeenth. 2. *Tuesday was the eighteenth of January.*

eighth   **1.** next after the seventh.   **2.** *August eighth is my birthday.*

eight i eth   next after the seventy-ninth: *Today is Grandfather's eightieth birthday.*

eighty   eight times ten.   **eight ies.**

ei ther   **1.** one or the other of two: *A door must be either shut or open.   Either come in or go out.*   **2.** each of two: *On either side of the river are fields of corn.*   **3.** *If you do not go, I shall not go either.*

el bow   **1.** the joint in the middle of the arm.   See the picture under **arm.**   **2.** any bend: *We came to an elbow in the river.*

elec tric   run by electricity: *We have electric lights.*

elec tri cian   a person whose business is repairing electric wires, lights, motors, and so on.

elec tric i ty   **1.** a kind of force that causes certain metals to pull together or push apart, that makes light and heat, and that runs motors.   **2.** electric current: *Many refrigerators are run by electricity.*

el e phant   the largest four-footed animal.

el e va tor   **1.** a vehicle for carrying people or things up and down.   **2.** a part of an airplane that helps lift it.   See the picture under **airplane.**   **3.** a building for storing grain.

elev en   **1.** one more than ten.   **2.** *I started at eleven o'clock.*

elev enth   **1.** next after the tenth.   **2.** *Today is the eleventh of May.*

elf   in stories, a tiny man that is full of mischief; a fairy.   **elves.**

elk   a large deer.

elm   **1.** a tall shade tree: *The American Elm is the State Tree of Massachusetts, of Nebraska, and of North Dakota.*   **2.** *Elm trees are beautiful.*

else   other; different; instead: *Will somebody else speak? Shall we go somewhere else tomorrow? What else could I say?*

emp ty   **1.** pour out or take out all.   **2.** flow out: *The river empties into the ocean.*   **3.** *Throw away the empty can.*   **emp tied, emp ty ing; emp ti er, emp ti est.**

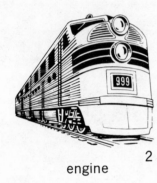

engine 2

end   **1.** the last part; the part where a thing begins or where it stops: *Every stick has two ends.*   **2.** finish something: *Let's end this fight right now.*   **3.** *Knock on the end door.*   **4.** *Drive to the end of this road.*   **5.** *The children were tired at the end of the day.*   **end ed, end ing.**

en e my   **1.** one who is against you or not a friend.   **2.** anything that will harm: *Frost is an enemy of flowers.*   **3.** *The soldiers watched for enemy aircraft day and night.*   **en e mies.**

en gine   **1.** a machine, run by gas, oil, electricity, or steam, that does work or makes something move: *Engines make automobiles go.*   **2.** the machine that pulls a railroad train.   See the picture.

en gi neer   **1.** a person who plans and builds or takes care of machines, roads, bridges, and buildings.   **2.** the man who runs a train engine.

en joy   be happy or have fun with: *We enjoy games.*   **en joyed, en joy ing.**

enor mous   very, very large.

enough   as many or as much as needed: *Has he had enough to eat?   Are there enough seats for all?   Have you played enough?*

en ter   go into; come into: *We enter a room through the door.*   **en tered, en ter ing.**

en trance   **1.** the act of coming in: *The fireman's entrance was swift.*   **2.** the place by which to enter: *Where is the entrance to the hall?*

en try   **1.** a word and how it is explained in a dictionary.   **2.** *Entry words are easy to find in this book.*   **en tries.**

en ve lope   a folded paper cover or case for a letter or for anything flat.

equal   the same in amount, size, or number: *Ten dimes are equal to one dollar.*

equal ly   *The two sisters are equally pretty.*

erase   rub out or scrape away: *He erased the wrong answer and wrote in the right one.*   **erased, eras ing.**

eras er   a thing used to rub out or to erase.

es ca la tor   moving stairs.

es cape **1.** act of getting away: *The escape was made at night.* **2.** get free or get out and away: *The bird escaped from its cage.* **es caped, es cap ing.**

Es ki mo **1.** one of the people who live on the most northern shores of North America and Asia.
2. *An Eskimo house is sometimes made of skins.*

Eu rope part of the largest mass of land on the earth.

eve **1.** the evening or day before some holiday or special day: *Carolers sing on Christmas Eve.*
2. evening.

even **1.** level, flat, or smooth: *See that the edges of the paper are even.* **2.** equal; no more or less than: *They divided the money in even shares.* **3.** that can be divided by two without a remainder: *Two, four, six, eight, and ten are even numbers.* **4.** at the same level: *The snow is even with the window.* **5.** *Even children can do it. You can read even better if you try.*

eve ning the time between day and night, between sunset and bedtime.

even ly *Spread the frosting evenly on the cake. Divide the money evenly.*

event something important that happens: *The king's visit was an exciting event.*

ev er at any time: *Is he ever at home?*

ev er green **1.** a plant that has green leaves all the year. **2.** *Pines are evergreen trees.*

eve ry **1.** each: *Every boy must have his own book.*
2. Every now and then means from time to time.
3. Every other one means every second one.

ewe a female sheep.

ex act without any mistake; correct: *Give the girl the exact amount of our bill.*

ex act ly *Your papers must be exactly right.*

ex am ine **1.** look at closely and carefully: *The doctor will examine the wound.* **2.** test; ask questions of. **ex am ined, ex am in ing.**

ex am ple one thing taken to show what the others are like or should be like: *New York is an example of a busy city. He is a good example to follow.*

235

ex cel lent very, very good or better than others: *He did excellent work.*

ex cel lent ly *The meal was excellently prepared.*

ex cept other than: *He works every day except Sunday.   Except for two things the party was fun.*

ex cit ed stirred up or eager: *The excited crowd clapped loudly.*

ex cit ed ly *The boys shouted excitedly when the ball was caught.*

ex cite ment feeling excited: *The baby's first step caused great excitement in the family.*

ex claim speak or cry out suddenly with strong feeling.   **ex claimed, ex claim ing.**

ex cla ma tion something said suddenly with strong feeling: *Her only exclamation was "Well!"*

ex cuse **1.** a reason given to explain something you said or did: *There is no excuse for bad manners.* **2.** *He brought an excuse from home.*   **3.** give a reason: *She excused herself by saying her watch was broken.*   **4.** pardon somebody: *She excused his lateness today.*   **5.** allow to leave: *May I be excused from the table?*   **6. Excuse me** means pardon me or I'm sorry.   **ex cused, ex cus ing.**

ex er cise **1.** something that gives practice: *Do the exercises in your book.*   **2.** use; practice: *An athlete exercises every day.*   **ex er cised, ex er cis ing.**

ex pect look for or think something will probably come or happen: *We expect hot days in summer.*   **ex pect ed, ex pect ing.**

ex per i ment **1.** a test to find out something: *Scientists test ideas by experiments.*   **2.** test or try something out: *A baby experiments with his fingers and toes.*   **ex per i ment ed, ex per i ment ing.**

ex plain **1.** make plain or clear: *The teacher explained the hard arithmetic problem.*   **2.** give reasons for: *Can somebody explain why she laughed at me?* **ex plained, ex plain ing.**

ex plore go over a place and examine it: *The children explored the new house from attic to cellar.*   **ex plored, ex plor ing.**

ex press   1. put into words: *Try to express your idea clearly.*   2. send by some quick means: *I'll express the package.*   3. *Take an express train home from the city.*   **ex pressed, ex press ing.**

ex press way   a highway, without traffic lights, for fast traveling.

ex tra   1. beyond what is usual, expected, or needed: *The men asked for extra pay for extra work.*
2. *Have you an extra nickel?*

eye   1. the part of the body by which you see. See the picture under **face**.   2. something like an eye: *Can you see the eye in the needle?*

F

face   1. the front part of the head.   See the picture.
2. *The boy made a face at his sister.*   3. *The face of the clock is silver.*   See the picture under **clock**.
4. have the front toward: *The house faces the street.*
5. meet bravely: *The man faced his problem and solved it.*   **faced, fac ing.**

fact   a thing known to be true.

fac to ry   a building or group of buildings where things are made, usually by machines.   **fac to ries.**

fade   1. lose color: *My dress faded when it was washed.*   2. die away: *The sound faded after the train went by.*   3. cause to fade: *Sunlight faded my new dress.*   **fad ed, fad ing.**

fad ed   1. See **fade**.   2. *He threw away his faded shirt.*

fail   1. not succeed; not be able to do: *He tried hard to learn to sing, but he failed.*   2. not do what should be done: *He failed to follow directions.*   3. **Without fail** means surely.   **failed, fail ing.**

faint   1. fall down and lie as if asleep, not knowing what is going on.   2. *The print was so faint I couldn't read it.*   3. *He called for help in a faint voice.*   **faint ed, faint ing; faint er, faint est.**

faint ly   *His voice was heard faintly inside the cave.*

fair[1]   a show or sale, often of farm animals and things such as clothes and canned food.

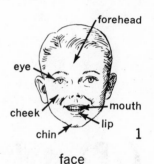

face

fair[2] **1.** not favoring one more than any other; honest: *A fair judge decided to let the man go.* **2.** going by the rules: *Be sure to play fair.* **3.** not good and not bad: *The crop of wheat this year is fair.* **4.** not cloudy or stormy: *The weather will be fair today.* **fair er, fair est.**

fair ly *The game was played fairly.*

fairy 1. in stories, a tiny person with magic power. **2.** *We like to read fairy stories.* **fair ies.**

fal con a hawk trained to hunt and kill other birds.

fall 1. dropping or coming down from a higher place: *The fall from his horse hurt him.* **2.** drop or come down from a higher place: *Snow is falling fast.* **3.** the part of the year between summer and winter; autumn. **4.** *This is going to be a beautiful fall day.* **fell, fall en, fall ing.**

fall en See **fall.** *Much rain has fallen.*

fam i ly 1. father, mother, and their children. **2.** all of a person's relatives. **3.** *She is a family friend.* **fam i lies.**

fa mous very well known; important.

fan 1. an instrument with which to stir the air in order to cool it or to blow dust away. See the pictures. **2.** stir the air; stir up. **fanned, fan ning.**

fan cy 1. the power to imagine: *Fairies and giants are creatures of fancy.* **2.** not plain: *She wore a fancy blue dress.* **fan cies; fan ci er, fan ci est.**

far 1. a long way; a long way off: *The moon is far from the earth, but the sun is farther. What planet is farthest of all?* **2.** much: *It is far better to go by train.* **far ther, far thest.**

fare the money that a person pays to ride.

farm 1. land used to raise crops or animals. **2.** raise crops or animals to eat or to sell. **3.** *We looked at all the farm animals.* **farmed, farm ing.**

farm er a man whose business is farming.

fash ion 1. the way a thing is shaped or done: *He walks in a straight fashion.* **2.** make, shape, or form: *He fashioned a whistle out of a piece of wood.* **fash ioned, fash ion ing.**

1

fan

fast[1] **1.** quick; rapid; swift: *The fastest runner will win.* **2.** quickly; rapidly; swiftly: *Airplanes go faster than cars.* **3.** showing a time ahead of the real time: *That clock is fast.* **4.** firmly: *The leaves stuck fast to the wall.* **fast er, fast est.**

fast[2] go without food. **fast ed, fast ing.**

fas ten tie, lock, or make hold together: *Fasten your cap before you go out.* **fas tened, fas ten ing.**

fat **1.** a white or yellow oily mass formed in the body of an animal. **2.** *That fat boy is fatter than his brother.* **fat ter, fat test.**

fa ther **1.** a male parent. **2.** *A priest is called "Father."*

fault **1.** something that is not as it should be. **2. Find fault with** means find things wrong with something or someone. **3.** cause for blame: *Whose fault was it?*

fa vor ite liked best: *What is your favorite flower?*

fawn a baby deer.

fear **1.** a feeling that danger or something bad is near. **2.** feel fear; be afraid of. **feared, fear ing.**

feast **1.** a big meal for some special party: *We went to the wedding feast.* **2.** eat many good things: *They feasted on chicken.* **feast ed, feast ing.**

feath er **1.** one of the light, thin objects that cover a bird's skin. **2.** *Feather pillows are soft.*

Feb ru ary the second month of the year.

fed See **feed.** *We fed the birds yesterday.*

fee ble weak: *A feeble old man was calling for help.* **fee bler, fee blest.**

fee bly *The sick girl raised her head feebly.*

feed **1.** food for animals: *You know where your chicken feed is.* **2.** give food to: *We feed babies from bottles.* **3.** eat: *Cows feed on hay.* **fed, feed ing.**

feel **1.** touch: *Feel the cloth.* **2.** try to find by touching: *He was feeling in his pocket for a marble.* **3.** find out by touching: *He could feel the cool breeze.* **4.** be; have in the mind: *She feels glad.* **felt, feel ing.**

feet more than one foot: *A dog has four feet.* *He is three feet tall.*

239

fence

fell See **fall.** *Snow fell last night.*

fel low *He looked at the poor fellow in the street.*

felt[1] **1.** cloth made by rolling and pressing wool, hair, or fur together. **2.** *A felt hat is warm.*

felt[2] See **feel.** *He felt the cat's soft fur.*

fe male **1.** a woman or girl; a kind of person or animal that brings forth young. **2.** *Cows and hens are female animals.*

fence something, usually made of wood, wire, or metal, put around a yard, garden, or field to show where it ends or to keep people and animals out or in. See the pictures.

fend er something that protects by being between: *Automobile fenders protect the car from bumps.*

fern a kind of plant that has no flowers.

fer ry **1.** a place where boats carry people and things across a river or narrow strip of water. **2.** the boat. **3.** carry people and things across a river or strip of water. **fer ries; fer ried, fer ry ing.**

fes ti val **1.** a day or special time of feasting. **2.** *Every year the city has a music festival.*

few **1.** not many: *Few men are seven feet tall.* **2.** a small number: *Winter in some places has only a few warm days.* **few er, few est.**

field **1.** land used for crops or for pasture. **2.** *Our school has a baseball field.* **3.** in baseball, stop a batted ball and throw it in. **4.** *We saw a small field mouse.* **field ed, field ing.**

fierce wild: *A fierce lion roared. A fierce wind blew down the tree.* **fierc er, fierc est.**

fierce ly *The lion roared fiercely.*

fife a musical instrument.

fif teen **1.** five more than ten. **2.** *It is fifteen minutes after two.*

fif teenth **1.** next after the fourteenth. **2.** *He went on the fifteenth of May.*

fifth **1.** next after the fourth. **2.** *Tomorrow is the fifth of February.*

fif ti eth **1.** next after the forty-ninth. **2.** *This is their fiftieth year in business.*

fif ty   **1.** five times ten.   **2.** *Fifty years ago his father began the business.*   **fif ties.**

fig   **1.** a small fruit that grows in warm places. **2.** *Fig bars are good cookies.*

fight   **1.** a struggle or contest.   **2.** a bad quarrel. **3.** take part in a struggle.   **fought, fight ing.**

fig ure   **1.** a mark or sign that stands for a number, such as 1, 2, 3, 4.   **2.** use numbers to find out the answer to some problem.   **3.** *A four-figure number is one like 2580.*   **4. Figure out** means think out; understand.   **fig ured, fig ur ing.**

file[1]   **1.** a place for keeping papers in order. **2.** persons or things one behind another: *The soldiers marched in single file.*   **3.** put away papers in order: *She filed the letters in a drawer.*   **filed, fil ing.**

file[2]   **1.** a tool with many fine, sharp edges on it, used to smooth or wear away hard surfaces. **2.** smooth or wear away with a file: *He filed the key until the edge was smooth and would not stick in the lock.*   **filed, fil ing.**

fill   **1.** put into until there is no more room; make full.   **2.** take up all the space in: *Children filled the room.*   **3.** stop up or close by putting something in: *The farmer dug out the stump and filled the hole with dirt.*   **filled, fill ing.**

film   **1.** a very thin surface or covering, often of liquid: *There was a film of oil on the water.*   **2.** a roll or sheet of thin material used to take pictures. **3.** a movie: *We saw a film about animals.*

fin   one of the parts of a fish with which it swims and balances itself.   See the picture.

fi nal   coming last; deciding; closing the question: *Here is the final report.*

fi nal ly   *We finally came to the river.*

finch   a small songbird: *The Eastern Goldfinch is the State Bird of Iowa and of New Jersey. The American Goldfinch is the State Bird of Minnesota.   The Purple Finch is the State Bird of New Hampshire, and the Willow Goldfinch is the State Bird of Washington.*   **finch es.**

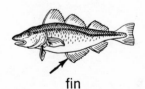

fin

241

find   **1.** meet; come upon: *Did he find a dollar?*
2. look for and get: *Please find my hat.*   **3.** get: *Can you find time to do this?*   **4.** learn; discover: *We may find that he could not swim.*   **found, find ing.**

fine[1]   **1.** *The man paid a fine for speeding.*
2. *The judge fined him ten dollars.*   **fined, fin ing.**

fine[2]   **1.** very small or thin: *Thread is finer than rope.   Sugar is ground fine.*   **2.** excellent: *We praised her fine singing.*   **fin er, fin est.**

fin ger   one of the five end parts of the hand. See the picture under **arm.**

fin ish   **1.** complete; bring to an end; get to the end of: *Finish your dinner before you go.*   **2.** *It was a close race from start to finish.*   **fin ished, fin ish ing.**

fir   **1.** a tree somewhat like a pine, often used for a Christmas tree: *The Douglas Fir is the State Tree of Oregon.*   **2.** *There are many kinds of fir trees.*

fire   **1.** flame, heat, and light that feed upon something and destroy it: *The fire burned the coal to ashes.*   **2.** *A fire truck came up the street.*

fire fly   a small insect that gives off flashes of light when it flies at night.   **fire flies.**

fire man   **1.** a man whose work is putting out fires.
2. a man who looks after fires in engines.   **fire men.**

fire works   skyrockets and other things that burst into bright lights and make a loud noise.

firm   not moving when pressed or pushed: *The men stood firm against the king.   He felt firm ground under his feet and stopped swimming.*   **firm er, firm est.**

firm ly   *She held her sister firmly by the hand.*

first   **1.** *He is first in his class.   What is your first name?*   **2.** *We eat first and then feed the cat.*
3. *At first he did not like school.*

fish   **1.** an animal that lives in the water and has fins but no legs.   **2.** fish used for food.   **3.** catch fish; try to catch fish.   **4.** *Give your fish some fish food.*   **fish es** or **fish; fished, fish ing.**

fist   the hand closed tightly: *He shook his fist at me.*

fit[1]   a sudden, short period of doing or feeling something: *The girls had a fit of laughing.*

fit[2] **1.** be right or correct: *The dress fits her well.*
2. try to make right: *She fitted the collar onto the dress.*
3. right: *Grass is a fit food for cows; it is not fit for men to eat.* **4.** feeling well and strong: *He is fit for work.* **fit ted, fit ting; fit ter, fit test.**

five **1.** one more than four. **2.** *Come at five o'clock.*

fix **1.** make firm or tight: *The man fixed the post in the ground. The boy fixed the date in his mind.*
2. put in order; arrange: *Fix your hair.* **3.** mend: *Can he fix a watch?* **fixed, fix ing.**

fixed **1.** See **fix.** **2.** *He looked at me with fixed eyes.*

flag a piece of colored cloth, usually almost square, that stands for some country or thing.

Flag Day June 14, the day in 1777 when the Stars and Stripes became the flag of the United States.

flake a flat, thin piece, usually not very large and easily broken loose or broken apart: *Flakes of rust fell off the old iron door.*

flame one of the hot glowing tongues of light, usually red or yellow, that come when a fire blazes up.

fla min go a wading bird with pink or red feathers.

flap **1.** *There is a flap on his pocket.* **2.** *With a flap of its wings the bird left the tree.* **3.** *The sail flapped against the side of the boat.* **4.** *The goose flapped its wings.* **flapped, flap ping.**

flare **1.** a bright, unsteady flame. **2.** blaze for a minute, sometimes with smoke. **flared, flar ing.**

flash **1.** a sudden light or flame. **2.** give out such a light or flame. **3.** come and go quickly: *A bird flashed across the road.* **flash es; flashed, flash ing.**

flash light a light run by batteries. See the picture.

flashlight

flat[1] an apartment or set of rooms on one floor.

flat[2] **1.** smooth and level; even: *This floor is flat.*
2. not very deep or thick: *A plate is a flat dish.*
3. *The boy fell flat on the ground.* **4.** in music, a tone one half step below; the sign (♭). **flat ter, flat test.**

flew See **fly**[2]. *The bird flew high in the air.*

flick er shine with an unsteady light: *The light from the fire flickered on the walls.* **flick ered, flick er ing.**

1

2

float

flight¹ **1.** act or manner of flying: *Watch the flight of a bird through the air.* **2.** a ride in an airplane: *We took the first flight after the weather cleared.* **3.** set of stairs or steps from one landing or one story of a building to the next: *We live one flight up.*

flight² running away; escape: *Their flight was discovered when he saw the broken lock.*

fling throw; throw with force: *Fling a stone into the water.* **flung, fling ing.**

flip toss or move by the snap of a finger and thumb: *The man flipped a coin.* **flipped, flip ping.**

float **1.** anything that stays up or holds up something in water: *A cork on a fish line is a float.* **2.** a flat car that carries something in a parade. See the pictures. **3.** stay on top of or be held up by air or water: *A cork will float.* **4.** move along without trying; be moved along in or on something: *The boat floated out to sea.* **float ed, float ing.**

flock **1.** *We watched a flock of geese fly past.* **2.** *Sheep usually flock together.* **flocked, flock ing.**

flood **1.** a flow of water over what is usually dry land; a large amount of water. **2.** fill over the top. **3.** flow over. **flood ed, flood ing.**

floor **1.** the part of a room to walk on. **2.** a story or one level of a building: *Five families live on the fourth floor.*

flop move, fall; drop loosely or heavily: *The fish flopped helplessly on the deck.* **flopped, flop ping.**

Flor i da one of the fifty states of the United States.

floun der a flat fish.

flour the fine powder, made by grinding wheat or rye, which is used in cooking.

flow run like water: *A stream flows past the house.* **flowed, flow ing.**

flow er **1.** the part of a plant or tree, often beautiful in color and shape, that produces the seed. **2.** *We have a flower box on the window sill.*

flow er ing *We took a flowering plant to our teacher.*

flown See **fly²**. *The bird has flown away.*

flung See **fling**. *The boy flung the ball.*

flute a musical instrument.
fly[1] an insect with two wings. **flies.**
fly[2] **1.** move through the air with wings: *These birds fly long distances.* **2.** float in the air: *Our flag flies every day.* **3.** cause to fly: *The boys are flying kites.* **4.** go through the air in an airplane: *We are flying to Mexico.* **flew, flown, fly ing.**
fly catch er a bird that catches insects while flying: *The Scissor-Tailed Flycatcher is the State Bird of Oklahoma.*
fog a cloud of fine drops of water just above the ground, thick and white, hard or sometimes impossible to see through.
fold[1] **1.** a layer of something folded: *Put two folds in this paper.* **2.** bend or double over on itself: *You fold a letter or a blanket.* **3.** bend close to the body: *You fold your arms.* **fold ed, fold ing.**
fold[2] a pen for sheep. See the picture.

fold[2]

fol low **1.** go or come after: *Let's follow him. Night follows day.* **2.** go along something: *Follow this road to the corner.* **3.** use or act as you are told: *He has followed the directions.* **fol lowed, fol low ing.**
fond loving; liking: *She is fond of children.* **fond er, fond est.**
fond ly *She kissed her baby brother fondly.*
food anything that plants, animals, or people eat or drink that makes them live and grow.
fool act foolish for fun; play; joke: *Don't fool around in school.* **fooled, fool ing.**
fool ish without sense; not wise; silly.
fool ish ly *When she spoke, she laughed foolishly.*
foot **1.** the end part of a leg; the part that you stand on. See the picture under **leg.** **2.** the lowest part; the bottom: *Meet me at the foot of the hill.* **3.** a measure of length: *Twelve inches are equal to one foot.* **feet.**
foot ball **1.** a leather ball used in a game. **2.** the game, in which two teams try to kick or carry a football past a line at either end of the field.
foot print the mark made by a foot.

for 1. *He gave me a new book for the old one.*
2. *He stands for honest government.* 3. *A party was given for him.* 4. *These apples are eight for a dollar. We thanked him for his kindness.* 5. *He went for a walk.* 6. *He was punished for stealing.* 7. *We walked for a mile.* 8. *We worked for an hour.*

force 1. power; being strong. 2. *They took the child from her by force.* 3. make a person act against his will. 4. get or take by being stronger than the thing or person against you: *He forced his way in.*
5. break through: *We forced a door that was locked.* **forced, forc ing.**

fore at the front; toward the beginning or front.

fore head the part of the face above the eyes. See the picture under **face.**

fore noon 1. the part of the day from sunrise to noon. 2. the time between early morning and noon.

for est 1. thick woods, often covering many miles.
2. *Forest fires can be stopped.*

for ev er 1. for ever; without ever coming to an end. 2. always; all the time.

for get 1. let go out of the mind; fail to remember.
2. fail to think of;
fail to do. **for got, for got ten** or **for got, for get ting.**

for get-me-not a small blue flower: *The Forget-Me-Not is the State Flower of Alaska.*

for got See **forget.** *He was so busy that he forgot to eat his lunch.*

for got ten 1. See **forget.** *Have you forgotten something?* 2. *Here is the forgotten book.*

fork 1. a tool having a handle and two or more long points, for lifting food or other things.
2. anything that separates into two branches: *He came to a fork in the road.* See the picture.

form 1. a shape: *The pupils learned that circles and cones are forms.* 2. shape; make: *The cook formed the cookies into stars.* 3. take shape: *Ice formed in the stream.* **formed, form ing.**

fort a strong building or place that can be held against an enemy.

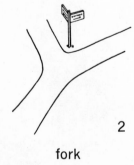

2

fork

forth   **1.** out; into view; away: *The sun came forth from behind the clouds.   Go forth and seek your fortune.*   **2.** *He strode back and forth on the deck.*

for ti eth   next after the thirty-ninth: *He is eating his fortieth pancake.*

for tune   **1.** a great deal of money or property: *He made a fortune when he discovered gold.*   **2.** *Did you have your fortune told?*

for ty   four times ten.   **for ties.**

for ward   **1.** a certain player on a basketball team. **2.** onward; ahead: *Forward, march!*   **3.** to the front: *He brought forward several new ideas.*   **4.** *He threw a forward pass.*

fought   See **fight.**   *He fought bravely yesterday.*

found   See **find.**   *We found the treasure.*

foun tain   **1.** water rising into the air in a spray. **2.** the pipes through which the water is forced and the container the water falls into.   **3.** a place to get a drink: *There's a drinking fountain in the park.*

four   **1.** one more than three.   **2.** *Leave at four o'clock.*

four teen   **1.** four more than ten.   **2.** *Fourteen days ago we arrived.*

four teenth   **1.** next after the thirteenth.   **2.** *The fourteenth of February is Valentine's Day.*

fourth   **1.** next after the third.   **2.** *This is his fourth year in high school.*

Fourth of July   a holiday; the birthday of the United States.

fowl   **1.** any bird; a rooster, hen, or turkey. **2.** the birds used for food.

fox   a small, sly, wild animal.   **fox es.**

fra grant   sweet-smelling: *This rose is fragrant.*

frame   **1.** the part over which something is stretched or built: *The frame of a house is built first.*   See the picture.   **2.** the outside edge in which a thing is set: *He put a frame on the picture.*   **3.** make; put together; plan: *He framed his speech the day before.* **4.** put an edge around: *I asked him to frame the picture.*   **framed, fram ing.**

frame

247

framed 1. See **frame**. 2. *The framed pictures were hung in the hall.*

frank furt er a red sausage made of beef or pork.

free 1. let go; let loose: *The boy freed the dog.* 2. loose; not fastened or shut up. 3. not under another person's control. 4. not held back from acting or thinking as one pleases: *We live in one of the freest nations in the world.* **freed, free ing; fre er, fre est.**

free ly *He gave away his money freely.*

freeze 1. turn into ice; harden by cold. 2. make or become very cold. 3. kill or hurt by frost. **froze, fro zen, freez ing.**

freight 1. the things that a ship or train carries. 2. **Freight train** means a train that carries things but no passengers. 3. *I saw two freight cars.*

fresh 1. newly made, grown, or gathered: *These are fresh vegetables.* 2. pure; cool: *A fresh breeze was blowing.* **fresh er, fresh est.**

fresh ly *These berries are freshly picked.*

fric tion the rubbing of one thing against another, such as skates on ice, hand against hand.

Fri day the sixth day of the week.

fried 1. See **fry**. 2. *We ate fried potatoes.*

friend a person who knows and likes you.

friend ly of a friend: *He sent a friendly greeting to us.* **friend li er, friend li est.**

fright sudden fear of something.

fright en make afraid: *Does a thunderstorm frighten you?* **fright ened, fright en ing.**

fright ened 1. See **frighten**. 2. *The frightened child began to cry.*

fringe 1. edging or trimming made of threads or cords, either loose or tied together in small bunches. 2. anything like this. 3. anything around the edge. 4. make a fringe for. **fringed, fring ing.**

fringed 1. See **fringe**. 2. *She bought her mother a fringed shawl.*

frisky playful; full of life: *We have a frisky puppy at our house.* **frisk i er, frisk i est.**

frog   a small, leaping animal that lives near water.

from   1. *Steel is made from iron.*   2. *Take the book from her.*   3. *Three weeks from today is a holiday.*   4. *He is suffering from a cold.*   5. *Anyone can tell apples from oranges.*   6. *Take a book from the table.*

front   1. the first part; the part that faces forward: *The front of the house was painted.*   2. *Someone is at the front door.*   3. *Meet me in front of the house.*

frost   1. water frozen on a surface, making a cold, white cover over it: *There was frost on the grass this morning.*   2. cover with frost.   3. *Mother is going to frost a cake.*   4. **Frosting** means a sweet top on a cake.   **frost ed, frost ing.**

frost ed   1. See **frost.**   2. *We like frosted cookies.*

frown   1. wrinkles in the forehead, usually when one is thinking hard or is angry: *He had a frown on his face when he saw the broken bike.*   2. look as though one is angry or thinking: *You frown when you are angry.*   **frowned, frown ing.**

froze   See **freeze.**   *The water in the pond froze.*

fro zen   1. See **freeze.**   *The milk has frozen in the bottle.*   2. *They came to a frozen river.*   3. **Frozen to the spot** means too frightened to move.

fruit   1. the part of a tree, bush, or vine that is formed after the blossoms die and that is usually good to eat.   2. *Fruit trees bloom in the spring.*

fry   cook in hot fat: *She is frying potatoes for supper.*   **fried, fry ing.**

ful crum   the thing on which a lever turns or is held up as it moves or lifts something.

full   able to hold no more: *The cup is full; don't try to put more in it.*   **full er, full est.**

ful ly   *Was he fully satisfied?*

fun   1. a good time; amusement: *We had fun at the party.*   2. **Make fun of** means laugh at someone.

fun nel   1. a cup, opening at the bottom into a tube and used to pour liquid, powder, or grain into a small hole.   2. the chimney on a ship.   See the picture.

fun ny   1. causing laughter.   2. strange; queer; odd in speech or acts.   **fun ni er, fun ni est.**

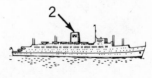

funnel

fur 1. the soft coat of hair that covers many animals. **2.** clothes made of fur: *Mother's furs keep her warm.* **3.** *She had a fur coat.*

fur nace a box in which a fire is made to melt iron, make glass, or heat a building.

fur ni ture things used in a house or room so people can live there, such as chairs, tables, and beds.

fu ture the time to come; what is to come.

G

gal lon a measure for liquids: *A gallon of milk is equal to four quarts.*

gal lop run in a fast, hopping way: *The horse galloped home.* **gal loped, gal lop ing.**

game something to play or a contest with certain rules: *This store sells games. We played a game of tag.*

ga rage a place for keeping or fixing automobiles.

gar bage 1. scraps of food to be thrown away. **2.** *Put this in the garbage can, please.*

gar den 1. a piece of ground in which vegetables or flowers are grown. **2.** *Stay on the garden walk.*

gar den ia 1. a plant with fragrant white flowers. **2.** *She uses gardenia perfume.*

gas 1. something that is like air, not hard or liquid: *We filled the balloon with gas to make it go up in the air.* **2.** the liquid that makes automobiles run. **3.** *We have a gas stove in the kitchen.* **gas es.**

gasp 1. a catching of the breath with the mouth open. **2.** take a short, quick breath through the mouth. **3.** talk while breathing this way: *"Help! Help!" gasped the drowning man.* **gasped, gasp ing.**

gate a door in a wall or fence. See the picture.

gath er 1. collect; bring or come into one place: *He gathered his books and papers after school.* **2.** pull together in folds: *When Mother made a skirt she gathered it at the top.* **gath ered, gath er ing.**

gave See **give.** *He gave me some of his candy.*

gay 1. happy and full of fun; merry: *It was a gay picnic.* **2.** bright-colored. **gay er, gay est.**

gate

gaze   **1.** a long, steady look.   **2.** look long and steadily.   **gazed, gaz ing.**

gear   a wheel with teeth around the edge that fits into another wheel and makes it turn.   See the picture.

geese   more than one goose.

gen tle   **1.** soft or low: *The rain made a gentle sound.*   **2.** kind or friendly: *We had a gentle dog.*   **gen tler, gen tlest.**

gen tly   *The rain fell gently.*

ge og ra phy   **1.** the study of the earth's surface, countries, and people.   **2.** a book about geography.   **ge og ra phies.**

Geor gia   one of the fifty states of the United States.

germ   a very tiny animal or plant, too small to be seen without a microscope: *Some germs make you sick.*

get   **1.** receive: *I expect to get a bike for Christmas.*   **2.** cause to be or do: *Can you get the window open?*   **3.** become: *It is getting colder.*   **got, get ting.**

ghost   **1.** in stories, one who is dead but who appears to living people.   **2.** *The girl told ghost stories.*

gi ant   **1.** in stories, a huge, very strong man.   **2.** *He saw three giant footprints in the snow.*

gift   something given; a present.

gig gle   laugh in a silly way.   **gig gled, gig gling.**

gin ger bread   **1.** a kind of cake or cookie.   **2.** *A gingerbread man is a cookie shaped like a man.*

ging ham   **1.** a cotton cloth made from colored threads.   **2.** *Her gingham dress had red stripes.*

gi raffe   an animal that has a very long neck.

girl   **1.** a female child.   **2.** a young, unmarried woman.

Girl Scout   a member of a group for girls called The Girl Scouts of the United States of America.

give   **1.** hand over as a present and without receiving anything in return.   **2.** pay: *I will give you three dollars for the wagon.*   **3.** do or make: *He gives the boy a good haircut.*   **gave, giv en, giv ing.**

giv en   See **give.**   *We have given him a book.*

glad   **1.** happy or pleased: *She is glad to be well again.*   **2.** bringing joy; pleasant: *The glad news made her happy.*   **glad der, glad dest.**

gears

glider

glad i o lus a plant with tall stalks of large, brightly colored flowers. **glad i o li** or **glad i o lus es.**

glad ly *I will gladly sing to you.*

glance look quickly: *I only glanced at him as he went by.* **glanced, glanc ing.**

glare 1. shine strongly enough to hurt the eyes. 2. look at someone angrily. **glared, glar ing.**

glass 1. material that you can usually see through: *Windows are made of glass.* 2. *Fill the glass with milk.* 3. a mirror. 4. *She put cherries in a glass dish.* 5. **Glasses** often means eyeglasses. **glass es.**

gleam send out a light; shine: *The flashlight gleamed in the dark.* **gleamed, gleam ing.**

glid er an airplane without a motor: *A glider coasts on the air currents.* See the picture.

glit ter shine with a bright, sparkling light: *Snow glittered in the sun.* **glit tered, glit ter ing.**

globe 1. anything that is round like a ball. 2. the earth; the world. 3. a ball with a map of the earth or the sky drawn on it.

gloomy dark and sad: *We felt better when we left that gloomy room.* **gloom i er, gloom i est.**

glo ry 1. great praise: *The pilot of the plane got all the glory.* 2. something that should be praised: *They saw the glory of the sky at night.* **glo ries.**

glove a covering for the hand, usually with a place for each finger and for the thumb.

glow 1. the shine from something that is hot or bright. 2. shine with a bright, warm color: *A fire glows in the stove.* **glowed, glow ing.**

glue 1. something used to stick or hold things together: *We fixed the broken chair with glue.* 2. stick together with glue: *We glued the parts of the model plane.* **glued, glu ing.**

gnaw bite at and wear away: *A mouse has gnawed right through this box.* **gnawed, gnaw ing.**

go 1. move along: *Cars go on the road.* *Don't go yet.* 2. pass: *Vacation goes quickly.* 3. have its place; belong: *This book goes on the top shelf.* 4. be about to: *Are you going to start now?* **went, gone, go ing.**

goat   a small animal with horns.

gob ble[1]   **1.** the noise a turkey makes.   **2.** make this noise or one like it.   **gob bled, gob bling.**

gob ble[2]   eat fast and noisily: *He gobbled his dinner.*   **gob bled, gob bling.**

gob lin   in stories, a mean or ugly elf.

God   *People worship God in different ways.*

goes   See **go.**   *He goes to school.*

gold   **1.** a heavy, bright-yellow metal. **2.** *She wore a gold ring.*

gold en   like gold: *The baby had golden hair.*

gold en rod   a plant with tall stalks of small yellow flowers: *The Goldenrod is the State Flower of Kentucky and of Nebraska.*

gold fish   a small fish of golden color often kept in a pool or fish bowl.   **gold fish** or **gold fish es.**

gone   See **go.**   *He has gone far away.*

good   **1.** excellent or well done: *He does good work.* **2.** doing what is right: *That's a good boy.*   **3.** pleasant: *Have a good time.*   **bet ter, best.**

good-by or **good-bye**   *We said "Good-by" and went home.*

good ness   **1.** being good.   **2.** *"My goodness!" cried Grandmother.*

goose   a bird like a duck but larger.   **geese.**

go pher   an animal like a rat.

go ril la   a very fierce, strong animal like a monkey.

got   See **get.**   *We got the letter yesterday.*

gourd   a kind of fruit, the hard shell of which can be used to make cups and bowls.

gov ern ment   the way of running and taking care of a country, a state, a county, or a city.

gov er nor   a man who is head of a state of the United States.

grab   take suddenly or snatch: *The dog grabbed the meat and ran.*   **grabbed, grab bing.**

grade   **1.** a class in school: *He is in the fifth grade.* **2.** a number or letter that shows how well one has done.   **3.** give a grade to: *The teacher graded the papers.*   **4.** *She is in grade school.*   **grad ed, grad ing.**

253

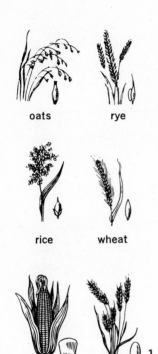

oats   rye

rice   wheat

corn   barley

grain

grain 1. the seed of plants like wheat, oats, and corn. See the picture. 2. one of the tiny bits of material that make up some things: *A beach is made of grains of sand.*

grand large and splendid; wonderful: *They lived in a very grand castle.* **grand er, grand est.**

grand child a child of one's son or daughter.

grand chil dren more than one grandchild.

grand daugh ter a daughter of one's son or daughter.

grand fath er the father of one's father or mother.

grand moth er the mother of one's mother or father.

grand son a son of one's son or daughter.

grand stand a place for people to sit while they are watching a game or a sport.

grant give what is asked: *The king granted our wish.* **grant ed, grant ing.**

grape 1. a small, round fruit, red, purple, or green, that grows on a vine: *The Oregon Grape is the State Flower of Oregon.* 2. *He likes grape jam best.*

grape fruit 1. a yellow fruit like an orange, but larger and more sour. 2. *Drink your grapefruit juice.*

grass a plant with leaves like blades: *The yard was covered with beautiful green grass.* **grass es.**

grass hop per an insect with wings and strong legs for jumping.

grassy covered with grass. **grass i er, grass i est.**

grate[1] a frame of iron bars to hold a fire or cover a window.

grate[2] 1. rub with a squeaky sound. 2. wear down or grind off in small pieces. **grat ed, grat ing.**

grat ed 1. See **grate**[2]. 2. *The cake was covered with grated chocolate.*

gra vy 1. the juice that comes out of meat when it is cooked. 2. a sauce made from this juice.
3. *Please bring me a gravy dish.* **gra vies.**

gray having a color between black and white: *We saw the gray clouds coming fast.*
Also spelled **grey.** **gray er, gray est.**

graze[1]   eat growing grass: *Cattle were grazing in the field.*   **grazed, graz ing.**

graze[2]   scrape or touch lightly in passing: *The car grazed the garage door.*   **grazed, graz ing.**

grease   **1.** fat or oil.   **2.** put grease on or in: *Please grease my car.*   **greased, greas ing.**

great   **1.** big; large: *We saw a great crowd.*   **2.** more than usual: *He was in great pain.*   **3.** important: *We saw a great picture.*   **great er, great est.**

green   **1.** having the color of most growing plants.   **2.** not ripe or ready to eat.   **green er, green est.**

greet   say "Hello" to someone: *My friend greeted me when I arrived.*   **greet ed, greet ing.**

grew   See **grow.**   *He grew two inches taller last year.*

grey hound   a tall, slim hunting dog.

grin   **1.** a broad smile.   **2.** smile with lips pulled back so teeth are showing.   **grinned, grin ning.**

grind   crush or cut into small pieces or into powder.   **ground, grind ing.**

groan   **1.** a sound made down in the throat when one is sad or in pain: *We heard the groans of the sick man.*   **2.** make this sound.   **groaned, groan ing.**

gro cer   a person whose business is to sell food and things for the house.

gro cery   **1.** a store that sells food and things for the house.   **2.** **Groceries** sometimes means food and things for the house.   **gro cer ies.**

ground[1]   **1.** the surface of the earth; soil: *The ground was hard and rocky.*   **2.** *They lived on the ground floor of this building.*

ground[2]   **1.** See **grind**   **2.** *Hamburger is made of ground beef.*

group   **1.** several persons or things together: *We saw a group of children playing tag.*   **2.** form or put several together: *The children grouped themselves on the steps.*   **grouped, group ing.**

grouse   a bird with feathers on its legs: *The Ruffed Grouse is the State Bird of Pennsylvania.*   **grouse.**

grove   a group of trees: *An orange grove is an orchard of orange trees.*

grow 1. *Our school is growing fast.* 2. *Few trees grow in the desert.* 3. *We grow carrots in our garden.* 4. *It is growing dark.* **grew, grown, grow ing.**

growl 1. a sound like that made by a fierce dog; a deep, warning sound. 2. make such a sound: *The dog growled at the birds.* **growled, growl ing.**

grown See **grow.** *The corn has grown very tall.*

grown-up 1. a grown person. 2. *He acted in a grown-up manner.*

gruff cross and unfriendly: *The old man spoke in a gruff voice.* **gruff er, gruff est.**

gruff ly *She answered him gruffly.*

grum ble complain; find fault: *She grumbled about the weather all day.* **grum bled, grum bling.**

grunt 1. a deep, hoarse sound that a hog makes or a sound like it. 2. make this sound. **grunt ed, grunt ing.**

guard 1. a person who keeps watch over something or someone: *The guard would not let us go into the building.* 2. a certain player in such games as football and basketball. 3. watch over; take care of; keep safe: *The dog guarded the child day and night.* **guard ed, guard ing.**

guess 1. an idea one has that may not be right: *My guess is that the tree is ten feet high.* 2. think without really knowing: *I guess it will rain tomorrow.* **guess es; guessed, guess ing.**

guest a person who is visiting at another's house: *She was our guest for dinner.*

guide 1. a person who leads you or shows the way: *We hired a guide.* 2. show the way or lead someone: *The Indian guided the men.* 3. *There are guide words on every page.* **guid ed, guid ing.**

guin ea hen a bird having dark-gray feathers with small white spots.

guin ea pig an animal often used by scientists for experiments.

gui tar a musical instrument.

gull a bird living on or near lakes and oceans: *The Sea Gull is the State Bird of Utah.*

gulp   swallow eagerly or noisily.   **gulped, gulp ing.**

gum[1]   **1.** the sticky juice of certain trees, which is used for sticking paper and other things together. **2.** something to chew without swallowing.   **3.** *Gum comes from a gum tree.*

gum[2]   the part of your jaws around the teeth.

gun   an instrument used to shoot: *He aimed the gun at the tree and shot.*

gup py   a small, brightly colored fish.   **gup pies.**

gym   gymnasium.

gym na si um   a room or building in which athletes and other people exercise and play some games.

H

hab it   something you do without thinking: *Biting your fingernails is a bad habit.*

had   See **have.**   *She had a party.   He had to go home.   Mother had the walls washed.*

had n't   had not.

hail[1]   **1.** small pieces of ice coming down like rain; frozen rain.   **2.** fall in frozen drops.   **hailed, hail ing.**

hail[2]   **1.** a loud call; a shout: *The ship moved on without hearing our hails.*   **2.** greet: *The crowd hailed the team that won.*   **3.** call loudly to; shout to: *The boys tried to hail a passing car.*   **hailed, hail ing.**

hair   fine, threadlike pieces growing from the skin of people and animals: *The little girl's hair was soft as silk.*   See the picture under **head.**   **hair.**

half   **1.** one of two equal parts: *A half of four is two.* **2.** *The glass was half full of milk.   The meat was half cooked.*   **3.** *Come in half an hour.*   **halves.**

hal i but   very large, flat fish, used for food.

hall   **1.** a narrow space in or through a building: *Leave your umbrella in the hall.*   **2.** a large room: *No hall in town was large enough for the crowd.*

Hal low een or **Hal low e'en**   October 31.

halt   stop.   **halt ed, halt ing.**

ham   salted and smoked meat from a hog's leg.

ham burg er **1.** ground beef, usually shaped into flat cakes. **2.** a sandwich made with hamburger.

ham mer **1.** a tool used to drive nails and to beat metal into shape. **2.** drive, hit, or work with a hammer. **ham mered, ham mer ing.**

ham mock a hanging bed.

ham ster a small animal often kept as a pet.

hand **1.** the end part of the arm, having four fingers and a thumb, which takes and holds things. See the picture under **arm**. **2.** *The hands of a clock show the time.* See the picture under **clock**. **3.** give with the hand; pass: *Please hand me a spoon.* **4.** *This is a hand-woven cloth.* **hand ed, hand ing.**

hand ful as much or as many as the hand can hold.

hand ker chief a square of cloth used for wiping the nose, face, and hands.

han dle **1.** a part of something made to be held or taken up by your hand. See the pictures. **2.** touch, feel, or use with the hand: *Don't handle that book until you wash your hands.* **han dled, han dling.**

hand some good-looking; pleasing to the eye: *That man is handsome.* **hand som er, hand som est.**

hand writ ing writing done by hand with pen or pencil: *He recognized the handwriting on the card.*

hand y **1.** easy to reach or use: *There were handy shelves near the kitchen sink.* **2.** skillful with the hands: *He is handy with tools.* **hand i er, hand i est.**

hang **1.** fasten or be fastened to something above: *Hang your cap on the hook.* **2.** put to death by hanging with a rope around the neck. **3.** bend down: *She should hang her head in shame.* **hung (hanged for 2), hang ing.**

hang ar a shed for airplanes.

Ha nuk kah a holiday, usually in December, when some people give gifts and light candles.

hap pen go on; take place: *Nothing interesting happens here.* **hap pened, hap pen ing.**

hap pi ly *The girls played happily together.*

hap pi ness being happy or glad: *We wish the bride much happiness.*

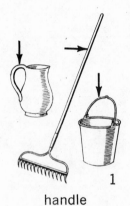

handle

hap py **1.** feeling as you do when you are having a good time; glad; pleased. **2.** showing that one is glad. **hap pi er, hap pi est.**

har bor a place of shelter for ships.

hard **1.** like steel, glass, and rock; not soft; not moving when touched. **2.** needing much work or time: *This was a hard job to do.* **3.** *It is raining hard.* **hard er, hard est.**

hard ly *We hardly had time to eat breakfast.*

hare an animal with long ears and long hind legs.

harm **1.** hurt: *I hope no harm comes to him.* **2.** cause pain: *The baby's fall did not harm him.* **harmed, harm ing.**

harp a musical instrument.

has See **have.** *Who has my book? He has been sick. Has she gone?*

has n't has not.

haste **1.** trying to be quick; hurry: *All his haste was of no use.* **2. Make haste** means hurry; be quick.

hast i ly *The boys hastily pitched their tents as the rain began to fall.*

hat a covering for the head.

hatch **1.** bring forth from an egg. **2.** come out from the egg: *Three of the chickens hatched today.* **3.** plan secretly; plot: *The soldiers were hatching a surprise move.* **hatched, hatch ing.**

hate not like very much. **hat ed, hat ing.**

haul pull or drag with force: *The logs were hauled by horses.* **hauled, haul ing.**

have **1.** hold: *I have a club in my hand.* **2.** own: *They have a big house and farm.* **3.** know; understand: *You have the right idea.* **4.** be forced: *All animals have to sleep.* **5.** *Please have the boy bring my mail.* **6.** *What have I done?* **has, had, hav ing.**

have n't have not.

Ha waii the fiftieth state of the United States.

hawk a bird with a strong bill and large claws.

haw thorn **1.** a small tree with thorns and red, pink, or white flowers: *The Hawthorn is the State Flower of Missouri.* **2.** *Hawthorn trees have red berries.*

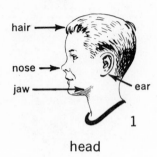

head

heart

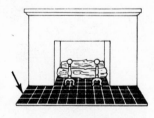

hearth

hay   **1.** grass cut and dried as food for cattle and horses.   **2.** *We rode on the hay wagon.*

hay loft   a place in a barn where hay is stored.

hay mow   a hayloft.

he   *He works hard.   He is a big boy.   He is going.*

head   **1.** the top part of the human body.   See the picture under **body.**   **2.** the front of an animal where the eyes, ears, and mouth are.   **3.** the top part; the front: *The head of the line is here.*   **4.** be at the front or the top of: *His name heads the list.*   **5.** move toward; face toward: *Our ship headed south.*
6. *She is the head clerk.*   **7. Over one's head** means too hard for one to understand.   **head ed, head ing.**

head quar ters   **1.** the place from which orders are sent out.   **2.** the main office.

health   being well or not sick: *Everyone's health is important.*

heap   **1.** *They made a heap of stones on the beach.*
2. *He was heaping his dish with ice cream.   Her clothes were heaped in a corner.*   **heaped, heap ing.**

hear   **1.** receive sounds through the ear: *Can you hear my watch tick?*   **2.** receive word or news: *Did you hear from your brother?*   **heard, hear ing.**

heard   See **hear.**   *I heard the noise.*

heart   **1.** the part of the body that pumps the blood.
2. feelings; mind: *She has a kind heart.*   **3.** the middle; the main part: *It is dark in the heart of the forest.*   **4.** a certain shape.   See the picture.

hearth   part of a floor where a fire can be made. See the picture.

heat   **1.** being hot: *The heat of a fire feels good on a cold day.*   **2.** make or become warm or hot: *The stove heats the room.*   **heat ed, heat ing.**

heav i ly   *The tired man walked heavily.*

heavy   **1.** hard to lift or carry; having much weight.
2. large; greater than usual.   **heav i er, heav i est.**

he'd   **1.** he had: *He'd gone when we got there.*   **2.** he would: *He'd wait if you asked him to.*

hedge   a thick row of bushes making a fence.

hedge hog   a porcupine.

heel **1.** the back part of a person's foot, below the ankle. See the picture under **leg**. **2.** the part of a stocking or shoe that covers the heel. **3.** the part of a shoe or boot that is under the heel or raises the heel. See the picture.

held See **hold**[1]. *Mother held the new baby.*

hel i cop ter aircraft that can move straight up and down.

he'll he will.

hel lo a call of greeting or surprise: *I said, "Hello!"*

hel met a covering usually made of metal to protect the head.

help **1.** *I need some help with my work. "Help!" cried the man in the boat.* **2.** *He helped me lift the board.* **3.** *Help yourself to milk and sugar.* **4.** *He cannot help going to sleep.* **helped, help ing.**

help ful giving help; useful: *The girls tried to be helpful at the party.*

help ful ly *The girls helpfully pitched in to do the spring cleaning.*

help less without help; not able to help oneself: *A little baby is helpless.*

hem lock **1.** an evergreen tree like a pine: *The Eastern Hemlock is the State Tree of Pennsylvania; the Western Hemlock is the State Tree of Washington.* **2.** *Hemlock trees grow in cool countries.*

hen a female chicken or other bird.

her **1.** *Have you seen her? Find her. Wait for her.* **2.** *She has left her book. She has hurt her arm.*

herd **1.** *We saw a herd of elephants in the movie.* **2.** *He herded the sheep on a hill.* **herd ed, herd ing.**

here in this place; at this place: *We live here in the summer. Bring the children here for their lesson.*

her on a wading bird with long legs.

hers of her; belonging to her: *This money is hers.*

her self **1.** *She herself did it. She herself brought the book.* **2.** *She hurt herself. She did it by herself.*

he's **1.** he is: *He's waiting for me.* **2.** he has: *He's taken all the money.*

hi another way of saying hello.

3

heel

hi bis cus   a plant with large flowers: *The Hibiscus is the State Flower of Hawaii.*   **hi bis cus es.**

hic cups   a catching of the breath that one cannot stop or control.

hick o ry   **1.** a North American tree with nuts that are good to eat.   **2.** *Mother made a cake with hickory nuts in it.*   **hick o ries.**

hid   See **hide²**.   *The dog hid his bone.*

hid den   **1.** See **hide²**.   *Where have you hidden the candy?*   **2.** *The story is about hidden treasure.*

hide¹   an animal's skin.

hide²   **1.** put out of sight; keep out of sight: *Hide it where no one will find it.*   **2.** get out of sight.   **hid, hid den** or **hid, hid ing.**

high   **1.** tall; sharp; great: *Snow was on the high mountains.   She had a higher voice than yours.*   **2.** up above the ground; near the top.   **3.** *The airplane flew a mile high.*   **4. High school** means the school you go to after finishing grade school.   **high er, high est.**

high ly   *The patient spoke highly of his doctor.*

high way   a main road.

hike   **1.** a long walk.   **2.** take a long walk; tramp; march.   **hiked, hik ing.**

hill   **1.** a raised part of the earth's surface, not so big as a mountain.   **2.** a little heap or pile: *Ants make hills to live in.*

him   *Don't hit him.   Give him a drink.   Go to him.*

him self   **1.** *Did he himself talk to you?*   **2.** *He cut himself.   He kept the toy for himself.*

hind   back; rear: *The horse cut his hind leg.*

hinge   a joint on which a door, gate, cover, or lid moves back and forth.

hint   **1.** a clue that helps you know something: *The black cloud gave a hint of the coming storm.*   **2.** suggest without really telling: *She hinted that she wanted to go home.*   **hint ed, hint ing.**

hip   **1.** the place where the leg joins the body. See the picture under **body**.   **2.** a part in animals where the hind leg joins the body.

hip po pot a mus   a huge, thick-skinned animal.   **hip po pot a mus es** or **hip po pot a mi.**

hire   pay for the use of something or the work of somebody: *He hired a car.*   **hired, hir ing.**

his   *His feet are cold.   This is his book.   My books are old; his are new.*

his to ry   **1.** an account of what has happened. **2.** the story of a man or a nation: *We studied the history of the United States.*   **his to ries.**

hit   **1.** a coming against something sharply.   **2.** in baseball, hitting the ball and running to first base: *The team got two hits.*   **3.** give a blow to; strike: *When boys fight, they hit each other.   One boy hit me twice.   He has hit the ball.*   **hit, hit ting.**

hitch   fasten with a hook, ring, rope, or strap: *He hitched his horse to a post.*   **hitched, hitch ing.**

hive   **1.** a house or box for bees to live in.   **2.** a large number of bees living together.

hoarse   sounding hard and not smooth: *A cold made his voice hoarse.*   **hoars er, hoars est.**

hoe   **1.** a tool with a small blade set across the end of a long handle, used for loosening soil, cutting weeds, and so on.   **2.** loosen soil around; dig or cut with a hoe.   **hoed, hoe ing.**

hog   a pig raised for food.

hold[1]   **1.** having one or two hands on something and not letting go: *Take a good hold of his rope.*   **2.** pick up or take up and keep: *Please hold my hat while I play this game.*   **3.** keep in some place or some way: *Hold the dish level.*   **4.** keep from acting; keep back: *Hold your breath.*   **5.** *This cup will hold water.*   **6.** *How much will it hold?*   **7.** *Shall we hold a meeting of the club?*   **held, hold ing.**

hold[2]   the lowest part of the inside of a ship: *A ship's load of freight is carried in its hold.* See the picture.

hole   **1.** an open place: *Here is a hole in the stocking.* **2.** a hollow place: *The car hit a hole in the road.*

hol i day   **1.** a day when one does not work or go to school; a day for having fun.   **2.** vacation.

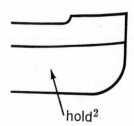
hold[2]

hol low   1. a place lower than the parts around it. 2. take out the inside parts.   3. *I sat on a hollow log.*   **hol lowed, hol low ing; hol low er, hol low est.**

hol ly   1. an evergreen bush or tree with shiny leaves and red berries: *The American Holly is the State Tree of Delaware.*   2. *Holly berries are pretty in winter.*   **hol lies.**

home   1. the place where a person or family lives. 2. the town or country where one was born or brought up: *His home is Virginia.   Alaska is the home of the fur seal.*   3. a place where people who are poor, old, sick, or blind may live.   4. in many games, the place where a player can rest and be safe: *The runner ran for home.*   5. *This is my home town.*

hon est   fair; telling the truth; not saying or doing anything that isn't true, right, or good.

hon es ty   the act of being fair and doing only what is right and saying only what is true.

hon ey   1. a thick, sweet liquid, good to eat, that bees make.   2. *Mother keeps honey in a honey pot.*

hon ey bee   a bee that makes honey.

honk   1. the cry of a wild goose.   2. any sound like that: *He was frightened by the honk of an automobile horn.*   3. make the cry of a wild goose or something like it.   **honked, honk ing.**

hood

hood   1. a soft covering for the head and neck: *My raincoat has a hood.*   2. the metal covering over the engine of an automobile.   See the pictures.

hoof   the hard part of the foot of some animals.

hook   1. a piece of hard material, curved or pointed, for catching hold of something or for hanging things on.   See the pictures.   2. catch or take hold of with a hook.   3. fasten with hooks.   4. catch fish with a hook.   **hooked, hook ing.**

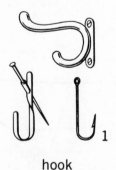

hook

hoop   1. a ring or a flat circle made of metal: *The hoops held the barrel together.*   2. *The child rolled his hoop along the ground.*   3. a frame, shaped like a circle, used to hold out a woman's skirt.

hoot   1. sound that an owl makes.   2. make this sound or one like it.   **hoot ed, hoot ing.**

hop   1. *Take three hops to the left.*   2. *How far can you hop on your right foot?*
3. *Many birds hop.*   **hopped, hop ping.**

hope   1. a feeling that what you want to happen will happen: *Her words gave me hope.*   2. the thing hoped for: *It is my hope that you will come.*   3. look for; expect: *I hope you'll like school.*   **hoped, hop ing.**

hope ful ly   *The boy hopefully asked if anyone had found his baseball.*

hope less   feeling no hope: *The boy had lost so often that he became hopeless.*   *I tried to help, but it was hopeless.*

horn   1. a hard mass, usually curved and pointed, on the heads of cattle, sheep, goats, and some other animals.   2. a musical instrument played by blowing into it.   3. a signal of danger: *The driver blew his horn loudly.*   See the pictures.

hor net   a large insect, like a wasp, that can sting.

horse   an animal with hard hoofs and a mane.

hose   1. stockings.   2. a long, hollow line for carrying liquid.

hos pi tal   a place where sick people are cared for.

hot   1. much warmer than the body; having much heat.   2. having a sharp, burning taste: *Pepper and mustard are hot.*   **hot ter, hot test.**

ho tel   a house or large building where people can rent rooms to sleep in.

hound   a dog that likes to hunt.

hour   1. one of the twelve equal parts of time between noon and midnight, or between midnight and noon: *Sixty minutes make an hour.*   2. *He left two hours ago.*   3. *Our lunch hour begins at twelve o'clock.*

hour ly   1. *The patient made hourly calls to his doctor.*   2. *Give two pills hourly.*

house   1. a building in which people live.
2. a building used for some special thing: *We built a chicken house.*

how   1. *How can it be done?   How did it happen?*
2. *How tall are you?   How long will it take?*   3. *How are you?*

horn

howl 1. a long, loud, sad cry. 2. give a long, loud, sad cry. **howled, howl ing.**

hub the center part of a wheel. See the picture under **wheel.**

hug 1. a tight squeeze with the arms: *Give Mother a hug.* 2. put the arms around and hold close: *She hugged the child.* **hugged, hug ging.**

huge very, very large: *A whale or an elephant is a huge animal.* **hug er, hug est.**

hum 1. a sound that doesn't stop: *We listened to the hum of bees in the field.* 2. without stopping, make a sound like that of a bee or of a spinning top: *The sewing machine hums when Mother sews.* 3. sing with closed lips, not sounding words: *She was humming a tune.* **hummed, hum ming.**

hu man being a person or persons; like a person: *Men, women, and children are human beings. The dog seemed almost human.*

hum ming bird a very small, brightly colored bird with wings that move so rapidly they make a humming sound in the air.

hun dred ten times ten.

hun dredth the next after the ninety-ninth: *This is the hundredth day of the year.*

hung See **hang.** *He hung his cap in the closet where he had hung it before.*

hun ger the pains caused by having had nothing to eat: *The little boy who ran away from home soon felt hunger.*

hun gri ly *The children hungrily ate all the hot dogs.*

hun gry 1. feeling a wish or need for food: *Mother says the boys in our family always seem to be hungry.* 2. *She is hungry for books.* **hun gri er, hun gri est.**

hunt 1. chase animals for food or for fun: *The men were hunting deer.* 2. look for; try to find: *Don't forget to hunt for that lost book.* **hunt ed, hunt ing.**

hur rah a shout of joy: *Give a hurrah for the team!*

hur ray hurrah.

hur ri cane a storm with heavy wind and very heavy rain.

hur ry   **1.** a quick move: *Her hurry caused the accident.*   **2.** a desire to have quickly or do quickly: *She was in a hurry to see her father.*   **3.** drive, carry, send, or move quickly: *They hurried the sick child to the doctor.*   **hur ries; hur ried, hur ry ing.**

hurt   **1.** a cut or sore; the breaking of a bone; any wound: *She has had many hurts in her life.*   **2.** suffer pain: *My hand hurts.*   **3.** do harm to: *Will it hurt this hat if it gets wet?*   **hurt, hurt ing.**

hus band   a man who has a wife; a married man.

husk   **1.** the dry outside covering of some seeds or fruits: *An ear of corn has a husk.*   See the picture.   **2.** dry or worthless covering of anything.   **3.** remove the husk from: *Husk the corn.*   **husked, husk ing.**

Husky or **husky**[1]   an Eskimo dog.   **Husk ies.**

husky[2]   **1.** dry in the throat; hoarse: *You certainly have a husky cough.*   **2.** big and strong: *He is a husky boy.*   **husk i er, husk i est.**

hut   a small cabin: *The boys built a hut in the woods.*

hy a cinth   a spring plant that grows from a bulb.

hy drant   a large pipe in the street from which firemen draw water.

husk

I

I   *I am ten years old.   I like my dog.   I will go with you.*

ice   **1.** water made hard by the cold; frozen water: *We skated on the ice.*   **2.** a frozen dessert.   **3.** make cool with ice; put ice in or around.   **4.** cover with icing: *Mother will ice the cake.*   **5. Icing** means frosting.   **6.** *We drank ice water.*   **iced, ic ing.**

ice cream   a dessert that is made of cream and sugar and then is frozen.

iced   **1.** See **ice.**   **2.** *She likes iced tea.*

ici cle   a pointed, hanging stick of ice formed when water drips and freezes.

I'd   **1.** I should; I would: *I'd go with you if I could.*   **2.** I had: *I'd forgotten the answer.*

Ida ho   one of the fifty states of the United States.

idea a plan, picture, or thought in the mind: *Whose idea was it to go to the zoo?   We had no idea it was true.*

if **1.** not certain or sure: *Come if you can.   If it rains tomorrow, we shall stay at home.*
2. whether: *I wonder if he will go.*

I'll **1.** I shall. **2.** I will.

Il li nois one of the fifty states of the United States.

I'm I am.

imag ine form a picture of something in the mind; have an idea: *The girl likes to imagine that she is a teacher.* **imag ined, imag in ing.**

im me di ate ly **1.** *I answered his letter immediately.*   **2.** *He came in but went out again immediately.*

im pa tient not patient; not wanting to wait.

im pa tient ly *He rang the doorbell impatiently.*

im po lite not polite; rude; having bad manners.

im por tant meaning a lot: *It is important to go to school.   The President is an important man.*

im pos si ble something that cannot be or happen: *It is impossible for two and two to make six.*

im prove make or become better: *You could improve your handwriting.* **im proved, im prov ing.**

in **1.** *We live in the country.   Is your father in today?* **2.** *You can do this in an hour.   In summer we do not go to school.* **3.** *In case of fire, don't run.*

inch a measure of length: *Twelve inches are equal to one foot.* **inch es.**

in cline be willing; lean toward: *Dogs are inclined to eat meat.   The board was inclined against the wall.* **in clined, in clin ing.**

in deed **1.** in fact; really: *War is indeed terrible.*
2. a word used to show surprise: *Indeed!   I never would have thought it.*

in dex a list at the end of a book telling on what pages to find each thing. **in dex es.**

In di an **1.** one of the people living in America before Columbus discovered it. **2.** a person living in a country in Asia. **3.** *There was an Indian camp near the forest.   An Indian prince rode by on an elephant.*

In di ana one of the fifty states of the United States.

In di an paint brush a plant with bright-red tips on its leaves: *The Indian Paintbrush is the State Flower of Wyoming.* **In di an paint brush es.**

ink a colored liquid used for writing or printing.

inn a building in which people who are traveling can sleep, rest, and eat: *We spent the night at a little inn.*

in quire try to find out something by asking questions: *I inquired about a room. A policeman was inquiring about the child.* **in quired, in quir ing.**

in sect a small animal with a body divided into three parts, having three pairs of legs and usually two pairs of wings: *Flies, mosquitoes, and bees are insects.*

in side 1. the part within; the surface not on the outside: *The inside of the box was lined with silk.* 2. the things within: *The inside of the book was more interesting than the cover.* 3. in: *The nut is inside the shell.* 4. *He wore his coat inside out.*

in sist keep saying or thinking something without changing your mind or giving up: *He insists that this is his book.* **in sist ed, in sist ing.**

in stant 1. a small bit of time: *He stopped for an instant.* 2. quick: *He made a cup of instant coffee.* 3. at an exact moment: *Stop talking this instant!*

in stant ly *He stopped instantly when he saw me.*

in stead 1. *Instead of studying, she read a story.* 2. *She stayed home, and her sister went instead.*

in stru ment 1. any tool, machine, or other thing that helps us do or make something. 2. a thing that produces sounds of music.

in sur ance *Father bought fire insurance, but when our house burned, he did not get enough money from it to build a new house.*

in ter est 1. a feeling of wanting to know or share in: *He has an interest in reading.* 2. extra money you pay if you borrow some money: *If you borrow from a bank, you pay interest.* 3. make someone want to know or share: *A good story interests us.* **in ter est ed, in ter est ing.**

269

in ter est ing   *He told an interesting story.*

in tro duce   **1.** make people known to each other: *May I introduce my father?*   **2.** bring in for the first time: *She introduced a new idea at the meeting.*   **in tro duced, in tro duc ing.**

in vent   **1.** make or think of something new: *Who invented the airplane?*   **2.** make up: *He invented an excuse for staying home.*   **in vent ed, in vent ing.**

in ven tion   the thing invented: *The radio is a wonderful invention.*

in ven tor   a person who invents.

in vis i ble   not able to be seen: *Germs are invisible without a microscope.   The man was invisible in the fog.*

in vi ta tion   *The children received invitations to the party.*

in vite   ask someone politely to come to some place or to do something: *We invited her to join our club. Shall we invite them to stay?*   **in vit ed, in vit ing.**

Io wa   one of the fifty states of the United States.

iris   **1.** a plant with long, pointed leaves, tall stalks, and big flowers: *The Iris is the State Flower of Tennessee.*   **2.** the colored part of your eye.   **iris es.**

iron   **1.** a metal from which tools and machines are made: *Steel is made from iron.*   **2.** an instrument that is heated and used to press clothing.   **3.** press with an iron.   **4.** *There was an iron fence around the park.*   **ironed, iron ing.**

is   *The earth is round.   She is a girl.   He is at school. A child is loved by his mother.   She is going to jump. It is four o'clock.*

is land   a mass of land surrounded by water.

is n't   is not.

it   *Here is your paper; read it.   I cut my hand and it hurts.   Look at it carefully.   It snows in winter.   It is my turn.   I lost my dog; have you seen it?*

itch   feeling something in the skin that makes one want to scratch: *My mosquito bites itch.   My finger itches.*   **itched, itch ing.**

item   one separate thing: *The list had twelve items on it.   I read a short item in the paper.*

it'll it will.

its of it; belonging to it: *The cat chased its tail. This chair has lost one of its legs.*

it's 1. it is: *It's a nice day.* 2. it has: *It's been raining all morning.*

it self 1. *The land itself is worth more than the old house. Work itself never hurt anyone.* 2. *The horse tripped and hurt itself.*

I've I have.

J

jack et 1. a short coat. 2. an outside covering: *New books have paper jackets.*

jack-o'-lan tern a pumpkin hollowed out and cut to look like a face, used as a lantern at Halloween.

jacks a game played with a ball and small, six-pointed metal objects. See the picture.

jag uar a wild animal that looks like a leopard.

jail a place where people are kept to punish them.

jam[1] 1. a crowded mass: *What a traffic jam!* 2. press or squeeze tight: *Jam this stick in the door. A crowd jammed into the bus.* 3. fill or block up the way by crowding: *Trucks jam the streets.* 4. stick or catch so that it cannot be worked: *The window has jammed; I can't open it.* **jammed, jam ming.**

jam[2] fruit boiled with sugar until it is thick.

James town the first settlement built in Virginia, in 1607.

jan i tor a person who takes care of a building.

Jan u ary the first month of the year.

jar[1] a deep container usually made of stone or glass, with a wide mouth.

jar[2] shake; rattle; send a shock through something: *Your heavy footsteps jar my table.* **jarred, jar ring.**

jas mine jessamine.

jaw 1. the lower part of the face. See the picture under **head.** 2. *The jaws of a tool are the parts that bite or grab.*

jeans strong cotton work pants.

jacks

jeep   a kind of small, powerful automobile.

jel ly   **1.** a food made of fruit juice and sugar boiled together: *Jelly is good spread on bread.*   **2.** *We ate jelly rolls for breakfast.*   **jel lies.**

jerk   **1.** pull or twist suddenly: *He jerked his hand out of the hot water.*   **2.** move with a jerk: *The old wagon jerked along.*   **jerked, jerk ing.**

jes sa mine or **jas mine**   a vine or bush with fragrant yellow, white, or red flowers: *The Yellow Jessamine is the State Flower of South Carolina.*

jet[1]   **1.** a stream of any liquid forced from a small opening: *A fountain sends up a jet of water.*
2. an airplane that is driven by a jet of air, gas, and so on.

jet[2]   **1.** a hard black mineral that is shiny when rubbed: *Jet is used for beads and jewelry.*
2. *She wore a jet bracelet.*

jew el   **1.** a rare stone, such as a diamond.
2. a piece of jewelry.

jew el ry   things to wear, such as bracelets, necklaces, rings.

jig saw   a narrow saw used to cut curves and so on.

jin gle   **1.** a sound like little bells ringing.
2. a verse that has a jingling sound: *Mother Goose rhymes are jingles.*   **3.** make such a sound: *He jingled the coins in his pocket.*   **jin gled, jin gling.**

job   **1.** work; anything a person has to do: *He had the job of painting the boat.*   **2.** work done for pay: *My father has a job in a factory.*

join   **1.** bring things together or make them connect: *We joined hands in a circle.*   **2.** take part with others: *He joined the Boy Scouts.*   **joined, join ing.**

joint   **1.** the place at which two things or parts are joined together.   **2.** the parts where two bones move on each other: *Your knee is a joint in your leg.*
See the pictures.   **3. Out of joint** means moved out of place at the joint.

joke   **1.** something funny said or done to make somebody laugh.   **2.** make jokes; say or do something funny.   **joked, jok ing.**

joint

jol ly merry; very cheerful. **jol li er, jol li est.**

Josh ua tree a yucca plant that looks like a short tree with twisted branches.

jour ney a trip.

joy a glad feeling; happiness.

joy ful glad; happy: *They had a joyful Christmas.*

joy ful ly *She waved her hand joyfully at her friends.*

judge **1.** a person who decides questions about the law or between two people who don't agree.
2. a person chosen to decide who wins a contest.
3. a person who can decide on how good a thing is: *He is a good judge of dogs.* **4.** act as a judge; decide questions of law. **judged, judg ing.**

jug gle do tricks that require skill in throwing, catching, or balancing: *Some people can juggle five balls at once.* **jug gled, jug gling.**

juice the liquid part of fruit, vegetables, and meat.

Ju ly the seventh month of the year.

jump **1.** a spring from the ground; a leap.
2. a sudden jerk of the body, usually when frightened.
3. leave the ground by pushing the body upward.
4. give a sudden jerk: *We often jump when we hear a loud noise.* **jumped, jump ing.**

June the sixth month of the year.

jun gle wild land with thickly grown bushes, vines, and trees: *There are jungles in Africa.*

ju ni per **1.** an evergreen bush or tree with purple berries. **2.** *Juniper trees look pretty on a lawn.*

just **1.** *That is just a pound.* **2.** *He just left me.* **3.** *I just caught the train.* **4.** *He is just a common man.* **5.** *The hat was just above him.*

K

kan ga roo an animal, living in Australia, that has small front legs and very strong hind legs, and carries its young in a pocket.

Kan sas one of the fifty states of the United States.

ka ty did a large green insect somewhat like a grasshopper.

keep **1.** have forever: *You may keep this book.* **2.** have and not let go: *Can she keep a secret?* **3.** have and take care of: *She keeps chickens.* **4.** hold back: *Keep the baby from crying.* **5.** *A refrigerator keeps food fresh.* **kept, keep ing.**

Ken tucky one of the fifty states of the United States.

kept See **keep.** *He kept the book I gave him.*

ket tle a metal pot, with a handle, for cooking.

key[1] **1.** a small metal instrument for opening or fastening a lock. **2.** the answer to a puzzle or problem. **3.** an explanation of abbreviations or signs used in a dictionary or a map. **4.** one of the parts pressed by the fingers on a piano, a typewriter, and other instruments. **5.** in music, a scale of notes: *The song is written in the key of B flat.*

key[2] a low island.

kick **1.** a blow with the foot. **2.** strike out with the foot: *Will that horse kick?* **3.** strike something with the foot. **kicked, kick ing.**

kid a young goat.

kill **1.** *The blow killed him.* **2.** *The farmer must kill the weeds in his fields.* **killed, kill ing.**

ki mo no **1.** a loose garment worn by men and women in some countries of Asia. **2.** a woman's loose housecoat.

kind[1] *What kind of book is that?*

kind[2] friendly; doing good, not harm: *A kind girl tries to help people.* **kind er, kind est.**

kind ly **1.** *She had a kindly smile.* **2.** *She spoke kindly to the children.* **kind li er, kind li est.**

king the man who rules a country and its people.

king fish er a bright-colored bird.

kiss **1.** a touch with the lips as a sign of love, greeting, or respect. **2.** touch with the lips as a sign of love, greeting, or respect. **kiss es; kissed, kiss ing.**

kitch en a room where food is cooked and prepared.

kite a light frame made of wood covered with paper or cloth: *Boys like to fly kites.* See the picture.

kit ten a young cat.

kite

knee   the joint between the thigh and the lower leg.
See the picture under **leg**.

kneel   go down on one's knees: *They often kneel in prayer*.   **knelt** or **kneeled, kneel ing**.

knelt   See **kneel**.   *She knelt and prayed*.

knew   See **know**.   *She knew the right answer*.

knife   a flat piece of steel or other metal with a handle and a sharp edge.   **knives**.

knight   a man given a title because of great service: *The knights fought for their king*.

knit   1. make a kind of cloth with long needles, usually out of wool yarn.   2. grow together: *The broken bone will knit quickly*.   3. *I like my knit dress*.   **knit ted** or **knit, knit ting**.

knob   1. a round lump.   2. the handle of a door or of a drawer.

knock   1. the sound made by hitting something: *A knock on the door made us all jump*.   2. hit something.   3. hit and cause to fall: *He ran against another boy and knocked him down*.   **knocked, knock ing**.

knot   1. strings or ropes twisted together in such a way that they will not pull apart: *He pulled the ends of the rope together and tied them in a knot*.   2. tie or fasten together in a knot: *If you knot the string, it won't slip*.   **knot ted, knot ting**.

knot ted   1. See **knot**.   2. *The knotted thread would not go through the needle*.

know   1. *How many kinds of birds do you know?*
2. *I know her very well, but I don't know her sister*.
3. *He knows arithmetic.   We know that two and two are four*.   **knew, known, know ing**.

known   See **know**.   *We have known many people*.

ko a la   a gray, furry animal of Australia that carries its young in a pocket.

ku kui   1. a large tree grown for its oil: *The Kukui is the State Tree of Hawaii*.   2. *The kukui tree is also called a candlenut tree*.

kum quat   1. a fruit like a small orange.   2. *He has kumquat jam on his bread*.

L

lab o ra to ry   a building or room where scientists work and do experiments.   **lab o ra to ries.**

La bor Day   a holiday, the first Monday in September.

lace   **1.** fine threads woven to make a delicate net. **2.** a cord, string, or strip for holding together: *These shoes need new laces.*   **3.** pull or hold together with laces.   **4.** *Here is a lace handkerchief.*   **laced, lac ing.**

lad   a boy; a young man.

lad der   a set of rungs or steps fastened into two long poles, for climbing up and down.   See the picture.

la dy   **1.** a woman.   **2.** a woman with nice manners: *She is a real lady.*   **la dies.**

la dy bug   a small, red beetle with black spots.

laid   See **lay**[1].   *He laid down the heavy bundle.*

lain   See **lie**[2].   *The dog has lain here all day.*

lake   water surrounded by land.

lamb   **1.** a young sheep.   **2.** meat from a lamb. **3.** *We had lamb chops.*

lame   **1.** not able to walk very well; having a hurt leg or foot.   **2.** stiff and sore.   **lam er, lam est.**

lame ly   *He hopped lamely across the yard.*

lamp   a thing that gives light, usually by burning oil or electricity: *We have a new shade for this lamp.*

land   **1.** the hard part of the earth's surface. **2.** ground; soil.   **3.** a country.   **4.** come to land: *The ship landed at the dock.*   **5.** *A rabbit is a land animal.*   **land ed, land ing.**

land lord   a person who owns land, buildings, or rooms that he rents to others.

lane   **1.** a path or narrow road in the country. **2.** any narrow way: *I see three lanes of traffic.*

lan guage   human speech, spoken or written.

lan tern   a light that can be carried.

large   big; of great size, amount, or number: *America is a large country.*   **larg er, larg est.**

lar i at   a long rope with a knot that slides tight, used by cowboys for catching horses and cattle.

rung

ladder

lass a girl; a young girl. **lass es.**

last[1] continue without being worn out or used up: *How long will our money last?* **last ed, last ing.**

last[2] **1.** coming after all others or at the end: *Z is the last letter in the alphabet.* **2.** *We stood last in the line.* **3.** *Last night we were home.*

latch **1.** something for fastening a door, gate, or window. See the picture. **2.** fasten with a latch. **latch es; latched, latch ing.**

late **1.** *I came home late.* **2.** *It was late in the evening.* **3.** *We had a late supper.* **lat er, lat est.**

late ly not long ago: *Have you been there lately?*

laugh **1.** the sound you make when you see or hear something funny: *The man had a loud laugh.* **2.** make these sounds. **laughed, laugh ing.**

laugh ing ly *She told the story laughingly.*

laugh ter the sound of laughing.

launch[1] a small boat run by a motor.

launch[2] **1.** cause to slide into the water to float. **2.** start or set going. **launched, launch ing.**

launch ing pad the surface on which a rocket is prepared and from which it is shot into the air.

laun dry **1.** clothes washed or to be washed. **2.** a place where clothes are washed and ironed. **laun dries.**

lau rel a small tree or bush with shiny leaves and bunches of pink blossoms: *The Mountain Laurel is the State Flower of Connecticut and of Pennsylvania.*

lav en der light purple.

law **1.** a rule for all the people: *Good citizens obey the laws.* **2.** the study of such rules: *Did he study law?* **3.** any rule: *Scientists study the laws of nature.*

lawn[1] a piece of land covered with grass.

lawn[2] a kind of thin linen or cotton cloth.

law yer a person who studies and knows the laws and gives advice about questions of law.

lay[1] **1.** put down: *Lay the baby down gently.* **2.** put in place: *We will lay the bricks tomorrow.* **3.** *Hens lay eggs.* **laid, lay ing.**

lay[2] See **lie**[2]. *She lay down and fell asleep.*

latch

lay er   one fold or a flat mass: *My birthday cake has two layers.   I am wearing three layers of clothes— a shirt, a sweater, and a coat.*

la zy   not willing to work or move fast: *I was too lazy to finish the lesson today.*   **la zi er, la zi est.**

lead[1]   **1.** a heavy gray metal.   **2.** *He used a lead weight on his fishing line.*

lead[2]   **1.** show the way by going along with or in front of.   **2.** be first.   **led, lead ing.**

leaf   **1.** one of the thin, flat, green parts of a tree or plant.   **2.** a thin sheet; a page.   **leaves.**

leak   **1.** *A leak in the paper bag lets the sugar run out.*   **2.** *Gas is leaking from this pipe.*   **leaked, leak ing.**

leaky   *Rain dripped on my head through the leaky roof.*   **leak i er, leak i est.**

lean[1]   **1.** stand slanting or bent: *The small tree leans over in the wind.*   **2.** rest against something: *Lean against the wall.*   **leaned, lean ing.**

lean[2]   thin or having little fat.   **lean er, lean est.**

leap   **1.** a jump or spring off the ground.   **2.** jump.   **leaped, leap ing.**

learn   find out about something; come to know how to do something.   **learned, learn ing.**

least   **1.** *He is the least friendly of the dogs.*   **2.** *The least I can do is go.*   **3.** *He liked that book least of all.*

leath er   **1.** a strong material made by tanning the skins of animals.   **2.** *These are leather gloves.*

leave[1]   *May I have your leave to go?*

leave[2]   **1.** go away: *We leave tonight.*   **2.** stop being in or working for: *Why did you leave the Boy Scouts?*   **3.** go without taking; let stay behind: *Don't leave your book on the table.*   **left, leav ing.**

led   See **lead**[2].   *A dog led the blind man.*

left[1]   **1.** See **leave**[2].   **2.** *How much is left?*

left[2]   on or to the side with the arm and hand most people use less than the other: *He sprained his left ankle.   She uses her left hand when she writes.*

leg   **1.** one of the limbs on which people and animals stand and walk.   See the picture under **body**.   **2.** anything shaped or used like a leg.

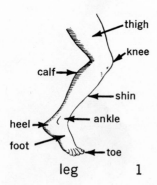

leg   1

278

lem on **1.** a sour, light-yellow fruit. **2.** *We made a lemon pie.*

lem on ade a drink made of lemon juice, sugar, and water.

lend let another person have or use for a time something you own: *Will you lend me your bicycle for an hour?* **lent, lend ing.**

length **1.** the longest way a thing can be measured: *My rug is two feet in length.* **2.** how long a thing lasts: *The length of the speech was an hour.* **3.** distance: *The length of the race is one mile.*

lent See **lend.** *I lent you my pencils.*

leop ard a fierce, spotted animal like a cat.

less **1.** *We had less rain this year than last. I paid less than five dollars for my bicycle.* **2.** *Five less two is equal to three.*

les son *Tomorrow we take the tenth lesson.*

let not stop someone or something from doing something: *Let the dog have a bone. Let him go. Will your mother let you stay?* **let, let ting.**

let's let us.

let ter **1.** *There are twenty-six letters in our alphabet.* **2.** *I wrote a letter to my aunt.*

let tuce **1.** a plant with large green leaves that are used for salad. **2.** *Here is a lettuce salad.*

lev el **1.** a surface having the same height everywhere: *We stopped at three different levels on the way up.* **2.** an instrument that shows whether a surface is level. **3.** having the same height everywhere: *This floor is not level.*

lev er a bar on a fulcrum for moving a weight.

li brar i an a person who works in a library.

li brary **1.** a collection of books: *Those two girls have libraries all their own.* **2.** a room or building where a collection of books is kept. **li brar ies.**

lick pass the tongue over or lap up with the tongue: *The kitten licked her paw.* **licked, lick ing.**

lic o rice **1.** the sweet root of a plant, dried and used in candy. **2.** *Licorice candy is usually black.*

lid a cover: *Take the lid off the pan, please.*

lie[1] **1.** something said that is not true: *His lie was discovered by his friends.* **2.** say something that is not true: *He never lied to anyone.* **lied, ly ing.**

lie[2] **1.** have one's body in a flat position. **2.** rest on a surface: *The book was lying on the table.* **lay, lain, ly ing.**

life **1.** *People, animals, and plants have life; rocks and metals do not.* **2.** *My uncle had a long life.* **3.** *Life in the country is good.* **4.** *Put more life in your work.* **lives.**

lift raise; move something up into the air; take up or pick up. **lift ed, lift ing.**

light[1] **1.** that by which we see: *The sun gives light to the earth.* **2.** a thing that gives light: *Bring a light into this room.* **3.** give light to; fill with light: *The room is lighted by six windows. We lit the candles.* **4.** become light: *The sky lights up at sunset.* **5.** bright; clear: *It is as light as day.* **6.** *She has light hair.* **light ed** or **lit, light ing; light er, light est.**

light[2] come down to the ground: *He lighted from his horse.* **light ed** or **lit, light ing.**

light[3] **1.** easy to carry; not heavy. **2.** having little weight for its size. **light er, light est.**

light ly *He tapped her lightly on the shoulder.*

light ning a flash of electricity in the sky.

like[1] be pleased or satisfied with. **liked, lik ing.**

like[2] **1.** *She is like her sister. She can sing like a bird.* **2.** *Isn't that just like a boy! I feel like working. It looks like rain.*

li lac **1.** a bush with lavender or white blossoms: *The Purple Lilac is the State Flower of New Hampshire.* **2.** *Lilac blossoms are fragrant.*

lily **1.** a plant that has flowers shaped like bells: *The Sego Lily is the State Flower of Utah.* **2.** *We planted lily bulbs.* **lil ies.**

limb **1.** a leg, arm, or wing. **2.** a large branch. See the picture.

lime[1] a powder used in building and in gardening.

lime[2] **1.** a fruit like a lemon but green and smaller. **2.** *We picked limes from our lime tree.*

limb

280

lime stone   a kind of rock used for building.

limp[1]   **1.** *The man walked with a limp.*   **2.** *The horse limped home.*   **limped, limp ing.**

limp[2]   *I am so tired I feel as limp as a rag.*

Lin coln's Birth day   February 12.

line[1]   **1.** *He used string for a fishing line.*   **2.** *Draw two lines on the paper.*   **3.** *Here is the line between your yard and ours.*   **4.** arrange in line: *Line up along the wall.*   **5.** mark with lines.   **lined, lin ing.**

line[2]   **1.** put a layer of something inside a dress, hat, box, or bag: *I lined the box with cotton before packing the dishes.*   **2. Lining** usually means the inside part of clothing.   **lined, lin ing.**

lin en   **1.** a kind of strong cloth.   **2. Linen** sometimes means tablecloths, napkins, sheets, towels, shirts, and collars.   **3.** *She wore her linen skirt.*

li on   a large, strong, wild animal.

lip   either of the two edges of the mouth.   See the picture under **face.**

liq uid   **1.** something that flows like water; not a hard mass or a gas: *A dark liquid was in the jar.* **2.** *We use liquid soap to wash dishes.*

list   **1.** items written one below the other: *Here is the shopping list.*   **2.** make a list of: *Will you list these words in order?*   **list ed, list ing.**

lis ten   try to hear: *The mother listens for her baby's cry.*   *I like to listen to music.*   **lis tened, lis ten ing.**

lit   **1.** See **light**[1].   *Have you lit the candles?* **2.** See **light**[2].   *Two birds lit on my window sill.*

lit tle   **1.** not big: *A grain of sand is little.* **2.** short; not long in time or in distance: *Wait a little while and I'll go a little way with you.* **3.** not much: *The littlest child eats the least food.*   **less** or **lit tler, least** or **lit tlest.**

live[1]   **1.** have life or be alive: *All animals and plants live; rocks do not.*   **2.** make your home: *Where do you live?*   **lived, liv ing.**

live[2]   **1.** having life; alive: *This is a live dog.* **2.** burning: *We cooked food over live coals.*   **3.** carrying an electric current: *Don't touch a live wire.*

liz ard   a small animal like a snake but with legs.

load   **1.** *The cart has a load of hay.*   **2.** *He loaded the truck with bricks.*   **3.** *Send us four loads of sand.*   **load ed, load ing.**

load ed   **1.** See **load.**   **2.** *A loaded truck went by.*

loaf[1]   **1.** bread baked as one piece: *We cut the loaf into slices.*   **2.** anything like a loaf in shape: *Mother baked a meat loaf for dinner.*   **loaves.**

loaf[2]   spend time doing nothing important: *I can loaf all day Saturday.*   **loafed, loaf ing.**

lob ster   a sea animal having two big claws.

lo cal   *The local newspaper gives news of our town.*

lo cal ly   *Her father is well known locally.*

lo cate   **1.** stay in a place: *Early settlers located near water.*   **2.** find out the position of: *The soldier tried to locate the enemy's camp.*   **lo cat ed, lo cat ing.**

lock[1]   **1.** something that holds doors, lids, or windows so they can't be opened.   **2.** fasten: *We lock our doors at night.*   **locked, lock ing.**

lock[2]   a curl of hair, wool, or fur.

lock et   a little case of gold, silver, or other metal for holding a picture or a lock of hair.

log   **1.** a long piece cut from the trunk or a branch of a tree.   **2.** *They built a log house.*

lone ly   **1.** *The little boy was lonely without his dad.*   **2.** *This is a lonely road.*   **lone li er, lone li est.**

lone some   **1.** *Were you lonesome at camp?*   **2.** *She heard the lonesome whistle of a train in the distance.*   **lone som er, lone som est.**

long[1]   wish very much or want badly: *He longed for his mother.   She longed to see him.*   **longed, long ing.**

long[2]   **1.** having great distance from end to end: *An inch is short; a mile is long.*   **2.** *My table is three feet long.*   **3.** *Summer will come before long.*   **4.** *A long vowel is a vowel like "a" in "late."*   **long er, long est.**

look   **1.** *He gave me an angry look.*   **2.** *Look at the pictures.*   **3.** *Did you look in the closet for your cap?*   **4.** *She looks happy.   It looked cold outside.*   **5. Look after** means take care of.   **looked, look ing.**

loon   a large diving bird.

loop 1. the shape of a curved line that crosses itself. 2. make a loop: *She looped the ribbon to make a bow.* **looped, loop ing.**

loose not tight; not firmly fastened: *She wore a loose coat.* **loos er, loos est.**

loose ly *The loosely tied package was easy to open.*

loos en make or become loose: *The knot loosened, and the dog ran away.* **loos ened, loos en ing.**

lope run with long, easy steps. **loped, lop ing.**

Lord God.

lose 1. *Try not to lose a friend.* 2. *Did you lose a book?* 3. *We won't lose the game.* **lost, los ing.**

lost 1. See **lose.** 2. *Here is the lost dog.*

lot 1. a piece of ground: *We play in an empty lot.* 2. a great many; very much: *He has a lot of marbles.*

lots *We ate lots of candy at the party.*

loud not quiet or soft; making a great sound. **loud er, loud est.**

loud ly *He called loudly for his dog.*

Lou i si ana one of the fifty states of the United States.

love 1. a deep feeling for a person or thing. 2. have such a feeling for. **loved, lov ing.**

love ly beautiful; good: *What lovely manners! She is the loveliest girl I know.* **love li er, love li est.**

low[1] 1. the sound a cow makes. 2. make the sound of a cow. **lowed, low ing.**

low[2] 1. *This is a low stool.* 2. *He bowed low.* 3. *The plane is flying low.* **low er, low est.**

luck what seems to happen or come to you; good fortune: *I am in luck. She gave me a penny for luck.*

luck i ly *Luckily, I remembered to bring the key.*

lucky having or bringing good luck: *Three is my lucky number.* **luck i er, luck i est.**

lum ber[1] wood that is cut and ready for use.

lum ber[2] move along heavily and noisily: *The old bear lumbered along.* **lum bered, lum ber ing.**

lump 1. *He modeled a dog from a lump of clay.* 2. *There is a lump on my head where I bumped it.*

lunch a light meal. **lunch es.**

lung   the part of your body that takes in air.

lus cious   very pleasing to taste, smell, hear, see, or feel: *This is a luscious peach.*

ly ing[1]   *We did not believe the lying man.*

ly ing[2]   See **lie**[2].   *He is lying down.*

M

mac a ro ni   a food in the form of long, hollow tubes made of flour paste.

ma chine   **1.** an instrument with moving parts for doing work.   **2.** *Levers and pulleys are machines.*

mack er el   a salt-water fish used for food.

mad   **1.** out of one's head; crazy: *She must have been mad to run away.*   **2.** very excited; wild: *The boy made a mad dash for the bus.*   **3.** angry: *He will be mad when he sees me.*   **mad der, mad dest.**

made   See **make.**   *The cook made the cake.*

mag a zine   a paper-covered book that is printed weekly or monthly.

mag ic   **1.** in stories, making things happen by secret charms and power: *The fairy's magic changed the brothers into swans.*   **2.** *She had a magic wand.*

ma gi cian   **1.** in stories, one who has magic power.   **2.** a person who does tricks that seem to be magic.

mag net   a stone or piece of iron or steel that attracts or pulls to it anything made of iron or steel.

mag nif i cent   beautifully colored; grand; splendid: *The king had a magnificent palace.*

mag nif i cent ly   *She was magnificently dressed.*

mag ni fy ing glass   a certain kind of glass that causes things to look larger.   **mag ni fy ing glass es.**

mag no lia   a tree with large white or pink flowers: *The Magnolia is the State Flower of Louisiana and of Mississippi; it is also the State Tree of Mississippi.*

mag pie   a noisy, black-and-white bird.

maid   **1.** a young girl.   **2.** a woman servant.

mail   **1.** letters and parcels to be sent from one person and place to another.   **2.** send by mail.   **mailed, mail ing.**

main **1.** a large pipe for water, gas, and so on: *When the water main broke, our cellar was flooded.* **2.** most important: *Where is the main road?*

Maine one of the fifty states of the United States.

maj es ty *A king and queen are called "His Majesty" and "Her Majesty."* **maj es ties.**

make **1.** *I can make a boat. Will you make a fire?* **2.** *Don't make a noise. Make him stop hitting me. Make room for me.* **3.** *She will make a good teacher.* **4.** *Will you make the beds?* **5.** *Two and three make five.* **6.** *They will make a trip to Canada. Don't make a mistake.* **7. Make believe** means pretend. **8. Make good** means succeed. **9. Make up** means become friends again after a quarrel. **made, mak ing.**

male **1.** a person who can be a father when he grows up. **2.** *A rooster is a male animal.*

mal lard a kind of wild duck.

ma ma mother.

mam ma mother.

mam mal an animal, with a backbone, that gives milk to its young: *Human beings, horses, cattle, dogs, and whales are mammals.*

mam moth **1.** a kind of elephant that lived thousands of years ago. **2.** very big: *What a mammoth tree!*

man a male human being. **men.**

man age control or direct: *They hired a man to manage the business.* **man aged, man ag ing.**

man do lin a musical instrument.

mane the long, heavy hair on the neck of a horse, a lion, and some other animals.

man go **1.** a fruit with a thick skin. **2.** *Mango trees grow in warm places.*

man ner **1.** a way of behaving: *She has a kind manner.* **2. Good manners** means being polite.

many a great number of: *Many years ago the house was new.* **more, most.**

map a drawing of the earth's surface or part of it, showing countries, towns, rivers, seas, mountains, lakes, and so on. See the picture.

map

ma ple   **1.** a tree thick with leaves that give much shade: *The Sugar Maple is the State Tree of New York, of Vermont, of West Virginia, and of Wisconsin. The Red Maple is the State Tree of Rhode Island.*
2. *Maple sugar comes from some maple trees.*

mar ble   **1.** a hard stone, white or colored, that shines beautifully when rubbed.   **2.** a small ball of marble, clay, glass, and so on, used in games.
3. *He climbed the marble stairs.*

march[1]   **1.** *It was a long march to the capital.*
2. *The band played a march.*   **3.** *The Cub Scouts marched down the street.*   **marched, march ing.**

March[2]   the third month of the year.

ma rine   a member of the Marine Corps.

Ma rine Corps   one part of the armed forces of the United States.

mar i o nette   a doll or puppet moved by strings.

mark   **1.** any line or dot made on a surface.
2. a grade: *My mark in arithmetic was B.*   **3.** put one's name on: *Mark the towels you will take to camp.*
4. make a line to show where a place is: *He is marking all the large cities on this map.*   **5. Mark off** means make lines to show where something is.
6. Mark time means move the feet as if marching but without going forward.   **marked, mark ing.**

mar ket   **1.** a place where people bring things to sell.   **2.** a store: *She went to the meat market.*

mar lin   a large fish with a big fin on its back.

mar ried   **1.** See **marry.**   **2.** *We know lots of married people.*

mar ry   **1.** join as husband and wife: *The minister marries many brides and grooms.*   **2.** take as husband or wife: *He will marry the girl he loves.*   **mar ried, mar ry ing.**

Mar y land   one of the fifty states of the United States.

mash   beat into a soft mass; crush to a uniform mass: *I'll mash the potatoes.*   **mashed, mash ing.**

mashed   **1.** See **mash.**   **2.** *Mother served mashed potatoes for dinner.*

mask a covering to hide or protect the face. See the picture.

mass **1.** a lump; something that sticks together: *An island is a mass of land.* **2.** a large amount together. **mass es.**

Mas sa chu setts one of the fifty states of the United States.

mas ter **1.** a person who rules or commands; the one in control. **2.** *The lights went off when I pulled the master switch.*

mat a thick piece of woven or braided material.

match[1] a short piece of wood or paper tipped with something that makes fire. **match es.**

match[2] **1.** *Those two colors are a good match.* **2.** *We played a tennis match.* **3.** *The rugs and the wallpaper match.* **4.** *Our team could not match the other team.* **5.** *Match the numbers in these two columns.* **match es; matched, match ing.**

mate **1.** a husband or wife. **2.** one of a pair. **3.** *Birds mate in the spring.* **mat ed, mat ing.**

ma te ri al what a thing is made from or done with: *He got his writing materials together.*

mat ter **1.** what things are made of: *The earth and all things on it are made of matter.* **2.** a thing or things written: *Books, papers, and other printed matter lay on the desk.* **3.** be important: *Nothing seems to matter to that boy. Will it matter if you go?* **4.** *What's the matter with you?* **5.** *I'm going no matter what she says.* **mat tered, mat ter ing.**

mat tress a case of heavy cloth stuffed with soft material and used on a bed. **mat tress es.**

May[1] the fifth month of the year.

may[2] **1.** *May I have an apple? You may go now.* **2.** *It may rain tomorrow. The train may be late.* **3.** *May you be very happy.* **might.**

may be perhaps, but not surely: *Maybe it will rain.*

may flow er[1] a plant that blooms in May: *The Mayflower is the State Flower of Massachusetts.*

May flow er[2] the ship on which the Pilgrims came to America in 1620.

mask

may or   the man at the head of a city government.

me   *Give the dog to me.   Let me go.   Come with me.*

mead ow.   a piece of land used for growing grass.

mead ow lark   a bird about the size of a robin:
*The Meadowlark is the State Bird of Wyoming.   The
Western Meadowlark is the State Bird of Kansas, of
Montana, of Nebraska, of North Dakota, and of Oregon.*

meal[1]   the food eaten or served at any one time.

meal[2]   grain ground to a powder.

mean[1]   **1.** *What does that sentence mean?*   **2.** *You
didn't mean to break the glass.*   **meant, mean ing.**

mean[2]   unkind; cruel: *It is mean to tease
a puppy.*   **mean er, mean est.**

meant   See **mean**[1].   *He explained what he meant.*

mea sles   having a cold, a high temperature, and
small red spots on the skin: *When she had the
measles, she was sick in bed.*

meas ure   **1.** the size or amount of something: *His
neck measure is fourteen inches.*   **2.** a bar of music.
3. find the size or amount of anything: *He measured
the boy with a ruler.*   **4.** mark off: *Measure out a
bushel of potatoes.*   **meas ured, meas ur ing.**

meat   **1.** the part of an animal used for food.
2. the part that can be eaten: *The meat of a nut is
the inside part.*   **3.** *We are having a meat pie tonight.*

me chan ic   a man who makes and repairs machines.

med i cine   something to make a sick person well.

meet   **1.** come face to face with: *Our car
may meet another on the narrow road.*   **2.** come
together; join: *Two roads meet near the church.*   **3.** be
introduced to: *I want you to meet my sister.*   **4.** receive
and welcome: *I must go to the station to meet my
mother.*   **met, meet ing.**

mel on   a large fruit, with lots of juice, that grows
on a plant like a vine: *A cantaloupe is a melon.*
See the picture.

melt   change from a hard mass to a liquid: *The ice
melts in the spring.*   **melt ed, melt ing.**

melt ed   **1.** See **melt**.   **2.** *Popcorn is good with
melted butter on it.*

melon

288

mem ber one who belongs to a group.

Me mo ri al Day a holiday, May 30.

men 1. more than one man: *Boys grow up to be men.* **2.** human beings; persons: *Men, animals, and plants need food.*

mend put in good shape again; repair or fix: *Father can mend your broken doll.* **mend ed, mend ing.**

men tion speak about: *Do not mention the accident again.* **men tioned, men tion ing.**

menu a list of the food served at a meal: *Look at the menu and choose what you want to eat.*

mer ry gay and happy. **mer ri er, mer ri est.**

mer ry-go-round wood animals and seats on a platform that goes round and round.

mes quite a low tree often found in the desert.

mes sage words sent from one person to another.

mes sen ger a person who carries a message.

met See **meet.** *My father met us this morning.*

met al 1. a material such as iron, gold, or silver. **2.** *A metal cover was put on the jar.*

me te or a mass of stone or metal that comes toward the earth from space; a shooting star.

Mex i can 1. a person who was born in Mexico **2.** *The children learned a Mexican dance.*

Mex i co a country in North America, south of the United States.

mice more than one mouse.

Mich i gan one of the fifty states of the United States.

mi cro phone a machine for making small sounds louder or for sending sounds over radio.

mi cro scope an instrument with a magnifying glass that helps us see very small things clearly.

mid dle halfway between; in the center: *We live in the middle of the block.* *The middle house is ours.*

mid night twelve o'clock at night; the middle of the night.

might[1] great power: *Work with all your might.*

might[2] See **may**[2]. *Mother said we might play here.*

mike a microphone.

mile   a distance equal to 5280 feet.

milk   **1.** the white liquid, from cows, which we drink.   **2.** a liquid produced by many female animals as food for their young.   **3.** draw milk from a cow, goat, or other animal.   **4.** *We found the milk pail in the barn.*   **milked, milk ing.**

mill   **1.** a machine for grinding grain into flour or meal.   **2.** the building containing such a machine. **3.** a factory: *A cotton mill makes thread.*

mil lion   one thousand thousand: *I wish I had a million dollars.*

mind   **1.** the part of a person that thinks and feels. *The boy has a good mind.*   **2.** take care of: *Please mind the baby.*   **3.** obey: *Mind your father and mother.* **4.** feel bad about: *Some people don't mind cold weather.*   **mind ed, mind ing.**

mine[1]   a large hole dug in the earth to get out minerals: *We saw a gold mine and a copper mine.*

mine[2]   **1.** *This book is mine.*   **2.** *Your shoes are black; mine are brown.*

min er   a man who works in a mine.

min er al   **1.** material dug from the earth: *Anything that is not a plant or an animal is a mineral.* **2.** *Some people drink mineral water for their health.*

min is ter   a person whose work is to help the people who go to the church he belongs to.

mink   a mammal that lives in water part of the time.

Min ne so ta   one of the fifty states of the United States.

mint   **1.** a sweet-smelling plant, the leaves of which are used in candy and jelly.   **2.** a piece of candy that tastes like mint. See the pictures.   **3.** *Mint jelly is usually green.*

mi nus   **1.** less: *Twelve minus three leaves nine.* **2.** without: *The book was returned minus its cover.* **3.** *The minus sign is —.*

min ute   **1.** one of sixty equal parts of an hour; sixty seconds.   **2.** a short time: *I'll be there in a minute.*   **3.** an exact point of time: *The minute you see him coming, tell me.*

mint

mir ror　a glass in which you can see yourself.

mis chief　conduct that causes harm or trouble, often without meaning it: *His mischief caused a fire.*

mis chie vous　full of tricks and teasing fun: *The mischievous children were climbing the apple trees.*

mis for tune　bad luck.

Miss[1]　a title given to a girl or to a woman who is not married.　**miss es.**

miss[2]　**1.** fail to hit: *He shot twice but missed.*
2. fail to find, get, or meet: *Don't miss the train.*
3. leave out or skip: *He missed a word when he read the sentence.*　**4.** notice or feel bad because something is gone: *I did not miss my purse till I got home. We miss you.*　**missed, miss ing.**

Mis sis sip pi　one of the fifty states of the United States.

Mis sou ri　one of the fifty states of the United States.

mis take　**1.** something that is not right or correct: *I made two mistakes on the spelling test.*　**2.** think something that is not right or true: *Don't mistake that stick for a snake.*　**mis took, mis tak en, mis tak ing.**

mis tak en　See **mistake.**　*I have mistaken you for your sister many times.*

mis tle toe　a plant that grows on trees: *The Mistletoe is the State Flower of Oklahoma.*

mis took　See **mistake.**　*I mistook you for your cousin yesterday.*

mit ten　a kind of glove that covers the four fingers together and the thumb separately.

mix　put or stir together.　**mixed, mix ing.**

moat　a deep, wide ditch, usually full of water, around a castle or town to protect it against enemies.

moc ca sin　a soft shoe, often made from buckskin.

moc ca sin flow er　a flowering plant also called the lady's-slipper: *The Pink-and-White Moccasin Flower is the State Flower of Minnesota.*

mock ing bird　a bird that sounds like other birds: *The Mockingbird is the State Bird of Arkansas, of Florida, of Mississippi, and of Tennessee.*

mod el   1. *He has made a model of a ship.*   2. *Let's model an elephant.*   3. *Model yourself on your father.*   4. *I like model airplanes.*   **mod eled, mod el ing.**

mo las ses   1. a sweet, thick liquid used in cooking.   2. *Have some molasses candy.*

mole   a small animal that lives underground.

mom   mother.

mo ment   1. a very short space of time; an instant: *In a moment all was changed.*   2. a certain point of time: *I started the very moment I got your message.*

Mon day   the second day of the week.

mon ey   coins and bills.

mon grel   an animal of no certain kind: *The puppy was a mongrel, part collie and part police dog.*

mon key   a small animal that looks quite human.

Mon tana   one of the fifty states of the United States.

month   1. one of twelve equal parts of a year: *January is the first month.*   2. *He'll be gone six months.*

month ly   1. *This is a monthly magazine.   The Camp Fire Girls hold monthly meetings at school.*   2. *He visits us monthly.*

moon   a body that revolves around the earth.

moose   an animal with antlers.   **moose.**

mop   1. a bundle of rags or a sponge with a long handle for cleaning floors.   2. wash or wipe up: *He mopped his forehead.   We should mop the floor this morning.*   **mopped, mop ping.**

more   1. *A foot is more than an inch.   This plant needs more sun.*   2. *Tell me more about your camping trip.   We need more than ten boys for the team.*

morn ing   the early part of the day, ending at noon.

mosque   a place to worship; a kind of church.

mos qui to   a small, thin insect: *There are many mosquitoes near the lake in summer.*

most   1. *I have the most fun on Saturday.   He had the most votes.*   2. the greatest amount or number: *Who gave the most?*   3. *Most people like ice cream.*   4. *This one is the most beautiful of all.*

mo tel a group of rooms or cottages for people to rent and sleep in when they travel.

moth a small, winged insect that lays eggs in wool and often causes holes in clothing.

moth er 1. the female parent. 2. *The mother duck watched over her baby ducks.*

mo tion *He made a quick motion with his hand to show the way.*

mo tor 1. a small engine, usually run by electricity or gas: *An electric motor turned the fan.* 2. *He wants a motor scooter for his birthday.*

mo tor cy cle a kind of bicycle run by a motor.

mound a bank or heap of earth or stones.

mount[1] 1. a mountain; a high hill. 2. **Mount** is often used before names of mountains: *Mount Washington is in New Hampshire.*

mount[2] 1. go up: *We'll mount the hill to look for berries.* 2. get up on: *The mayor is mounting the platform.* **mount ed, mount ing.**

moun tain 1. a very high hill. See the picture. 2. *Mountain air is always fresh.*

mount ed 1. See **mount**[2]. 2. *The mounted policeman rode his horse through the park.*

mouse a small, gray, gnawing animal. **mice.**

mouth 1. an opening through which food is taken in. See the picture under **face.** 2. an opening like a mouth: *The boys entered the mouth of the cave.*

move 1. change the place or position of: *Move your chair to the table. The child moved in his sleep.* 2. change one's place of living. **moved, mov ing.**

mov ie a moving picture.

mow cut down: *It is time to mow the grass again.* **mowed, mowed** or **mown, mow ing.**

mow er *The lawn mower needs to be oiled.*

Mr. a title put in front of a man's name.

Mrs. a title put in front of a married woman's name.

much 1. *I do not have much money. You gave me too much cake.* 2. *I was much pleased with the toy.* **more, most.**

mud wet earth that is soft and sticky.

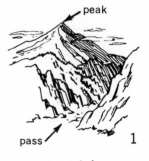

mountain

muff

muff   a covering, usually of fur, into which a girl puts her hands to keep them warm.   See the picture.

muf fler   1. a wrap or scarf worn around the neck. 2. a thing used to take away noise.

mule   an animal which is half donkey and half horse.

mul ti ply   take some number a given number of times: *To multiply six by three means to take six three times, making eighteen.*   **mul ti plied, mul ti ply ing.**

mumps   a swelling of the neck and face that makes it hard to swallow food: *He is sick in bed with mumps.*

mus cle   *You can feel the muscles in your arm.*

mu se um   the building or rooms in which a collection of objects is shown: *Our class saw paintings at the art museum and bones at the history museum.*

mush room   a small plant, shaped like an umbrella.

mu sic   1. different sounds arranged so that they are pleasing to hear: *He studied music at school.   I hear music in the next room.*   2. written or printed signs for different sounds: *Can you read music?*

mu si cal   *The bell made a musical sound.   Violins, pianos, and trumpets are musical instruments.*

mu si cian   a person who sings or who plays a musical instrument.

mus kie   a large fish: *The Muskellunge, or Muskie, is the State Fish of Wisconsin.*

must   *All men must eat to live.   I must keep my promise.   You must read this story.   The man must be crazy to talk so.   I must seem very rude.*

mus tache   the hair growing on a man's top lip.

mus tard   1. a plant whose seeds have a sharp, hot taste.   2. a powder or paste made from these seeds.

my   of me; belonging to me: *I learned my lesson. My house is around the corner.   My book is on the shelf; yours is here.*

my self   1. *I did it myself.*   2. *I can cook for myself. I hurt myself.*   **our selves.**

mys te ri ous   1. *Electricity is mysterious to most people.*   2. *He had a mysterious look on his face.*

mys tery   a secret; something that is hidden or not understood.   **mys ter ies.**

N

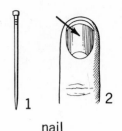

nail

nail **1.** a pointed length of wire used to hold pieces of wood together. **2.** the hard surface at the end of a finger or toe. See the pictures. **3.** fasten with nails. **nailed, nail ing.**

name **1.** *Our dog's name is King. She knows all her chickens by name.* **2.** *"Oak" is the name of one kind of tree.* **3.** *They named the baby after his father.* **4.** *Can you name these flowers?* **named, nam ing.**

nap a short sleep.

nap kin a piece of cloth or paper used at meals to protect the clothing and to wipe the lips and fingers.

nar ra tor a person who tells a story.

nar row **1.** not wide. **2.** *We used narrow ribbon to tie the package.* **3.** *He had a narrow escape.* **nar row er, nar row est.**

nar row ly *He narrowly missed being hit by the ball.*

na tion a group of people in the same country, having the same government, and mostly speaking the same language.

na ture the world; all things except those made by man.

naugh ty bad; not doing what one is supposed to do. **naugh ti er, naugh ti est.**

Na vy **1.** one part of the armed forces of the United States. **2.** all the ships of war of a country, with their crews and the department that manages them. **3.** *I have a navy-blue coat.* **na vies.**

near **1.** *We live near New York.* **2.** *It must be near five o'clock.* **3.** *Take the nearest cookie on the plate.* **near er, near est.**

near ly **1.** *It is nearly bedtime.* **2.** *As nearly as I can guess, it will not rain.*

neat **1.** *Her room was always neat.* **2.** *He is a neat child.* **neat er, neat est.**

neat ly *Write your name neatly.*

Ne bras ka one of the fifty states of the United States.

nec es sary *It is necessary to study in order to learn.*

295

neck **1.** the part of the body between the head and shoulders.   See the picture under **body**.
2. the part of a piece of clothing that fits the neck.
neck lace a chain or string of beads, worn around the neck.
neck tie a narrow band or a tie, worn around the neck and tied in front.
need be in want of; ought to have; not be able to do without.   **need ed, need ing.**
nee dle **1.** a thin, pointed tool with a hole, or eye, at one end, through which thread is passed for sewing.
2. a thin, pointed rod for knitting.   **3.** a thin steel pointer on a compass or dial.   **4.** a sharp, hollow tool used by doctors to give shots.   **5.** the thin, pointed leaf of some evergreen trees.
neigh bor someone who lives nearby.
neigh bor hood **1.** *She lives in our neighborhood.*
2. *We like to play with our neighborhood friends.*
nei ther *Neither you nor I will go.   Neither sentence is true.   Neither of the sentences is true.*
ne ne a kind of goose: *The Nene is the State Bird of Hawaii.*
neph ew a son of one's brother or sister.
nest a thing shaped like a bowl, built out of sticks, straw, and other material, by birds as a place in which to lay their eggs.   See the picture.
net an open material made of string, cord, thread, or hair, knotted together in such a way as to leave large or small holes: *A net holds her hair in place.*
Ne vada one of the fifty states of the United States.
nev er not ever; at no time.
new **1.** never having been made or used before.
2. not old or used up.   **new er, new est.**
New Hamp shire one of the fifty states of the United States.
New Jer sey one of the fifty states of the United States.
new ly *Our house has newly painted walls.*
New Mex i co one of the fifty states of the United States.

nest

news   facts about something which has just happened or will soon happen.

news pa per   sheets of paper printed every day or week, telling the news and useful facts.

newt   a small animal like a lizard.

New Year's Day   a holiday, January 1.

New York   one of the fifty states of the United States.

next   **1.** *The next train goes tomorrow morning.* **2.** *We live in the house next to the church.* **3.** *I am going to do my arithmetic problems next.*

nib ble   **1.** eat away with quick, small bites. **2.** bite gently or lightly.   **nib bled, nib bling.**

nice   pleasing; good; satisfying.   **nic er, nic est.**

nice ly   *She answered the question very nicely.*

nick el   **1.** a hard metal that looks like silver. **2.** a United States or Canadian coin worth five cents. **3.** *He bought a nickel candy bar.*

niece   a daughter of one's brother or sister.

night   **1.** the time between evening and morning. **2.** *He took the night train home.*

nine   **1.** one more than eight.   **2.** *Come at nine o'clock.*

nine teen   **1.** nine more than ten.   **2.** *We were here nineteen minutes ago.*

nine teenth   **1.** next after the eighteenth.   **2.** *This is the nineteenth of May.*

nine ti eth   next after the eighty-ninth: *Today is Grandfather's ninetieth birthday.*

nine ty   nine times ten.   **nine ties.**

ninth   **1.** next after the eighth.   **2.** *Her birthday is June ninth.*

no   **1.** *Father said no to our question.   No, I don't care for any more.   How many vote "No"?*   **2.** *Dogs have no wings.   Eat no more.*   **noes.**

nod   **1.** bow the head a little bit and raise it again quickly.   **2.** say yes by nodding.   **3.** let the head fall forward when sleepy or falling asleep.   **nod ded, nod ding.**

noise   a sound, often one that is not pleasant.

news

noise

nois i ly   *He walked along laughing noisily.*

noisy   **1.** *He is a noisy boy.*   **2.** *I live on a noisy street.*   **nois i er, nois i est.**

none   not any: *We have none of that paper left.*

non sense   **1.** *The clown's nonsense made us laugh.*   **2.** *"Nonsense!" she said.*

noon   twelve o'clock; the middle of the day.

nor   **1.** and no: *There was neither river nor stream in that desert.*   **2.** and not: *I have not gone there nor will I ever go.*

north   **1.** the direction to which a compass needle points; the direction to your right as you face the setting sun.   **2.** *Drive north for the next mile.*   **3.** coming from the north: *A north wind is often cold.*   **4.** *Follow the north branch of the river.*

North Amer i ca   one of the large masses of land on the earth.

North Car o li na   one of the fifty states of the United States.

North Da ko ta   one of the fifty states of the United States.

north east   **1.** the direction halfway between north and east: *Our house is in the northeast part of town.*   **2.** toward the northeast.   **3.** *A northeast wind was blowing.*

north ern   **1.** toward the north: *We took the northern road.*   **2.** from the north: *A northern wind shook the trees.*

North Pole   the point farthest north on the earth.

north ward   toward the north.

north west   **1.** the direction halfway between north and west: *Many of the northwest states have mountains.*   **2.** toward the northwest.   **3.** *A northwest wind blew.*

nose   the part of the face or head just above the mouth.   See the picture under **head.**

not   *Cold is not hot.   Six and two do not make ten.*

note   **1.** words written down to help you remember what you have heard or read.   **2.** a very short letter.   **3.** a single sound in music or the written sign to show the sound.

noth ing   **1.** not anything.   **2.** zero.

no tice   **1.** *This is beneath her notice.*   **2.** *There was a notice about the game in the paper.*   **3.** *I noticed a hole in my stocking.   The boy didn't notice the car that passed.*   **no ticed, no tic ing.**

no tion   idea; a thought about something.

noun   the name of a person, place, or thing.

No vem ber   the eleventh month of the year.

now   **1.** at this time or by this time.   **2.** since; now that: *Now I am older, I have changed my mind.*   **3.** *By now the coffee should be ready.*   **4.** *Now, you knew that was wrong.   Oh, come now!*

noz zle   a tip on a hose that shoots liquid out in a stream.

num ber   **1.** a word that tells exactly how many: *Two, thirteen, twenty-one, fifty, and one hundred are numbers.*   **2.** the sum of a group of things or persons: *The number of boys in our class is twenty.*   **3.** give a number to: *The pages of this book are numbered.   We numbered the boxes.*   **4. Numbers** sometimes means arithmetic.   **num bered, num ber ing.**

nu mer al   a figure or group of figures standing for a number.

nurse   **1.** a person who takes care of the sick.
2. a woman who cares for and brings up other people's children.   **3.** wait on or try to cure the sick: *He nursed his sick dog back to health.*   **nursed, nurs ing.**

nut   **1.** a dry fruit or seed with a hard shell.
2. a small block, usually of metal, with a hole in the center into which a screw fits.   See the picture.

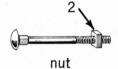

nut

O

oak   **1.** a tree having hard wood and nuts called acorns: *The Oak is the State Tree of Illinois and of Iowa.   The White Oak is the State Tree of Connecticut and of Maryland.   The Live Oak is the State Tree of Georgia.   The Northern Red Oak is the State Tree of New Jersey.*   **2.** *Oak leaves covered the ground.*

oar a long pole with one flat end, used in rowing.

oat **1.** a plant. **2. Oats** means the grain of the oat plant: *Horses like to eat oats.* **3.** *Oat flour is ground from oats.* See the picture under **grain.**

oat meal **1.** a breakfast food. **2.** *Oatmeal cookies are my favorite.*

obe di ent doing as one is told.

obe di ent ly *The dog followed obediently.*

obey do what one is told to do: *The dog obeyed and went home. We obey our father.* **obeyed, obey ing.**

ob ject **1.** anything that can be seen or touched. **2.** not like something or be against: *Many people object to loud noise.* **ob ject ed, ob ject ing.**

ob serv a to ry a place with a telescope for looking at the stars. **ob serv a to ries.**

oc ca sion **1.** a certain time: *We have met your father on several occasions.* **2.** a special event: *The jewels were worn only on a great occasion.*

oc ca sion al ly *We go fishing occasionally.*

ocean the great body of salt water that covers almost three fourths of the earth's surface.

o'clock of the clock; by the clock: *It is one o'clock.*

Oc to ber the tenth month of the year.

oc to pus a sea animal having a soft, thick body and eight arms. **oc to pus es.**

odd **1.** left over; extra: *There seems to be an odd stocking in the wash.   The boy did odd jobs.* **2.** leaving a remainder of one when divided by two: *Three, five, and seven are odd numbers.* **3.** strange or queer: *He has an odd name.* **odd er, odd est.**

odd ly *He was oddly dressed.*

odor smell: *The odor of roses came from the garden.*

of **1.** *The members of the team went home.* **2.** *They built a house of bricks.* **3.** *She is a woman of good sense.* **4.** *The state of Texas is very big.* **5.** *Texas is north of Mexico.* **6.** *His teachers think well of him.*

off **1.** *He pushed me off my seat.   You are off the road.   He went off in his car.* **2.** *The electricity is off. A button is off his coat.* **3.** *Turn the water off.   The game was called off.* **4.** *She cleared off her desk.*

of fer   **1.** holding out something to be taken: *Ten dollars for the bike was the best offer he had.* **2.** hold out to be taken or refused: *He offered me his coat.   Is he offering us his help?*   **3.** suggest: *She may offer a few ideas to improve the plan.*   **of fered, of fer ing.**

of fice   the place in which some people work.

of fi cer   **1.** a person who commands others in the Army or Navy.   **2.** *A police officer stopped the car.*

of ten   many times: *It often snows in January.   We have been here often.*   **of ten er, of ten est.**

oh or **Oh**   a word used to express surprise, joy, pain, and other feelings: *Oh, dear me!   Oh! Joy!*

Ohio   one of the fifty states of the United States.

oil   **1.** thick liquid from animal fat or vegetable fat or taken from the earth.   **2.** put oil on or in. **3.** *Where is the oil can?*   **oiled, oil ing.**

oily   **1.** containing oil or covered with oil.   **2.** like oil; smooth; slippery.   **oil i er, oil i est.**

Okla ho ma   one of the fifty states of the United States.

old   not young or new.   **old er, old est.**

ole o mar ga rine   something like butter but made from animal fat and vegetable oils.

ol ive   **1.** a small, round fruit with a hard stone. **2.** *Olive trees grow in warm places.*

on   **1.** *This book is on the table.*   **2.** *Put the ring on her finger.*   **3.** *The picture is on the wall.*   **4.** *The race is on.*   **5.** *From that day on he was never late to school.*   **6.** *He was reading a book on animals.* **7.** *He went on a trip.*   **8. On and on** means without stopping.   **9. And so on** means and more of the same.   **10. On time** means not too late nor too early.

once   **1.** *Read it once more.*   **2.** *That man was once a little baby.*   **3. At once** means immediately or at the same time.   **4. Once upon a time** means long ago.

one   **1.** the number 1.   **2.** a single thing; not two or more.   **3.** *I was sick one day last week.* **4.** the same: *All face one way.*

onion

orange blossom

on ion a vegetable eaten raw and used in cooking.

on ly **1.** no other or no more: *Water is his only drink. This is the only road along the shore. Only he remained.* **2.** just: *He sold only two.* **3. If only** often means I wish: *If only the sun would shine!*

open **1.** spread out or unfold: *Open your books.* **2.** start or begin: *We open our meetings with a song. School opens in September.* **3.** *The open windows let in fresh air.* **4.** *We cooked over an open fire. The box was open.* **5.** not hiding something or keeping something secret: *Please be open with me.* **opened, open ing.**

open ly *He openly confessed that he had eaten all the cake.*

op era a play in which the characters sing instead of speak.

op er ate **1.** run: *The machines operate night and day.* **2.** manage: *The boy operates the elevator.* **3.** *A doctor operates on a sick person if he thinks it is necessary.* **op er at ed, op er at ing.**

op er a tion **1.** doing something or making something work: *The operation of a railroad needs many men.* **2.** *The operation of this machine is simple.* **3.** *Taking out the tonsils is a common operation.*

op er a tor a person who makes something work: *She wants to be a telephone operator.*

opos sum a small mammal that lives in trees.

op po site **1.** placed against; face to face; back to back: *The house straight across the street is opposite to ours.* **2.** as different as can be: *North and south are opposite directions.*

or **1.** *Is it sweet or sour? Are you going to walk or ride?* **2.** *Either eat this or go hungry. Hurry, or you will be late.* **3.** *An author, or a man who writes books, is visiting school today.*

or ange **1.** a round, yellowish-red fruit, full of juice, that is good to eat. **2.** *There are many orange trees in Florida.*

or ange blos som the blossom of the orange tree: *The Orange Blossom is the State Flower of Florida.*

or bit   **1.** the path of a satellite around a planet or star.   See the picture.   **2.** the path of a man-made satellite around the earth.   **3.** start going around a planet in a nearly round path: *The capsule began to orbit at midnight.*   **or bit ed, or bit ing.**

or chard   **1.** a piece of ground on which fruit trees are grown.   **2.** the trees in an orchard: *The orchard is producing many apples this year.*

or ches tra   **1.** musicians playing together: *Her father is a member of the orchestra.*   **2.** all the instruments played together by the musicians in an orchestra: *An orchestra has violins, cellos, and horns.*

or der   **1.** the way a group of things is placed or arranged: *The children lined up in order of size.*   **2.** a command: *The orders of the captain must be obeyed.*   **3.** give directions: *He ordered steak for dinner.*   **4.** tell what to do: *The policeman ordered him to stop.*   **or dered, or der ing.**

Or e gon   one of the fifty states of the United States.

or gan   **1.** a musical instrument.   **2.** any part of an animal or plant fitted to do certain things in life: *The eyes, stomach, heart, and lungs are organs of the body.*

or gan ize   **1.** put into order or arrange: *Please organize your work so you can do it well.*   **2.** combine in a company, club, or other group: *We organized a music club.*   **or gan ized, or gan iz ing.**

ori ole   a bird with yellow-and-black feathers: *The Baltimore Oriole is the State Bird of Maryland.*

os trich   a large, long-legged bird that can run fast but cannot fly.   **os trich es.**

oth er   **1.** what is remaining or the rest: *We are here, but the other boys are at school.*   **2.** different: *I have no other place to go.   Come some other day.*   **3.** *She helps others.   Here are two books, but where are the others?*

ot ter   a mammal that lives in water part of the time.

ouch   an exclamation expressing sudden pain.

ought   **1.** should; be right or wise: *You ought to obey your parents.*   **2.** be likely or expected: *At your age you ought to know better.*

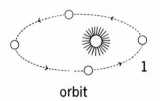

orbit

ounce 1. a measure of weight for dry material: *Sixteen ounces are equal to one pound.* 2. a measure for liquids: *Sixteen ounces are equal to one pint.*

our belonging to us: *We need our coats now.*

ours 1. *This garden is ours.* 2. *Ours is a large house. I like ours better than yours.*

our selves 1. *We ourselves will do the work.* 2. *We cook for ourselves. We help ourselves.* 3. *We cannot see ourselves as others see us.*

out 1. in baseball, the end of a player's turn at bat: *Three strikes make an out.* 2. away; forth: *The water will rush out. Come out the door. Spread the rug out.* 3. not in or at a place: *My mother is out just now. We are going out of town next week.* 4. not burning; no longer lighted: *The fire is out. Turn out the light.* 5. aloud; plainly: *Speak out so that all can hear.*

out fit 1. all the things necessary for any planned event. 2. get together everything necessary for any planned event: *He outfitted himself for a camping trip.* **out fit ted, out fit ting.**

out side 1. the side or surface that is not in: *The outside of my coat is worn.* 2. *Run outside and play.* 3. *We pulled off the outside leaves of the cabbage.* 4. out of; beyond the limits of: *Stay outside the house.*

ov en 1. a space in a stove for baking food. 2. a small furnace for heating or drying.

over 1. above: *The sky is over our heads. Pull the blanket over the baby.* 2. on or to the other side of: *Don't cross over the road. Can you climb over the hill?* 3. across a space or distance: *Go over to the store for me.* 4. out and down from; down from the edge of: *He fell over the edge of the cliff.* 5. all through: *I want to travel over the United States. He went over everything twice.* 6. at an end: *The play is over.* 7. about: *Think that over. He is troubled over his health.* 8. more than: *It cost over ten dollars.* 9. **Over again** means once more. 10. **Over and over** means again and again.

owe have to pay: *I owe the grocer a dollar for what we bought.* **owed, ow ing.**

owl   a bird with big eyes and a short, hooked bill.
own   1. have: *I own many books.*   2. belonging to oneself or itself: *This is my own book.   She makes her own dresses.*   3. *I'd like a room of my own.*   4. *That dog has its own house.*   **owned, own ing.**
ox   the full-grown male of cattle when fitted and trained for farm work.   **ox en.**
oys ter   a kind of shellfish often used as food and sometimes containing a pearl.

P

pace   1. walk with steps that are the same in size and speed: *He paced the floor as he talked.*   2. measure by paces: *We paced off the distance for the race.*
3. **Keep pace with** means keep up with; go as fast as.   **paced, pac ing.**
Pa cif ic   the great ocean west of America.
pack   1. a bundle of things tied together for carrying.
2. a case to be carried on the back. See the picture.
3. put together in a box or bag.   **packed, pack ing.**
pack age   things packed or wrapped together and tied or fastened; a parcel.
pad   1. a mass of soft material used for protection or stuffing; a cushion: *The baby's play pen has a pad made to fit it.*   2. fill with something soft: *We padded the box with cotton.*   3. a tablet of writing paper.   **pad ded, pad ding.**
pad ded   1. See **pad.**   2. *He sat down on the padded bench.*
pad dle¹   1. a short oar that is broad at one or both ends, used to move a canoe: *Pulling a paddle through the water moves the canoe forward.*   2. move a boat or a canoe with a paddle: *He paddled the canoe up the river.*   **pad dled, pad dling.**
pad dle²   move the hands or feet about in water.   **pad dled, pad dling.**
page   one side of a leaf or sheet of paper: *A page in this book is torn.*
paid   See **pay.**   *I have paid my bills.*

pack

305

palm¹

palm²

pail   a deep, round container, with a handle, for carrying liquids.

pain   **1.** a feeling of being hurt; suffering: *A cut gives pain.*   **2. Take pains** means be careful.

paint   **1.** a thick liquid that can be put on a surface to color it.   **2.** cover with paint.   **3.** draw in colors: *The artist will paint a country scene.*   **4.** *Don't drop the paint bucket.*   **paint ed, paint ing.**

paint ed   **1.** See **paint.**   **2.** *A painted chair was in the corner.*

paint er   **1.** a person who paints pictures; an artist.   **2.** a person who paints houses.

pair   **1.** a set of two; two things that go together: *I need a pair of shoes.*   **2.** a thing with two parts that cannot be used separately: *Bring me a pair of scissors.   He put on a pair of trousers.*

pa ja mas   clothes to sleep in, with a coat or shirt and loose trousers.

pal ace   a grand house for a king or queen to live in.

palm¹   the inside of the hand between the wrist and the fingers.   See the picture.

palm²   **1.** a tree that grows in warm places, usually having a tall trunk and a bunch of large leaves at the top.   See the picture.   **2.** *Some palm trees have coconuts.*

pal met to   **1.** a kind of palm with fan-shaped leaves: *The Cabbage Palmetto is the State Tree of South Carolina.   The Sabal Palmetto Palm is the State Tree of Florida.*   **2.** *Leaves from palmetto trees make good fans.*

pa lo ver de   **1.** a tree that grows in dry places: *The Blue Paloverde is the State Tree of Arizona.*   **2.** *Paloverde trees have many blossoms.*

pan   a dish for cooking and other uses, usually made of metal, sometimes with a long handle: *We put a pan of water on the floor for the dog.*

pan da   an animal like a bear, but black and white.

pane   a sheet of glass in a window or door: *The hail broke several panes in the window.*

pan sy   a flower somewhat like a violet but larger and with several colors in it.   **pan sies.**

pan try   a small room in which food, dishes, silver, and table linens are kept.   **pan tries.**

pants   a common name for trousers.

pa pa   father; dad.

pa pa ya   1. a fruit, yellowish and like a melon. 2. *Papaya trees grow in warm places.*

pa per   1. material used as a surface for writing, printing, or drawing, and also used for wrapping packages and covering walls.   2. a piece or sheet of paper with writing or printing on it: *Important papers were stolen.*   3. a newspaper: *Have you seen today's paper?*   4. *Here is a paper cup.*

pa poose or **pap poose**   a North American Indian baby carried on his mother's back.

par a chute   a piece of cloth like a big umbrella, used to bring a person down safely through the air.

pa rade   a march for some special event: *Clowns, floats, and bands were in the circus parade.*

par a graph   a group of sentences that belong together: *Paragraphs usually begin on a new line, and the first line is set farther in from the left edge than the others.*

par a keet   a kind of small parrot with bright-colored feathers and a long tail.

par cel   a bundle of things wrapped or packed together; a package: *The postman brought me a parcel.*

par don   1. being excused from blame for something: *I beg your pardon for bumping you.* 2. being free from being punished: *After two years in jail the man got a pardon.*   3. excuse: *Grandmother pardons us when we are naughty.*   4. set free from being punished: *The governor pardoned the man.* 5. *Pardon me, please.*   **par doned, par don ing.**

par ent   a person's father or mother.

park   1. land used for the pleasure of the people: *Many cities have beautiful parks.*   2. leave a vehicle in a certain place: *Park your bicycle here.*   3. *We sat on a park bench.*   **parked, park ing.**

par lor   a room where people sit and talk or receive guests: *After dinner the family sat in the parlor.*

par rot a bird, with bright-colored feathers, that can be taught to say words.

part **1.** each of several equal amounts into which a whole may be divided. **2.** a thing that helps make up something. **3.** a dividing line left when combing one's hair. **4.** divide or force apart: *The policeman on horseback parted the crowd.* **5.** separate: *The friends parted in anger.* **6.** less than the whole: *He ate part of an apple.* **part ed, part ing.**

part ly not completely: *The answer is partly right.*

part ner **1.** one who does something with another person: *She was my tennis partner. Who was your partner at the dance?* **2.** a wife or husband.

par ty **1.** a group of people having a good time: *She had a party on her birthday.* **2.** a group of people doing something together: *A scouting party explored the woods.* **3.** *Wear your party dress.* **par ties.**

pasque flow er a flower that blooms in early spring: *The American Pasqueflower is the State Flower of South Dakota.*

pass **1.** a free ticket: *He gave me a pass to the circus.* **2.** a way through: *The scout looked for a pass through the mountains.* See the picture under **mountain.** **3.** go by; move beyond: *We passed the truck. The days pass slowly.* **4.** hand from one to another: *Please pass the butter.* **5.** be successful in a test: *He passed arithmetic.* **pass es; passed, pass ing.**

pas sen ger a traveler in a train, bus, boat, or other vehicle, usually one who pays a fare: *There were only six passengers on the bus.*

Pass o ver for some people a yearly church holiday.

past **1.** gone by; ended: *Summer is past. Our troubles are past.* **2.** just gone by: *The past year was wonderful.* **3.** beyond: *It is half past two. I ran past the house. The arrow went past the mark.* **4.** passing by: *The buses go past once an hour.*

paste **1.** something that will stick paper together: *Flour and water mixed together make a good paste.* **2.** stick with paste: *He pasted the picture in his book.* **past ed, past ing.**

pas tor   a minister of a church.

pas ture   a grassy field or hillside where cattle, sheep, or horses can feed.

pat   **1.** strike or tap lightly with something flat: *She will pat the mud into a flat cake.*   **2.** tap gently with the hand: *He patted the dog.*   **pat ted, pat ting.**

patch   **1.** a piece put on to mend a hole or a tear.   **2.** a piece of cloth or tape put over a wound or a sore eye.   **3.** anything like a patch: *There is a patch of sunlight on the lawn.*   **4.** put patches on to mend or protect.   **patch es; patched, patch ing.**

path   **1.** a road made by people or animals walking, usually too narrow for automobiles.   **2.** *The moon moves along a path through the sky.*

pa tient   **1.** a person who is being treated by a doctor: *The doctor took care of three patients that afternoon.*   **2.** being ready to wait for something: *She was very patient as she stood in line.*

pa tient ly   *She waited patiently for the late bus.*

pat io   a small yard that is closed in by walls on one or more sides but is open to the sky.

pat ter   make rapid taps: *The rain pattered on the window.*   **pat tered, pat ter ing.**

pause   **1.** a short stop: *There was a pause in the talking as he stepped into the room.*   **2.** stop for a time; wait: *The dog paused in his barking when he heard me.*   **paused, paus ing.**

paw   the foot of an animal having claws. See the picture.

paw

pay   **1.** money given for things or work: *He gets his pay every Saturday.*   **2.** give money for things or for work done: *Pay the doctor.*   **3.** give or offer: *He always pays attention to the teacher.*   **paid, pay ing.**

pea   **1.** a round, green seed used as a vegetable.   **2.** *I like pea soup.*

peace   **1.** being free from war of any kind: *After the war there were many years of peace.*   **2.** quiet or calm; being still: *We enjoy the peace of the country.*

peach   **1.** a yellowish-red fruit full of juice and with a pit in the center.   **2.** *We have a peach tree.*   **peach es.**

peach blos som   the flower of a peach tree: *The Peach Blossom is the State Flower of Delaware.*

pea cock   a large beautiful bird with a long, splendid tail.

peak   **1.** the pointed top of a mountain or hill. See the picture under **mountain.**   **2.** a mountain that stands alone.

pea nut   **1.** a seed like a nut that is good to eat when roasted.   **2.** *We like peanut butter.*

pear   **1.** a sweet fruit round at one end and smaller toward the stem end, full of juice and good to eat.   **2.** *Our pear tree is in bloom.*

pearl   **1.** a white or nearly white jewel that has a soft shine like satin: *Pearls are found inside the shells of some oysters.*   **2.** *She wore a pearl necklace.*

pe can   **1.** a nut shaped like an olive and with a smooth shell.   **2.** the tree it grows on.   **3.** *The Pecan Tree is the State Tree of Texas.*

ped al   **1.** a lever worked by the foot: *Pushing the pedals of a bicycle makes it go.*   **2.** work or use the pedals of; move by pedals: *He pedaled his bicycle slowly up the street.*   **ped aled, ped al ing.**

ped dle   travel about with things to sell: *He peddled from house to house.*   **ped dled, ped dling.**

peek   look quickly and slyly; peep: *Close your eyes and do not peek.*   **peeked, peek ing.**

peel   **1.** the outside covering of fruit: *Throw away the orange peel.*   **2.** strip the skin, bark, or other covering from.   **3.** come off: *The paint on the barn is peeling.*   **peeled, peel ing.**

peep[1]   **1.** a look through a small hole or crack; a little look: *He took a peep in the oven to see the cake.*   **2.** look through a hole or crack; take a little look: *He peeped over the fence.*   **peeped, peep ing.**

peep[2]   **1.** the cry of a young bird or chicken; a sound like a squeak.   **2.** make such a sound: *The baby birds peeped loudly.*   **peeped, peep ing.**

pel i can   a large water bird with a pouch under its bill for storing food: *The Eastern Brown Pelican is the State Bird of Louisiana.*

pen[1]   a tool used in writing with ink. See the picture.
pen[2]   **1.** a small, closed place to keep babies or animals in: *We put the baby in the play pen.* See the picture.   **2.** shut in a pen: *He pens his dog in the back yard.*   **penned, pen ning.**
pen cil   a pointed tool for writing or drawing.
pen guin   a sea bird that swims but does not fly.
Penn syl va nia   one of the fifty states of the United States.
pen ny   **1.** a cent; a copper coin of the United States and Canada.   **2.** *One hundred pennies are equal to one dollar.*   **pen nies.**
pe o ny   a garden plant with large red, pink, or white flowers: *The Peony is the State Flower of Indiana.*   **pe o nies.**
peo ple   **1.** men, women, and children; persons: *There were ten people present.*   **2.** family or relatives: *His people live in another town.*
pep per   **1.** a coarse powder, with a hot taste, used to season food.   **2.** a hollow red or green vegetable that is baked, fried, or used in pickles.
perch[1]   a small fresh-water fish, used by many people for food.   **perch es** or **perch.**
perch[2]   **1.** a bar, branch, or anything on which a bird can come to rest.   **2.** come and rest; sit: *A robin perched on our roof.*   **3.** sit rather high: *He perched on a stool.*   **perch es; perched, perch ing.**
per fect   **1.** having no faults or mistakes; not spoiled anywhere: *He turned in a perfect spelling paper.*   **2.** having all its parts; complete: *The set of dishes was perfect; nothing was broken.*
per fect ly   *She was perfectly right.*
per form   **1.** do; carry out an act: *The doctor performed an operation.*   **2.** act, play, sing, or do tricks in public: *Three musicians will perform tonight.*   **per formed, per form ing.**
per form ance   **1.** a thing performed; an act.   **2.** carrying out; doing: *She was careful in the performance of her work.*   **3.** the giving of a show: *The evening performance is over.*

pen[1]

1

pen[2]

per fume 1. a sweet smell: *We enjoyed the perfume of the flowers.* 2. liquid having the sweet smell of flowers.

per haps able to happen but not sure to happen: *Perhaps a letter will come today. He will bring one, perhaps two, boxes. Perhaps we'd better leave.*

pe ri od 1. a length of time. 2. a dot (.) marking the end of most sentences or an abbreviation.

per ma nent 1. curls or waves put into the hair to stay: *Her new permanent is very pretty.* 2. meant to last: *The dentist put a permanent filling in my tooth.*

per son a man, woman, or child.

pest a thing or person that causes trouble.

pet 1. an animal kept as a favorite and treated with love. 2. treat as a pet; stroke or pat lovingly and gently. 3. *That girl has a pet rabbit.* **pet ted, pet ting.**

pheas ant a bird with a long tail and brightly colored feathers: *The Ring-Necked Pheasant is the State Bird of South Dakota.*

phone a telephone.

pho to a photograph.

pho to graph a picture made with a camera.

pho tog ra pher a person who takes photographs.

pi ano a musical instrument.

pick 1. a pointed tool for breaking hard material. 2. break up something with a pointed tool. 3. pull away with the fingers: *We pick flowers.* 4. choose: *I picked brown shoes.* **picked, pick ing.**

pick et 1. a person guarding a place: *Pickets around the camp watched for the enemy.* 2. a stake driven into the ground to make a fence or tie a horse to. See the picture under **fence.** 3. tie to a picket: *Picket your horse here.* 4. watch or guard: *The workers picketed the store to keep away customers.* **pick et ed, pick et ing.**

pick le 1. salt water, vinegar, or other liquid in which food can be kept from spoiling. 2. food kept in salt water, vinegar, and spices: *Sweet pickles are good with a hamburger.* 3. trouble; difficulty: *I got into a bad pickle today.* 4. put food in such a liquid: *I helped Mother pickle beets.* **pick led, pick ling.**

312

pic nic   a trip or party with a meal outdoors.

pic ture   **1.** a drawing, painting, or photograph.
2. a scene: *The trees and brook make a lovely picture.*
3. *We are going to have a picture show.*

pie   any food served in a baked crust made of flour, water, and oil: *We had chicken pie for dinner.*

piece   **1.** one of the parts into which a thing is divided or broken; a bit or scrap: *The cup broke in pieces.*   **2.** a small amount or a single thing: *Take a piece of this cloth with you.   Put a piece of wood on the fire.   I lost one piece from my puzzle.*

pig   a hog; an animal raised for its meat: *Bacon, ham, and pork come from a pig.*

pi geon   a bird with a plump body and short legs.

pike   a large fresh-water fish with a long, narrow, pointed head.   **pike.**

pile   **1.** a lot of things lying one upon another.
2. a mass: *There is a pile of dirt near the door.*
3. a large amount: *I have a pile of work to do.*
4. make into a pile; heap up: *Ask the boys to pile the blankets in a corner.*   **piled, pil ing.**

Pil grim   one of the English settlers who came to Plymouth, Massachusetts, in 1620.

pill   medicine made up into a tiny ball to be swallowed without being chewed.

pil low   a bag or case filled with feathers or other soft material, usually to put under your head.

pi lot   **1.** a man whose business is to steer a ship or an airplane.   **2.** act as a pilot of; steer: *He used to pilot ships up the river.*   **pi lot ed, pi lot ing.**

pin   **1.** a short piece of wire with one sharp end to stick through things and fasten them together.
2. *She wore her class pin.*   **3.** fasten with a pin: *Pin his mittens to his coat.*   **4.** hold fast in one position: *When the tree fell, it pinned his shoulder to the ground.*   **pinned, pin ning.**

pinch   **1.** sharp pressure that hurts; a squeeze: *The pinch of his tight shoes made him limp.*   **2.** squeeze with thumb and finger.   **3.** press; squeeze: *He pinched his finger in the door.*   **pinch es; pinched, pinch ing.**

pine **1.** a tree with evergreen leaves shaped like needles: *The Pine Cone and Tassel are the State Flower of Maine.* *The Southern (longleaf) Pine is the State Tree of Alabama; the Southern (shortleaf) Pine is the State Tree of Arkansas.* *The Western White Pine is the State Tree of Idaho; the Eastern White Pine is the State Tree of Maine; the White Pine is the State Tree of Michigan.* *The Norway or Red Pine is the State Tree of Minnesota; the Ponderosa Pine is the State Tree of Montana.* **2.** *Many pine trees are used for lumber.*

pine ap ple **1.** a large fruit, looking like a big pine cone. **2.** *The pineapple sundae tasted good.*

pink light red; the color obtained by mixing red with white. **pink er, pink est.**

piñ on **1.** a kind of small pine tree: *The Single Leaf Piñon is the State Tree of New Mexico and of Nevada.* **2.** *Piñon trees do not grow as tall as some other trees.*

pint a measure specially used for liquids: *Two cups are equal to one pint.* *Two pints are equal to one quart.*

pi o neer **1.** a person who settles in a part of the country where few people have lived before. **2.** a person who goes first or does something first and so prepares a way for others: *He was a pioneer in space.*

pipe **1.** a tube through which a liquid or gas flows. **2.** a tube with a bowl at one end, for smoking. **3.** a musical instrument. **4.** part of an organ.

pi rate a man who robs ships at sea.

pit[1] **1.** a hole in the ground. **2.** a hole, dent, or hollow in any surface: *The old table had many pits and scratches on it.* **3.** mark with small holes. **pit ted, pit ting.**

pit[2] **1.** the stone of a cherry, peach, plum, date, or other fruit. **2.** remove the pits from fruit: *We helped Mother pit cherries.* **pit ted, pit ting.**

pitch er[1] in baseball, the player who throws the ball for the batter to hit. See the picture under **baseball.**

pitch er[2] a container made of glass or metal, with a handle and a place for pouring. See the picture.

pitcher[2]

pitch fork   a large fork with a long handle for lifting and throwing hay, grass, and so on.

piz za   1. a food made of a large, round crust spread with tomatoes, cheese, meat, and spices, and then baked.   2. *Pizza pies are good to eat.*

place   1. the part of space a person or thing is in. 2. a city, town, village, island, and so on.   3. a building: *A church is a place of worship.   They have a place in the country.*   4. a spot: *I have a sore place on my foot.*   5. a position: *He won first place in the contest.*   6. a space: *Find a place and sit down.* 7. put in a position: *Place the books on the table.* 8. **In place of** means instead of.   9. **Take place** means happen.   **placed, plac ing.**

plaid   1. a long piece of wool cloth, usually having crossed stripes in several colors, worn about the shoulders.   2. any cloth with crossed stripes. 3. *She wore a plaid dress.*

plain   1. clear; easy to understand; easily seen or heard: *The meaning of this sentence is plain.*   2. *She wore a plain dress.*   3. *He was a plain man of the people.*   **plain er, plain est.**

plan   1. something you have thought out and will do: *What are your summer plans?*   2. a drawing to show how anything is arranged: *He drew a plan of the first floor of the house.*   See the picture.   3. think out how something is to be made or done: *We are planning the class party.*   **planned, plan ning.**

plane[1]   an airplane.

plane[2]   1. a carpenter's tool for making wood or metal smooth.   2. shave the edges of wood or metal with a plane to smooth them.   **planed, plan ing.**

plan et   one of the bodies, like the earth, that move around the sun.

plank   a long, flat piece of sawed wood thicker than a board: *We walked on a plank to get across the stream.*

plant   1. any living thing that is not an animal. 2. a living thing with leaves, roots, and a soft stem that is smaller than a tree or bush.   3. put into the ground to grow.   **plant ed, plant ing.**

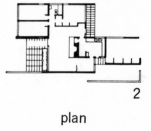

plan

plate   **1.** a dish, usually round, that is almost flat.
2. in baseball, the home base.   See the picture
under **baseball.**

plat form   a raised, level surface: *The auditorium
has a platform at one end.*

plat ter   a flat dish that is longer than it is wide,
used for serving food.

play   **1.** fun; something done to amuse oneself:
There will be time for play after school.   **2.** a story
acted on the stage: *We saw a play about fairies and
witches.*   **3.** have fun; do something in sport: *The
kitten plays with its tail.   Our team played the
sixth-grade team.*   **4.** act a part: *My sister played the
part of the queen.*   **5.** make believe: *Let's play that
this is a boat.*   **6.** perform on a musical instrument:
Can you play the piano? **played, play ing.**

play mate   a person who plays with another.

pleas ant   **1.** *We had a pleasant swim on a hot day.*
2. *She has a pleasant manner.*   **3.** *After the rain it was
pleasant and sunny.* **pleas ant er, pleas ant est.**

pleas ant ly   *The lady smiled pleasantly.*

please   **1.** give pleasure to: *Toys please children.*
2. be happy or delighted: *She was pleased with the
flowers.*   **3. Please** is a polite way of asking
something.   **4. If you please** means if you like or if
you will allow it.   **5. Do what you please** means do
what you think is fitting. **pleased, pleas ing.**

pleas ure   **1.** the feeling of being made happy;
delight; joy: *The boy's pleasure in the gift was good to
see.*   **2.** something that pleases; cause of delight:
The sunshine was a pleasure after so much rain.

plen ty   full enough; all that one needs: *You have
plenty of time to catch the train.*

plot   **1.** a secret plan, usually to do something
wrong: *Two men hatched a plot to steal the money.*
2. the plan of a play, poem, or story: *Boys like plots
that have adventure.*   **3.** a small piece of ground: *In the
back yard we have a garden plot.*   **4.** plan secretly with
others to do something: *They plotted against the
government.* **plot ted, plot ting.**

plow   1. a machine that cuts and turns up soil.
2. a machine that moves snow.   3. turn up with
a plow.   **plowed, plow ing.**

pluck   1. pick; pull off: *She plucked flowers in
the garden.*   2. pull at; tug: *She plucked at the loose
threads of her coat.*   **plucked, pluck ing.**

plum   1. a round fruit with a smooth skin, lots of
juice, and a pit.   2. *We have two plum trees.*

plumb er   a man whose work is putting in and
repairing water pipes, sinks, bathtubs, and so on.

plump   round; fat in a pleasing way: *A baby
usually has plump cheeks.*   **plump er, plump est.**

plunge   1. throw with force: *Plunge your hand into
the water.   He plunged the knife into the watermelon.*
2. rush or throw oneself into: *He plunged into the
river and saved the boy.*   **plunged, plung ing.**

plu ral   the form of a word that shows it means
more than one: *"Books" is the plural of "book."*

plus   1. *Three plus two is equal to five.*   2. *The work
of a spy requires brains plus courage.*   3. *His mark
was B plus.*   4. *The plus sign is* $+$.

Plym outh   a town in Massachusetts settled by the
Pilgrims in 1620.

pneu mo nia   *They took the boy to the hospital when
he got pneumonia.*

pock et   1. a small bag sewed into clothing for
carrying things.   2. *Do you have a pocket handkerchief?*

po em   an idea expressed in words of great beauty,
usually with accents repeated in each line and with
words that rhyme.

point   1. a sharp end: *Don't hurt yourself on the point
of this needle.*   2. a place or position: *Find the middle
point of the line.*   3. the main idea or purpose: *I did
not get the point of his story.*   4. an amount in scoring:
Our team won by three points.   5. a piece of land
sticking out into the water.   6. aim: *Don't point your
gun at me.*   7. show with the finger.   8. **Point out**
means show or call attention to: *Please point out my
mistakes.*   9. **Point of view** means what you think
about something.   **point ed, point ing.**

317

point ed   **1.** See **point.**   **2.** *The clown wore a pointed hat.*

point er   a short-haired hunting dog.

poke   **1.** *He gave his sister a poke with his finger.*
2. a bag.   **3.** push against with something pointed.
4. *A gossip pokes her nose into other people's business.*
5. go in a lazy way: *Don't poke along on the way to school, or you'll be late.*   **poked, pok ing.**

pole[1]   a long, thin piece of wood, or something like it: *These logs will be used for telephone poles.*

pole[2]   **1.** either end of the earth: *The North Pole and the South Pole are opposite each other.*   **2.** *A battery has two poles.*

po lice   **1.** the men who protect us and lock up people who break the law.   **2.** the department of government that keeps order.   **3.** *A police car was parked near the police station.*   **po lice.**

po lice dog   a large dog that looks like a wolf.

po lice man   a member of the police force; a police officer.   **po lice men.**

po lite   behaving correctly; having good manners: *The polite boy gave the lady his seat in the bus.*   **po lit er, po lit est.**

po lite ly   *He politely offered her a chair.*

pond   a body of still water, smaller than a lake.

po ny   **1.** a kind of small horse.   **2.** *We had a pony ride.*   **po nies.**

poo dle   a smart pet dog with thick, curly hair.

pool[1]   **1.** a small pond: *She took the children to the wading pool.*   **2.** a place, either inside or outside, to swim: *Our school has a new swimming pool.*

pool[2]   a game played on a special table with balls and a long stick.

poor   **1.** having few things or nothing: *The family was very poor.*   **2.** *This is very poor soil.*   **3.** *This poor child has hurt himself.*   **poor er, poor est.**

poor ly   *He did poorly in the test.*

pop   **1.** make a short, quick, bursting sound: *The fire popped, and sparks flew out.*   **2.** burst open; cause to burst open: *The bag popped.*   **popped, pop ping.**

pop corn   a kind of corn that bursts open and puffs out when heated: *Popcorn is good to eat.*

pop lar   **1.** a tree that grows rapidly: *The cottonwood is one kind of poplar.*   **2.** *This chest is made of poplar wood.*

pop py   a plant having many red, yellow, or white flowers: *The Golden Poppy is the State Flower of California.*   **pop pies.**

porch   a covered entrance on the outside of a building: *Our house has a big porch in front.   The children were playing on the porch.*   **porch es.**

por cu pine   an animal covered with stiff, sharp quills that are like needles.

pork   **1.** the meat of a hog used for food. **2.** *Mother cooked a pork roast.*

por poise   a kind of dolphin.

po si tion   **1.** the place where a thing or person is. **2.** a way of being placed: *The table is in its position against the wall.*   **3.** a job: *He held a high position in the bank.*

pos si ble   **1.** that can be; that can be done; that can happen: *Come if possible.   It is possible to cure pneumonia.*   **2.** *You have two possible choices.*

pos si bly   *I cannot possibly go.*

post   a piece of timber or iron firmly set into the ground usually to hold up something else: *The men put up a post and nailed a sign on it.*

post er   a large printed sheet or notice put up for everyone to see: *I saw a poster announcing the circus.*

post man   a man who delivers mail.   **post men.**

post of fice   the place where mail is handled.

pos ture   the way you stand and hold your body: *Good posture is important to health.*

pot   **1.** a kind of deep dish or bowl: *Mother made a big pot of soup.*   See the pictures.   **2.** put into a pot to grow: *We must pot these bulbs before winter.*   **pot ted, pot ting.**

po ta to   **1.** a vegetable that grows underground: *We eat white potatoes and sweet potatoes.*   **2.** *Potato salad is good in summer.*   **po ta toes.**

pot

pot ted   **1.** See **pot.**   **2.** *We bought some potted plants.*

pouch   **1.** a bag or sack: *The postman's pouch was full of letters.*   **2.** a fold of skin that is like a bag: *A kangaroo carries its young in a pouch.*   **pouch es.**

poul try   birds that are raised for meat, such as chickens, turkeys, geese, and ducks.

pound[1]   a measure of weight: *Sixteen ounces are equal to a pound.*

pound[2]   strike or beat something heavily again and again.   **pound ed, pound ing.**

pour   **1.** cause to flow in a steady stream.   **2.** flow in a steady stream: *The crowd poured out of the church. The rain poured down.*   **poured, pour ing.**

pow der   material turned to dust by pounding or grinding: *Buy baby powder and tooth powder.*

pow er   **1.** how strong someone or something is; how much someone or something can do: *I will give you all the help in my power.   The fairy had power to change into different shapes.*   **2.** a force that can do work: *Electric power runs many machines.*   **3.** *Father cuts the lawn with a power mower.*

pow er shov el   a machine that can dig and move dirt.

prac tice   **1.** something done many times over for skill: *They spent an hour a day on football practice.*   **2.** *The skater was out of practice.*   **3.** do something again and again: *She practices on the piano for at least an hour every day.*   **prac ticed, prac tic ing.**

prai rie   a large piece of almost level land, with grass but not many trees.

prai rie dog   an animal like a woodchuck.

praise   **1.** saying that a thing or person is good; words that tell how good a thing or person is: *Courage deserves praise.*   **2.** speak well of: *Everyone praised the athlete.*   **praised, prais ing.**

prance   **1.** spring about on the hind legs: *Horses prance when they feel lively.*   **2.** move happily or proudly: *The children pranced across the lawn pretending they were horses.*   **pranced, pranc ing.**

pray   *She knelt to pray.*   **prayed, pray ing.**

prayer   **1.** the act of praying: *Say a prayer before you go to bed.*   **2.** the thing prayed for: *Our prayers were granted.*   **3.** a form of words to be used in praying: *Do you know how the Lord's Prayer begins?*

preach er   a minister.

pre fix   a syllable, syllables, or word put at the beginning of a word to change its meaning or to make another word: *"Dismount" is made by adding the prefix "dis" to the word "mount."*   **pre fix es.**

pre pare   **1.** make ready; get ready: *He prepares his lessons.*   **2.** make in a special way: *Mother prepared a new kind of sauce for the vegetables.*   **pre pared, pre par ing.**

pre sent[1]   **1.** a gift; something given: *Here is a Christmas present for you.*   **2.** give: *They are going to present flowers to their teacher.*   **3.** introduce; make known; bring a person to meet somebody: *She was presented to the queen.*   **pre sent ed, pre sent ing.**

pres ent[2]   **1.** being here, not gone: *The whole class was present when the teacher came in.*   **2.** at this time; being or happening now: *Stories of the present are as exciting as stories of the past.*   **3.** now; this time; the time being: *That is enough for the present time.*
4. At present means now.

pres i dent   the chief officer of a country, company, club, or other group: *The president gave a speech to the group.   The highest officer of the United States is the President.*

press   **1.** use force or weight against; push with steady force: *Press the button to ring the bell.*
2. squeeze; squeeze out: *Press all the juice from the oranges.*   **3.** hug: *Mother pressed the baby to her.*
4. make smooth; flatten: *You press clothes with an iron.*   **pressed, press ing.**

pres sure   a steady pushing of a weight or force: *The pressure of the wind filled the sails of the boat.*

pre tend   **1.** make believe: *Let's pretend we are soldiers.*   **2.** claim: *I don't pretend to be a musician.*
3. claim without truth: *She pretends to like you, but she is not your friend.*   **pre tend ed, pre tend ing.**

pret ty   pleasing; sweet; charming: *She wore a pretty dress.*   **pret ti er, pret ti est.**

prey   hunt and kill for food: *Cats prey upon mice and birds.*   **preyed, prey ing.**

price   the amount for which a thing is sold or can be bought; the cost to the one who buys.

pride   **1.** a feeling of being pleased or satisfied with yourself or anything that you have: *Pride in our city should make us help to keep it clean.   He took pride in his fine garden.*   **2.** too high an idea of oneself: *His pride may get him into trouble.*

priest   a minister in certain churches.

prim   very neat; almost too tidy or careful about one's dress or conduct.   **prim mer, prim mest.**

pri ma ry   **1.** first in time; first in order: *We start school in the primary grades.*   **2.** from which others have come: *Red, blue, and yellow are primary colors.*

prim rose   any of a large group of plants with flowers of different colors.

prince   **1.** the son of a king or queen.   **2.** a ruler of a small country.

prin cess   **1.** the daughter of a king or queen.   **2.** the wife of a prince.   **prin cess es.**

prin ci pal   **1.** the head of a school; the chief person.   **2.** *This is the principal city of the state.*

print   **1.** words stamped on paper by a machine: *This book has clear print.*   **2.** a mark made on something by pressing or stamping: *The dog left prints in the snow as it walked.*   **3.** stamp words on paper, to make books, newspapers, and other written matter.   **4.** make letters the way they look in print instead of writing them: *Print your name clearly.*   **print ed, print ing.**

print er   a person whose work is printing or helping to print newspapers, magazines, and so on.

prize   **1.** a reward won in a contest: *Prizes will be given for the three best stories.*   **2.** *He grows prize vegetables in his garden.*

prob a ble   **1.** *Cooler weather is probable after this shower.*   **2.** *He is the probable cause of the noise.*

prob a bly   *We probably should wait for her.*

prob lem   a question or difficult matter to be thought about and worked out: *Our teacher gave us a problem in arithmetic.   That family has many problems.*

pro duce   1. make; bring into being: *This factory produces stoves.   Hens produce eggs.*   2. bring about; cause: *Hard work produces success.*   3. *Our class produced a play.*   **pro duced, pro duc ing.**

pro duc tion   1. *Our class play was a big production.*   2. *The production of a newspaper is hard work.*

pro gram   1. a list of items or events or performers: *I dropped my program.   She was next on the program.*   2. a plan of what is to be done: *We had a Christmas program.   The program for the week was very full.*

prom ise   1. words said or written, saying a person will do or not do something: *He always keeps his promise.*   2. give one's word; make a promise: *He promised to stay with the children till we came home from school.*   **prom ised, prom is ing.**

proof   the way of showing that something is true: *Do you have proof that he took it?*

pro pel ler   revolving blades that make boats and airplanes move. See the picture under **airplane.**

prop er ty   the thing or things someone owns: *This house is the property of our family.*   **prop er ties.**

pro tect   keep from harm or danger; shelter or guard: *Protect yourself from danger.   Protect the baby's eyes from the sun.*   **pro tect ed, pro tect ing.**

pro tec tion   protecting; being kept from harm: *We locked the door for protection.   This coat will be protection from the wind.*

proud   1. thinking well of oneself: *He was a strong, proud man.*   2. thinking too well of oneself: *He had few friends because of his proud manner.*   3. causing pride; being pleasing to one's feelings: *He was proud of his son.*   **proud er, proud est.**

proud ly   *He looked proudly at what he had drawn.*

prove   1. show that a thing is true or right: *Prove these answers.*   2. turn out to be: *The book proved interesting.*   **proved, prov ing.**

pro vide **1.** give: *Sheep provide us with wool.*
2. arrange for something in the future: *He saved money to provide for his old age.* **pro vid ed, pro vid ing.**

ptar mi gan a kind of bird found in mountains and cold lands: *The Alaska Willow Ptarmigan is the State Bird of Alaska.*

pub lic **1.** having something to do with the people; belonging to the people: *The courthouse is a public building. Public libraries and public schools serve the people.* **2. In public** means openly; not secret.

puff **1.** a short, quick breath of air: *A puff of wind blew away the letter.* **2.** let out short, quick breaths of air: *She puffed as she climbed the stairs.* **3.** swell with air: *He puffed out his cheeks.* **puffed, puff ing.**

pull **1.** a tug; a motion toward you: *I gave one pull at the rope.* **2.** move toward yourself; tug. **3.** move with force: *The dentist will pull your tooth. Don't pull my hair.* **pulled, pull ing.**

pul ley a wheel with a hollow edge in which a rope can move to lift or lower weights: *We used a rope and pulley to lift the big box.*

pump¹ **1.** a machine for forcing liquids, air, or gas into or out of things: *A pump brings water up from a well.* See the pictures.
2. move liquids, air, or gas: *We pumped air into the bicycle tires.* **pumped, pump ing.**

pump² a shoe having no laces, straps, or buttons.

pump kin a large fruit that grows on a vine.

punc tu a tion the use of periods, commas, and other marks in writing to help make the meaning clear: *Punctuation tells us where to pause when we read aloud.*

pun ish cause pain or loss to someone who did wrong: *Father sometimes punishes us when we are naughty.* **pun ished, pun ish ing.**

pu pil¹ a person who is learning in school or is being taught by someone: *The music teacher has many pupils.*

pu pil² the black center of the eye: *The pupil is the only place where light can enter the eye.*

pup pet a small doll moved by someone's hands.

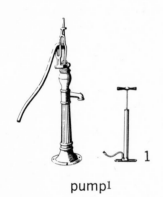

pump¹

pup py a young dog. **pup pies.**

pure **1.** not mixed with anything else; the real thing: *Mother's ring is made of pure gold.* **2.** perfectly clean: *We should drink only pure water.* **3.** *The sky was pure blue.* **pur er, pur est.**

pur ple a dark color made by mixing red and blue: *Purple lilacs are beautiful.* **pur pler, pur plest.**

purse a little bag or case for carrying money.

push **1.** press against something to make it move away from you. **2.** go by force: *We tried to push through the crowd that gathered around the door at the theater.* **pushed, push ing.**

put **1.** place; lay; set: *I put sugar in my tea. Did you put your toys on the shelf?* **2.** *Have you put your room in order? I put away my hat yesterday.* **3. Put off** means make something wait: *She put off her work until tomorrow.* **4. Put out** means make an end to: *Put out the fire.* **5. Put up** means keep until it is needed; give room to: *Mother puts up fruit for winter. The man asked if we could put him up for the night.* **6. Put up with** means bear: *He will not put up with her rude manner.* **put, put ting.**

puz zle **1.** a hard problem: *How to get all my things into one trunk is a puzzle.* **2.** a problem or task to be done for fun: *He was working a puzzle.* **3.** be unable to understand something: *How the cat got out puzzled us. They puzzled over their arithmetic for an hour.* **puz zled, puz zling.**

Q

quack **1.** the sound a duck makes. **2.** make such a sound. **quacked, quack ing.**

quail a small bird that builds its nest on the ground: *The California Valley Quail is the State Bird of California.* **quail.**

quar rel **1.** an angry talk or fight with words. **2.** fight with words; speak angrily to each other. **3.** stop being friends: *They haven't spoken since they quarreled.* **quar reled, quar rel ing.**

quart   a measure specially for liquids: *Four quarts are equal to one gallon.*

quar ter   **1.** a silver coin of the United States and Canada worth 25 cents: *Do you have change for a quarter?*   **2.** one of four equal parts; half of a half; one fourth: *Each of the four boys ate a quarter of the apple.   A quarter of an hour is fifteen minutes.*   **3.** *We left at quarter past three.*

queen   **1.** the wife of a king.   **2.** a woman ruler.   **3.** a woman who is very beautiful and important: *The May Queen rode on a float in the parade.*

queer   **1.** strange: *We heard a queer sound upstairs.*   **2.** not well: *I felt queer.*   **queer er, queer est.**

ques tion   a thing asked to find out something: *The teacher asks the children questions about the lesson.*

quick   fast and sudden; swift: *We made a quick trip to the store.*   **quick er, quick est.**

quick ly   *The girls quickly arranged for the party.*

qui et   **1.** making no sound; with little or no noise: *It was a quiet night.*   **2.** not moving; still: *We sat by a quiet pond.*   **qui et er, qui et est.**

qui et ly   *The boys and girls quietly left the room.*

quill   **1.** a large, stiff feather.   **2.** a pen made from a feather.   **3.** a stiff, sharp hair like the end of a feather: *A porcupine has quills on its back.*

quilt   a cover for a bed, usually made of two pieces of cloth sewed together with a soft pad between them.

quit   **1.** stop: *The men always quit work at five. Yesterday one man quit early.*   **2.** leave: *His big brother is quitting his job tomorrow.   He had quit once before.*   **quit, quit ting.**

quite   **1.** completely: *I am quite alone.   Are you quite satisfied?*   **2.** really; truly: *There was quite a change in the weather.*   **3.** very; rather: *It is quite hot.*

quo ta tion   **1.** somebody's words repeated exactly by another person; something repeated from a book, speech, and so on: *From what book does this quotation come?*   **2.** Quotation marks (" ") are put at the beginning and end of any quotation: *"Thank you very much," she said.*

R

rab bi   a teacher and pastor in one kind of church.

rab bit   an animal with soft fur and long ears.

rac coon   a small animal that lives mostly in trees.

race   **1.** a contest to see who can go fastest: *Ten boys entered the race.*   **2.** run to get ahead of someone: *They raced from the wall to the house.*   **3.** run; move fast: *Race to the doctor for help.*   **raced, rac ing.**

ra dio   an instrument for sending and receiving sound by electric waves without wires.

rad ish   a small, crisp root that has red or white skin and is good to eat.   **rad ish es.**

rag   a torn or old piece of cloth.

rage   being very angry: *Mad with rage, he dashed into the fight.*

rail   a bar of wood or metal: *Railroad trains run on steel rails.*   See the picture under **fence.**

rail road   **1.** a road or track on which trains go. **2.** the tracks, stations, trains, and the people who manage them: *Which railroad can take me west?*

rain   **1.** water falling in drops from the clouds. **2.** fall in drops of water.   **rained, rain ing.**

rain bow   a part circle of colors seen sometimes in the sky after or during a rain.

raise   **1.** lift up; put up: *Raise your hand if you know the answer.*   **2.** cause to rise: *The car raised a cloud of dust.*   **3.** make grow: *The farmer raises chickens and corn.*   **raised, rais ing.**

rai sin   **1.** a sweet, dried grape.   **2.** *He likes raisin pie.*

rake   **1.** a long-handled tool having a bar at one end with teeth in it.   **2.** make clean or smooth with a rake.   **raked, rak ing.**

ran   See **run.**   *The dog ran after the cat.*

ranch   a large farm and its buildings.   **ranch es.**

rang   See **ring**². *The telephone rang.*

rang er   a person who guards a forest against fires.

rap   **1.** a quick, light blow: *I heard a rap on the door.*   **2.** knock sharply.   **rapped, rap ping.**

rap id   very quick; swift: *He is a rapid worker.*

rap id ly   *The frightened boy ran rapidly toward home.*

rare[1]   **1.** not often found; few.   **2.** not happening often.   **rar er, rar est.**

rare[2]   not cooked much.   **rar er, rar est.**

rare ly   *He rarely comes to meetings.*

rasp ber ry   **1.** a small fruit that grows on bushes. **2.** *He likes raspberry ice cream.*   **rasp ber ries.**

rat   a gnawing animal like a mouse, but larger.

rath er   **1.** quite; more than a little: *He was rather tired.*   **2.** *I would rather go now than later.*

rat tle   **1.** short, sharp sounds: *I hear the rattle of milk bottles.*   **2.** a baby's toy that makes a noise when it is shaken.   **3.** make a number of short, sharp sounds: *The window rattled.*   **rat tled, rat tling.**

raw   **1.** not cooked.   **2.** damp and cold: *A raw wind was blowing.*   **3.** sore: *The horse had a raw spot on its back.*   **raw er, raw est.**

ra zor   a tool with a sharp blade for shaving.

reach   **1.** get to; come to: *Your letter reached me today.*   **2.** stretch: *She reached for the milk.*   **3.** touch: *I can reach the top.*   **reached, reach ing.**

read[1]   **1.** get the meaning of writing in print: *We read books.   The blind girl reads by touching special raised print.*   **2.** speak out loud the words of writing or print: *Please read it to me.*   **read, read ing.**

read[2]   See **read**[1].   *I read that book last year.   Have you read it?   Which book has he read?*

read er   a book for learning and practicing reading.

read y   **1.** *Dinner is ready.*   **2.** *She will be ready to go in a minute.*   **read i er, read i est.**

re al   **1.** *She did not tell the real reason.*   **2.** *Are these real diamonds?*

re al ize   understand clearly: *The teacher realizes now how hard you worked.*   **re al ized, re al iz ing.**

re al ly   **1.** *Did you really see him?*   **2.** *Oh, really?* **3.** *She didn't, really.*

rear[1]   **1.** make grow; help to grow; bring up. **2.** of an animal, rise on the hind legs: *The horse reared as the fire truck went past.*   **reared, rear ing.**

rear[2] **1.** back part; the back: *The kitchen is in the rear of the house.* **2.** *Look out the rear window. Leave by the rear door.* **3.** behind; in back of: *The garage is at the rear of the house.*

rea son cause: *Tell me your reason for not going.*

re ceive get or be given something: *We receive presents at Christmas.* **re ceived, re ceiv ing.**

re cess **1.** the time during which work stops: *We'll talk at recess.* **2.** a part in a wall, set back from the rest: *This seat will fit in that recess.* **re cess es.**

rec i pe a set of directions for preparing something, usually something to eat.

rec og nize know again: *I didn't recognize my old friend.* **rec og nized, rec og niz ing.**

re cord **1.** a round, flat object that gives off sounds when its top surface is touched by a kind of needle: *We played some records.* **2.** facts set down in writing: *We kept a record of the money we spent.* **3.** the facts about what someone has done: *He has a fine record at school.* **4. Break a record** means do something better than it has ever been done. **5.** put sounds on a record: *We are going to record the school song tomorrow.* **6.** keep an account of something: *Great events are recorded in history books. Photographers record great battles in pictures.* **7.** *Have you a record player?* **re cord ed, re cord ing.**

rec re a tion play; amusement: *Walking, gardening, and reading are quiet kinds of recreation.*

red **1.** the color of blood or of the lips. **2.** *She wore a red dress. He has hair redder than mine.* **red der, red dest.**

red bud **1.** a tree with heart-shaped leaves: *The Eastern Redbud is the State Tree of Oklahoma.* **2.** *We have a redbud tree in our yard.*

red wood **1.** a very tall evergreen tree: *The California Redwood is the State Tree of California.* **2.** *Redwood trees are giants of the forest.*

reel **1.** a spool to hold things like thread, yarn, film, rope, or hose: *Our hose is wound on a reel.* **2.** something wound on a reel: *Here is a reel of film.*

329

ref er ee   a judge in some games and sports.

re flect   throw back light, heat, or sound: *The mirror reflects my face.*   **re flect ed, re flect ing.**

re fresh ing   making you feel cool and fresh: *After our work we had a refreshing drink.*

re frig er a tor   a large container that keeps things cool and keeps food from spoiling.

ref u gee   a person who escapes from his home or country during dangerous times.

re fuse   say no to.   **re fused, re fus ing.**

rein deer   a kind of large deer.   **rein deer.**

rel a tive   a person who belongs to the same family as another, such as a father, brother, aunt, or cousin.

re lease   **1.** let go: *Release the lock, and the box will open.*   **2.** let loose; set free: *She released the rabbit from its cage.*   **re leased, re leas ing.**

re main   **1.** *We shall remain at the beach this summer.*   **2.** *The town remains the same year after year.*
3. *If you take two apples from five apples, three remain.*   **re mained, re main ing.**

re main der   the part left over; the rest: *If you take two from nine, the remainder is seven.*

re mark   **1.** something said in a few words.
2. say; speak.   **re marked, re mark ing.**

re mark a ble   not common; unusual: *It is remarkable that he came at all.*

re mem ber   **1.** call back to mind : *Can you remember my name?*   **2.** take care not to forget : *Remember to take your lunch.*   **re mem bered, re mem ber ing.**

rent[1]   **1.** *He paid the rent every month.*   **2.** *We rented a house at the beach.*   **3.** *He rents his house to us while he travels.*   **rent ed, rent ing.**

rent[2]   a tear; a torn place.

re open   open again.   **re opened, re open ing.**

re pair   fix; mend.   **re paired, re pair ing.**

re peat   **1.** *Don't repeat your mistake.*   **2.** *Please repeat that word.*   **3.** *Repeat the words after me.*
4. *Promise not to repeat this.*   **re peat ed, re peat ing.**

re ply   **1.** *What is your reply?*   **2.** *Reply to his question.*   **re plies; re plied, re ply ing.**

re port **1.** an account of something: *His report of the trip was interesting.* **2.** *He wrote a report about trees for class.* **3.** repeat what one has heard or seen; describe; tell. **re port ed, re port ing.**

re port er a person who finds news for a newspaper.

rep tile *Snakes, lizards, and alligators are reptiles.*

re quest ask or ask for: *He requested a pencil from the teacher.* **re quest ed, re quest ing.**

re quire **1.** need: *We require more spoons for our party.* **2.** demand; order; command: *The rules required us all to be present.* **re quired, re quir ing.**

res cue save from harm. **res cued, res cu ing.**

res er voir **1.** a place where water is collected and stored for use. **2.** anything to hold a liquid.

re spect **1.** *The teacher has the respect of her class.* **2.** *We respect an honest person.* **3.** *Don't you respect your father?* **re spect ed, re spect ing.**

rest[1] **1.** sleep. **2.** a pause after hard work. **3.** in music, a pause. **4.** be still: *My mother rests for an hour every day.* **5.** be held up by: *The roof rests on beams.* **rest ed, rest ing.**

rest[2] what is left; the remainder: *He ate half the apple and threw away the rest.*

res tau rant a place to buy and eat a meal.

re turn **1.** coming back: *We look forward to the return of spring.* **2.** go back; come back: *He will return in a moment.* **3.** bring back; pay back: *Return that book to the library.* **re turned, re turn ing.**

re volve move in a circle; turn around a center: *The moon revolves around the earth. The wheels of a moving car revolve.* **re volved, re volv ing.**

re ward **1.** something given for something done. **2.** give a reward to. **re ward ed, re ward ing.**

rhi noc er os a large, thick-skinned animal of Africa and Asia. **rhi noc er os es** or **rhi noc er os.**

Rhode Is land one of the fifty states of the United States.

rho do den dron an evergreen bush somewhat like an azalea: *The Western Rhododendron is the State Flower of West Virginia and of Washington.*

report

rhododendron

331

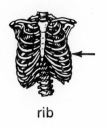

rib

rhyme   **1.** *"Kitten" is a rhyme for "mitten."*   **2.** a short poem having many lines ending in words that sound alike.   **3.** *"Long" and "song" are two words that rhyme.*   **rhymed, rhym ing.**

rib   one of the bones that curve round the chest. See the picture.

rib bon   **1.** a strip or band of cloth: *Ribbons are used to make bows for the hair.*   **2.** anything like this.

rice   **1.** the grain of a plant used for food.   See the picture under **grain.**   **2.** the plant itself.   **3.** *We had rice cakes for lunch.*

rich   **1.** having much money.   **2.** having plenty of what is needed: *The soil is rich.*   *This dessert is very rich.*   **rich er, rich est.**

rid   **1.** make free: *We have rid our barn of mice.*
2. Get rid of means get free from or do away with: *I can't get rid of this cold.*   *We got rid of the weeds by pulling them all up.*   **rid** or **rid ded, rid ding.**

rid den   See **ride.**   *The horseman has ridden all day.*

rid dle   a puzzling question or problem.

ride   **1.** a trip on a horse or vehicle: *We took a ride.*
2. sit on something and make it go: *Some people ride camels.*   **3.** be carried along: *We ride to school on rainy days.*   **rode, rid den, rid ing.**

right   **1.** that which is fair, good, honest, true: *Do right, not wrong.*   **2.** correct; true; fair: *He gave the right answer.*   **3.** correctly; truly: *I guessed right.*
4. opposite of left; the side to the east when you are facing north: *Make a right turn at the corner.*   *He turned to his right.*   **5.** exactly: *Your cap is right where you put it.*   *Stop playing right now.*   **6.** *Will your foot be all right now?*   **7.** *All right, have it your way.*   **8. Right away** means at once or immediately.

ring[1]   **1.** a circle: *The fairies danced in a ring.*
2. a thin circle of metal or other material: *Mother wears a wedding ring.*   **3.** a closed-in space for races or games: *The horses pranced around the circus ring.*

ring[2]   **1.** the sound of a bell: *Did you hear a ring?*
2. give forth a sound like a bell: *Did the phone ring?*
3. *Did you ring the bell?*   **rang, rung, ring ing.**

ripe full-grown and ready to be gathered; not green: *The ripe fruit was put in baskets.* **rip er, rip est.**

rise **1.** get up from a lying, sitting, or kneeling position: *Please rise from your seat when you speak.* **2.** get up from bed: *The farmer's wife rises at six.* **3.** go up; come up: *The kite rises in the air.   The sun rises in the morning.*   **4.** go higher: *The price of food is rising.* **rose, ris en, ris ing.**

ris en See **rise.** *The sun had risen before I went.*

riv er a large stream of running water.

road a highway or any way made to travel on from one place to another: *Our road went through the woods.*

road run ner a bird that can run very fast: *The Road Runner is the State Bird of New Mexico.*

roar **1.** a loud, deep sound: *The roar of the wind woke me.* **2.** make a loud, deep sound: *The audience roared with laughter at the clown.* **roared, roar ing.**

roast **1.** a piece of meat baked or to be baked: *Mother cooked a roast.*   **2.** cook by dry heat in an oven; bake: *We roasted corn.*   **3.** *We had roast beef for dinner.* **roast ed, roast ing.**

rob take away from by force; steal: *The bank was robbed.* **robbed, rob bing.**

robe a long piece of clothing like a loose coat.

rob in a large American thrush: *The Robin is the State Bird of Connecticut and of Michigan.*

rock[1] **1.** a large, hard mass found in the earth: *The ship crashed on the rocks.*   **2.** *This piece of candy is hard as a rock.*   **3.** *Father made a rock garden.*

rock[2] move backward and forward or from side to side; sway: *Mother rocked the baby.* **rocked, rock ing.**

rock et a long tube that can shoot rapidly upward or forward: *Large rockets are used to explore space.*

rocky[1] full of rocks or made of rock: *The ship neared the rocky shore.* **rock i er, rock i est.**

rocky[2] shaky; not steady; rocking back and forth: *That table is rocky; put a piece of wood under one leg.* **rock i er, rock i est.**

rod a thin, straight bar of metal or wood: *Have you seen my fishing rod?* See the picture.

rod

rode   See **ride**.   *We rode ten miles yesterday.*

ro dent   *Rats, mice, and squirrels are rodents.*

ro deo   a contest or show of skill in roping cattle, riding horses, and other cowboy skills.

roll   **1.** something rolled up: *Here's a roll of film.* **2.** a kind of bread: *He had a sweet roll for breakfast.* **3.** move along by turning over and over.   **4.** turn round on something; wrap: *She rolled the string into a ball.   The boy rolled himself up in a blanket.* **5.** make flat by rolling over it: *Mother rolls out pie crust.*   **6.** make deep, loud sounds: *Thunder rolls.*   **rolled, roll ing.**

roof   **1.** the top of a building.   **2.** something like it: *The roof of the car was dented.   I have a sore place on the roof of my mouth.*

room   **1.** a part of a building: *Step into the next room.*   **2.** space: *There is room for one more in the car.*

roost   **1.** a bar, pole, or perch on which birds sleep. **2.** a shed for birds to roost in.   **3.** sit as birds do on a roost.   **roost ed, roost ing.**

roost er   a male fowl, specially a chicken.

root   **1.** the part of a plant under the ground. **2.** something like a root: *The root of this tooth hurts.* **3.** a word from which other words are made.

rope   **1.** a thick cord made by twisting smaller cords together.   **2.** close in or mark off with a rope: *We have roped off a space in the garden for the flowers.* **3.** catch and tie with a lariat.   **roped, rop ing.**

rose[1]   **1.** a flower that grows on a bush and has long stems: *The Rose is the State Flower of New York; the American Beauty Rose is the Flower of Washington, D. C.; the Cherokee Rose is the State Flower of Georgia.   The Wild Rose is the State Flower of Iowa, and the Wild Prairie Rose is the State Flower of North Dakota.*   **2.** *The rose bush is blooming.*

rose[2]   See **rise**.   *The cat rose and stretched itself.*

rosy   rose-red.   **ros i er, ros i est.**

ro tate   **1.** move around a center; turn in a circle: *Wheels, tops, and the earth rotate.* **2.** take or make take turns: *Farmers rotate their crops.*   **ro tat ed, ro tat ing.**

rot ten 1. no longer good; spoiled: *He threw a rotten egg.* 2. not sound; weak; ready to break: *The rotten wood gave way, and he fell into the pond.* **rot ten er, rot ten est.**

round 1. shaped like a ball or circle or tree trunk: *The earth is round. A wheel is round. A telephone pole is round.* 2. *He walked round the block.* 3. *Wheels go round.* 4. **Round up** means gather cattle. **round er, round est.**

row[1] a line of people or things: *The children stood in a row in front of the row of chairs. Corn is planted in rows. Sit in the first row.*

row[2] move a boat by pulling oars through the water. **rowed, row ing.**

rub move one thing back and forth against another: *Rub your hands to warm them.* **rubbed, rub bing.**

rub ber 1. a material made from the juice of certain trees: *Rubber can stretch and bounce and will not let air or water through.* 2. a shoe covering made of rubber: *We wear rubbers on our feet when it rains.* 3. *She wore rubber gloves to clean house.*

rude having bad manners. **rud er, rud est.**

rude ly *He laughed rudely when she fell.*

ruf fle a strip of cloth, ribbon, or lace gathered along one edge and used for trimming things.

ruf fled *She wore a ruffled blouse.*

rug a heavy floor covering: *Don't spill milk on the rug.*

rule 1. something that tells what to do and what not to do: *Obey the traffic rules.* 2. decide which is right or which to do: *The judge ruled against our team.* 3. control: *In the United States, the people rule.* 4. mark with lines: *He ruled the paper with a ruler.* 5. **As a rule** means usually. **ruled, rul ing.**

rul er 1. a king, queen, or person who controls a government: *Rulers from several countries met to talk.* 2. a straight strip of wood or metal used in drawing lines or in measuring.

rum ble 1. a deep rolling sound. 2. make a deep rolling sound. **rum bled, rum bling.**

run   **1.** *The dog came on the run.*   **2.** *Our team had two runs.*   **3.** *Run for help.*   **4.** *Does your watch run well?*   **5.** *He runs a machine.*   **6.** *Who will run for President?*   **7.** *I have run a mile.*   **8. Run down** means stop going or working.   **9. Run out** means come to an end or use up.   **ran, run, run ning.**

rung[1]   a rod or bar used as a step of a ladder. See the picture under **ladder.**

rung[2]   See **ring**[2].   *The bell has rung.*

ru ral   of the country: *Rural life is pleasant.*

rush   **1.** a hurry: *What is your rush?*   **2.** move with speed, force, or haste.   **rushed, rush ing.**

rust   **1.** the red-brown coat that sometimes forms on iron or steel.   **2.** become covered with this: *Don't let your tools rust.*   **rust ed, rust ing.**

rusty   *He found a rusty knife.*   **rust i er, rust i est.**

rye   **1.** the grain of a plant, used for flour.   See the picture under **grain.**   **2.** the plant itself.   **3.** *Some people eat rye bread.*

S

Sab bath   the day of the week used for rest and worship: *Many people celebrate the Sabbath on Sunday.*

sack   a large bag made of paper or coarse cloth.

sad   unhappy; not glad.   **sad der, sad dest.**

sad dle   **1.** a seat for a rider.   **2.** put a saddle on: *Saddle the horse.*   **sad dled, sad dling.**

sad ly   *He picked up the broken toy sadly.*

safe   **1.** a place or container for keeping things safe.   **2.** *A rubber ball is a safe plaything.*   **saf er, saf est.**

safe ly   *The plane landed safely in a field.*

safe ty   **1.** being out of danger: *Cross the street in safety at the corner.*   **2.** *Mother uses safety matches.*

sage brush   a plant common to the dry plains: *The Sagebrush is the State Flower of Nevada.*

said   See **say.**   *He said he would come.*

sail   **1.** a piece of canvas that catches the wind.   **2.** a trip on a sailboat.   **3.** *The boys are going to sail in the race today.*   **sailed, sail ing.**

sail or   1. a member of the United States Navy.
2. a member of a ship's crew.

sal ad   1. raw vegetables or other food served with a dressing.   2. *We often eat salad with a salad fork.*

sale   1. *The sale of his old home made him sad.*
2. *This store is having a sale on hats.*

salm on   1. a large salt-water fish.   2. *Salmon salad is delicious.*

salt   1. a material of white grains found in the earth and in sea water.   2. *Where is the salt shaker?*

salty   *This meat tastes salty.*   **salt i er, salt i est.**

same   1. *We came back the same way we went.*
2. *Her name and mine are the same.*   3. *I feel the same.*

sand   1. tiny grains of worn-down rocks: *The beach is covered with sand.*   2. *Our room has a sand table.*

san dal   a kind of shoe fastened to the foot by straps.

sand wich   slices of bread with meat, jelly, or some other food between them.   **sand wich es.**

sandy   containing or covered with sand:
We found a sandy beach.   **sand i er, sand i est.**

sang   See **sing.**   *The bird sang for us yesterday.*

sank   See **sink.**   *The ship sank before help came.*

San ta Claus   *Santa Claus is pictured as a jolly old man who brings presents at Christmas.*

sat   See **sit.**   *I sat in a train all day yesterday.*

sat el lite   a thing that revolves around a planet.

sat in   1. cloth with one very smooth, shiny side.
2. *She wore a satin hat.*

sat is fy   give enough to; fill a need completely.
Does this satisfy you?   **sat is fied, sat is fy ing.**

Sat ur day   the seventh day of the week.

sauce   a liquid, served with or on food.

sau cer   a small dish with its edge curved up.

sau sage   chopped pork, beef, or other meats, seasoned and usually stuffed into a thin case.

save   1. make safe from harm; rescue: *The dog saved his life.*   2. collect; keep: *He saves stamps and old coins.*   **saved, sav ing.**

saw[1]   1. a tool for cutting.   See the picture.
2. cut with a saw.   **sawed, saw ing.**

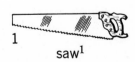

1
saw[1]

337

scale³

saw² See **see.** *I saw a robin yesterday.*

sax o phone   a musical instrument.

say   speak; put into words.   **said, say ing.**

scale¹   **1.** one of the thin, flat, hard plates that form the outside covering of fish and snakes. **2.** *Scales of paint were peeling off the old barn.*

scale²   a balance; an instrument for weighing.

scale³   **1.** a way of measuring some things.   **2.** an instrument used to measure.   **3.** in music, a group of notes that go up or down like steps.   See the picture.

scalp   **1.** the skin and hair on the top of the head. **2.** cut or tear the scalp from.   **scalped, scalp ing.**

scam per   scurry.   **scam pered, scam per ing.**

scare   frighten: *He scares me.*   **scared, scar ing.**

scare crow   *Scarecrows in fields frighten birds away.*

scarf   a cloth worn on the neck or head.   **scarves.**

scar let   very bright red.

scary   making one afraid.   **scar i er, scar i est.**

scat ter   **1.** *The farmer scattered corn on the ground for the chickens.*   **2.** *The police scattered the crowd.*   **scat tered, scat ter ing.**

scene   **1.** *The first scene is a city street.*   **2.** *I looked out the window at a country scene.*

scent   a smell: *The scent of roses filled the air.*

school   **1.** a place for teaching and learning.   **2.** *Our school visited the zoo.*   **3.** *This is our school song.*

sci ence   a careful study of facts about the earth or anything on it: *Science tells us the world is round.*

sci en tist   a person who studies science.

scis sors   a tool for cutting, with two sharp blades that move toward each other.   **scis sors.**

scold   speak to angrily.   **scold ed, scold ing.**

scoop   **1.** a tool like a shovel.   **2.** a large, deep spoon to dip out things.   **3.** take up or out with a scoop, or as a scoop does.   **scooped, scoop ing.**

scoot er   a child's vehicle moved by pushing one foot against the ground.

scorch   burn a little bit.   **scorched, scorch ing.**

Scotch ter ri er   a small dog with short legs.

Scot ty   a Scotch terrier.

scout mas ter   a man in charge of Boy Scouts.

scowl   **1.** an angry or hurt look; a frown.   **2.** look angry or hurt; frown.   scowled, **scowl ing.**

scram ble   **1.** make one's way by climbing and crawling.   **2.** struggle with others for something. **3.** mix together.   **scram bled, scram bling.**

scram bled   **1.** See **scramble.**   **2.** *Mother fixed scrambled eggs for breakfast.*

scrap   **1.** a small piece; a small part left over. **2.** *The man had a load of scrap iron.*

scrape   **1.** *Scrape your muddy shoes.   Scrape off the mud.*   **2.** *Don't scrape your heels.* **scraped, scrap ing.**

scratch   **1.** *The scratch on my leg hurts.*   **2.** rub or scrape.   **scratch es; scratched, scratch ing.**

scream   **1.** a loud, sharp cry.   **2.** make a loud, sharp cry.   **screamed, scream ing.**

screen   **1.** *She keeps her trunk behind a screen.* **2.** *We have screens at the windows to keep out flies.* See the pictures.

screw   a kind of nail that is turned, not pounded.

scrub   **1.** rub hard; wash or clean by rubbing. **2.** *She filled her scrub bucket.*   scrubbed, **scrub bing.**

scur ry   run quickly; hurry: *We could hear the mice scurry about in the walls.*   **scur ried, scur ry ing.**

sea   **1.** a great body of salt water; the ocean. **2.** *The sea breeze was cool.*

sea horse   a small fish that looks like a horse.

seal[1]   a mammal living in and around the sea.

seal[2]   **1.** a tool that stamps a picture on something. **2.** the picture.   **3.** close very tightly; fasten: *She sealed the letter.*   **sealed, seal ing.**

search   **1.** *He found his book after a search.* **2.** *We searched all day for a lost kitten.*   **3.** *The police searched the man.*   **search es; searched, search ing.**

sea son   **1.** one of the four parts of a year. **2.** improve the taste of.   **sea soned, sea son ing.**

seat   **1.** *Have a seat.*   **2.** *Our seats are in the first row.*   **3.** *This bench has a broken seat.*   **4.** *He seated himself in the chair.*   **seat ed, seat ing.**

sec ond[1]   one sixtieth of a minute.

screen

seesaw

segment

sec ond[2] **1.** next after the first. **2.** *Her birthday is the second of December.*

se cret **1.** something that others are kept from knowing about. **2.** *The club had a secret code.*

se cret ly *He took the money secretly.*

see **1.** look at. **2.** understand. **3.** find out. **4.** visit. **saw, seen, see ing.**

seed **1.** the thing from which a plant grows. **2.** scatter seed over. **seed ed, seed ing.**

seem **1.** *Does this room seem hot to you?* **2.** *I still seem to hear the music.* **seemed, seem ing.**

seen See **see.** *Have you seen the teacher?*

see saw *Our playground has two seesaws.* See the picture.

seg ment a piece cut off; a part. See the picture.

self *Your self is you. My self is I.* **selves.**

self ish caring too much for oneself.

self ish ly *He selfishly ate all the candy himself.*

sell trade a thing for money. **sold, sell ing.**

sem a phore an instrument for signaling: *The railroad semaphore showed that a train was coming.*

send **1.** *Mother sends me to the store.* **2.** *I send letters by mail.* **3.** *Send for a doctor.* **sent, send ing.**

sense *A blind man has a good sense of touch.*

sent See **send.** *They sent the trunks last week.*

sen tence a group of words that expresses a complete thought: *Read this sentence.*

sep a rate **1.** be between. **2.** put or come apart. **3.** *We had separate desks.* **sep a rat ed, sep a rat ing.**

sep a rate ly *We wrapped the two books separately.*

Sep tem ber the ninth month of the year.

se ri ous thoughtful; not joking.

serv ant **1.** a person hired to work for someone. **2.** *Policemen and firemen are public servants.*

serve **1.** *Soldiers serve their country.* **2.** *The waiter served the soup.* **3.** *One pie will usually serve six persons.* **served, serv ing.**

set **1.** *Set the box on end.* **2.** *Have you set the table?* **3.** *He set a good example.* **4.** *The sun sets in the west.* **5.** *A spark set the woods on fire.* **set, set ting.**

set ter a hunting dog.

set tle **1.** *Will you settle the question for us?*
2. *The Pilgrims settled in Plymouth.* **3.** *The cat settled itself for a nap.* **set tled, set tling.**

set tle ment a group of buildings and the people living in them: *Pioneers lived in early settlements.*

set tler a person who settles in a new country.

sev en **1.** one more than six. **2.** *After seven weeks we saw her.*

sev en teen **1.** seven more than ten. **2.** *It is seventeen minutes past eight.*

sev en teenth **1.** next after the sixteenth.
2. *Today is the seventeenth of May.*

sev enth **1.** next after the sixth. **2.** *My birthday is October seventh.*

sev en ti eth next after the sixty-ninth: *This was our seventieth day without rain.*

sev en ty seven times ten. **sev en ties.**

sev er al more than two or three but not many.

sew **1.** work on material with a needle and thread.
2. fasten or close with stitches. **sewed, sew ing.**

sew er an underground drain to carry off waste.

sew ing ma chine a machine for sewing.

shade **1.** *He sat in the shade of a big tree.* **2.** *Pull down the shades.* **3.** *I like a dark shade of blue.*

shad ow **1.** *Sometimes my shadow is very long.*
See the picture. **2.** *We made a shadow box in school.*

shad owy **1.** *Shadowy woods are cool.* **2.** *I saw a shadowy shape.* **shad ow i er, shad ow i est.**

shady **1.** *We found a shady spot.* **2.** *We ate under a shady tree.* **shad i er, shad i est.**

shag gy covered with a thick mass of hair, wool, or fur: *He has a shaggy dog.* **shag gi er, shag gi est.**

shake move quickly back and forth, up and down, or from side to side. **shook, shak en, shak ing.**

shak en See **shake.** *I have shaken the snow off.*

shaky **1.** *He spoke in a shaky voice.* **2.** *There was a shaky porch on the old house.* **shak i er, shak i est.**

shall *I shall come soon. Shall we go? You shall go to the party, I promise you. She shall drink her milk.*

1

shadow

shame 1. *He turned red with shame.* 2. *My mistake shamed me.* 3. *Shame on you.* **shamed, sham ing.**

shan't shall not.

shape 1. *The shape of her vase is square. An apple is different in shape from a banana.* 2. *The child shapes clay into balls.* **shaped, shap ing.**

share 1. *He did more than his share of the work.* 2. *The sisters share a room.* 3. *He shared his candy with me.* **shared, shar ing.**

shark any of a group of large, fierce fishes.

sharp 1. *I will need a sharp knife and a sharp pin.* 2. *Policemen must have sharp ears.* 3. in music, a tone one half step above; the sign (#). **sharp er, sharp est.**

sharp ly *"Stop that!" he said sharply.*

shave 1. cut hair off very close to the skin, usually with a razor. 2. cut off in thin slices: *She shaved the chocolate bar.* **shaved, shav ing.**

shawl a square or long piece of cloth to be worn about the shoulders or head.

she *She has many books. She is my sister.*

shed a building used for shelter or storing things.

she'd 1. she had: *She'd been there an hour.* 2. she would: *I'd wait if she'd wait, too.*

sheep an animal raised for wool and meat. **sheep.**

sheep dog a dog trained to help take care of sheep.

sheep ish shamed and timid: *He gave a sheepish smile when he saw that he was in the wrong place.*

sheet 1. a large piece of cloth used to sleep on or under. 2. a broad, thin piece of anything.

shelf 1. a flat piece of wood or metal to hold things. 2. *A shelf of rock hung over the cliff.* **shelves.**

shell 1. the hard covering of some animals. 2. the hard covering of a nut or egg. 3. take out of a shell: *I'll shell peas.* **shelled, shell ing.**

she'll she will.

shel ter something that covers or protects.

sher iff a county police officer.

she's 1. she is: *She's going with me.* 2. she has: *She's wanted to go for a long time.*

shin the front part of the leg from the knee to the ankle. See the picture under **leg**.

shine **1.** send out light; glow: *The sun shines.* **2.** make bright: *Shine your shoes. We shined the silver.* **shone** or **shined, shin ing.**

shiny bright; shining. **shin i er, shin i est.**

ship **1.** a large boat. **2.** send or carry by a ship, train, truck, or plane: *Will you ship the packages?* **shipped, ship ping.**

shirt a piece of clothing for the upper part of the body, worn specially by men and boys.

shiv er shake with cold or fear: *The noise made us shiver with fear.* **shiv ered, shiv er ing.**

shock[1] **1.** a sudden hard shake, blow, or crash. **2.** *An electric current can give you a shock.* **3.** *The boy's bad manners shock everyone.* **shocked, shock ing.**

shock[2] stalks of corn or bundles of grain set up on end. See the picture.

shock[3] a bushy mass: *He has a shock of red hair.*

shoe a covering for a person's foot.

shoe lace a cord or strip for fastening a shoe.

shone See **shine**. *The sun shone all last week.*

shook See **shake**. *They shook hands.*

shoot **1.** *See the new shoots on that bush.* **2.** *A bow shoots an arrow.* **3.** *Can you shoot this gun?* **4.** *Flames shoot up from a burning house.* **5.** *Corn shoots up in warm weather.* **shot, shoot ing.**

shop **1.** a place where things are sold. **2.** *He works in a carpenter's shop.* **3.** visit stores to buy things: *We shopped all morning.* **shopped, shop ping.**

shop ping *We went to the shopping center.*

shore the land at the edge of a sea or lake.

short **1.** not tall: *He is the shortest boy in class.* **2.** not long: *Summer seems short.* **short er, short est.**

shot[1] **1.** the sound of shooting. **2.** act of shooting.

shot[2] See **shoot**. *Many years ago he shot a lion.*

should **1.** *He should be here by now.* **2.** *We should have known better.* **3.** *If it should rain, we won't go.*

shoul der the part of the body from which an arm grows. See the picture under **body**.

shock [2]

should n't   should not.

shout   **1.** a loud call.   **2.** call loudly.   **3.** talk or laugh loudly.   **shout ed, shout ing.**

shove   **1.** *He gave the wagon a shove.*   **2.** *He shoved the cupboard into place.*   **shoved, shov ing.**

shov el   **1.** a tool used to lift loose material. **2.** *The man shoveled the dirt.*   **3.** *They shoveled a path through the snow.*   **shov eled, shov el ing.**

show   **1.** *We watched a good TV show.*   **2.** *She showed us her dolls.*   **3.** *The hole in his stocking shows.*   **4.** *A boy showed us the way to town.*   **showed, shown** or **showed, show ing.**

show er   **1.** a bath in which water pours down in small jets.   **2.** a short rain: *We had a shower this evening.*   **3.** *A shower of sparks fell from the engine.*

shown   See **show.**   *She has shown me the dress.*

shrank   See **shrink.**   *That shirt shrank in the wash.*

shrew   a small animal with a pointed nose.

shrill   having a high, sharp sound: *Crickets and katydids make shrill noises.*   **shrill er, shrill est.**

shrimp   **1.** a small shellfish with a long tail. **2.** *Shrimp salad is good to eat.*   **shrimp.**

shrink   **1.** draw back: *Any dog will shrink from a blow.*   **2.** *Wool shrinks in hot water.*   **3.** *Hot water shrinks wool.*   **shrank, shrunk, shrink ing.**

shrunk   See **shrink.**   *His socks have shrunk.*

shut   **1.** cover by pushing or pulling some part into place: *You can shut a door, a window, or a box.* **2.** *Shut your eyes.*   *Shut the book.*   **shut, shut ting.**

shy   **1.** uneasy in company: *He is shy and does not like parties.*   **2.** *Deer are shy animals.*   **shi er, shi est.**

sick   not feeling well.   **sick er, sick est.**

side   **1.** *A square has four sides.*   **2.** *Write only on one side of the paper.*   **3.** *My left side hurts.*   **4.** *We live on the east side of the city.*   **5.** *It is pleasant to be on the winning side.*   **6.** *The policeman sided with the boys.*   **7.** *There is a door at the side of the house.*   **sid ed, sid ing.**

sift   separate large pieces from small by shaking through a screen: *Sift the flour.*   **sift ed, sift ing.**

sigh   1. *She gave a loud sigh.*   **2.** let out a long, deep breath.   **sighed, sigh ing.**

sight   1. the power of seeing.   **2.** *At first sight, I thought it was you.*   **3.** *A sunset is a lovely sight.*

sign   1. any mark or thing used to tell or stand for something: *Those clouds are a sign of rain.   The signs to add, subtract, multiply, and divide are +, −, ×, ÷.*   **2.** put one's name on.   **signed, sign ing.**

sig nal   1. *A red light is a signal of danger.*   **2.** *He signaled the car to stop by raising his hand.*   **3.** *The man waved a signal flag.*   **sig naled, sig nal ing.**

si lent   1. *He entered the silent house.*   **2.** *Pupils must be silent in the library.*   **3.** *He made a silent wish.*

si lent ly   *The cat crept silently through the grass.*

silk   1. a fine, soft thread spun by some worms.   **2.** cloth made from it.   **3.** *She used silk thread.*

sill   a piece of wood or stone across the bottom of a door or window: *Your book is on the window sill.*

sil ly   without sense; foolish.   **sil li er, sil li est.**

si lo   a round building for storing food for cattle.

sil ver   1. a shiny, white metal.   **2.** tools for eating: *Please put the silver on the table.*   **3.** *She has silver hair.*

sim ple   easy to do.   **sim pler, sim plest.**

since   1. *We have been up since dawn.*   **2.** *She left, and I have not seen her since.*

sin cere ly   *He was sincerely sorry.*

sing   1. *He sings on the radio.*   **2.** *Birds sing.*   **3.** *We sing the baby to sleep.*   **sang, sung, sing ing.**

sin gle   1. only one.   **2.** not married.

sink   1. *The dishes are in the kitchen sink.* See the picture.   **2.** *The sun sinks in the west.*   **3.** *We saw the swimmer sink twice.*   **sank, sunk, sink ing.**

sip   1. drink little by little: *She sipped her tea.*   **2.** *She drank it sip by sip.*   **sipped, sip ping.**

sir   a title that shows respect to a man.

si ren   a whistle that makes an up-and-down sound.

sis ter   1. a girl who has the same parents as you.   **2.** *Mother bought us sister dresses.*

sit   1. rest on the lower part of the body.   **2.** *The clock will sit on that shelf for years.*   **sat, sit ting.**

sink

six **1.** one more than five. **2.** *It is almost six o'clock.*

six teen **1.** six more than ten. **2.** *Sixteen days ago our vacation began.*

six teenth **1.** next after the fifteenth. **2.** *The sixteenth of May is my birthday.*

sixth **1.** next after the fifth. **2.** *This is the sixth of November.*

six ti eth next after the fifty-ninth: *It was the sixtieth day of my vacation.*

six ty six times ten. **six ties.**

size *The two boys are the same size.*

skate **1.** a blade fastened to a shoe so a person can slide over ice. **2.** a roller skate. **3.** slide or move along on skates. **skat ed, skat ing.**

skel e ton *The skeleton is a frame for the body.*

ski **1.** one of a pair of boards on which a person can slide over snow. **2.** slide on skis. **skied, ski ing.**

skid slip or slide sideways. **skid ded, skid ding.**

skill *It takes skill to play the piano.*

skim **1.** remove from the top: *She skims the fat off the soup.* **2.** read hastily. **skimmed, skim ming.**

skin the covering of the body.

skip **1.** leap lightly; jump. **2.** pass over: *Skip the hard words.* **skipped, skip ping.**

skirt **1.** the lower part of a dress. **2.** a piece of clothing for women and girls.

skunk a bushy-tailed animal about the size of a cat.

sky space; the air above us. **skies.**

slacks long trousers. See the picture.

slam **1.** shut with force and noise. **2.** hit hard and with noise. **slammed, slam ming.**

slant **1.** lean to one side. **2.** not level: *Our house has a slant roof.* **slant ed, slant ing.**

slap **1.** a blow with the open hand. **2.** strike with a hand or something flat. **slapped, slap ping.**

sled a vehicle for sliding on ice and snow. See the picture.

sleep **1.** *He needs eight hours of sleep.* **2.** *We sleep at night.* **slept, sleep ing.**

sleep i ly *He yawned sleepily and closed his eyes.*

slacks

sled

sleepy 1. *This boy is always sleepy.* 2. *It was a sleepy little town.* **sleep i er, sleep i est.**
sleeve the part of clothing covering the arm.
sleigh *Sleighs are larger than sleds and have seats.*
slept See **sleep.** *The baby slept soundly all night.*
slice 1. a thin, flat, broad piece. 2. cut into thin, flat pieces. sliced, **slic ing.**
sliced 1. See slice. 2. *We ate sliced peaches.*
slick smooth; easy to slide on. **slick er, slick est.**
slid See slide. *The minutes slid rapidly by.*
slide 1. the act of sliding. 2. a smooth surface on which to slide. 3. a picture shown on a screen. 4. move smoothly. slid, **slid ing.**
slim thin; narrow. **slim mer, slim mest.**
sling 1. a loop of cloth around the neck to hold a hurt arm. 2. throw; cast. **slung, sling ing.**
slip[1] 1. *His broken leg was caused by a slip on the ice.* 2. *The girl wore a pink slip under her party dress.* 3. *That remark was a slip of the tongue.* 4. *Time slips by.* 5. *The knife slipped and cut him.* 6. *He slipped on the ice.* **slipped, slip ping.**
slip[2] a narrow strip of paper.
slip per a light, low shoe.
slope land or any surface that slants.
slow 1. *Slow down! Step on the brakes to slow the car.* 2. *Take the slower train.* 3. *The clock was slow.* 4. *The old man walked slowest of all the people.* **slowed, slow ing; slow er, slow est.**
slow ly *He turned slowly.*
slung See **sling.** *They slung some stones and ran.*
sly 1. *That girl is as sly as a fox.* 2. *She cast a sly look at the box.* **sly er, sly est** or **sli er, sli est.**
sly ly *You can tell he is slyly planning something.*
smack 1. *He smacked his lips when he saw food.* 2. kiss loudly. **smacked, smack ing.**
small 1. not large. 2. not much. 3. not important. **small er, small est.**
smart 1. feel or cause sharp pain. 2. clever; bright. **smart ed, smart ing; smart er, smart est.**
smash break into pieces. **smashed, smash ing.**

smell　1. *The smell of burning rubber is not pleasant.* 2. *We smell with our noses.* **smelled, smell ing.**

smile　1. the act of curving the corners of the mouth up to show you are pleased. 2. *Smile when you are happy.* **smiled, smil ing.**

smog　smoke and fog in the air.

smoke　1. gases that rise in a cloud from anything burning. 2. *The stove smokes.* 3. *Dad smokes a pipe.* 4. *Look at that big smoke cloud.* **smoked, smok ing.**

smoked　1. See **smoke.** 2. *Smoked fish is good.*

smoky　1. *He built a smoky fire.* 2. *The fireman ran into the smoky house.* 3. *It was difficult to see through the smoky glass.* **smok i er, smok i est.**

smooth　1. make even and flat; take out wrinkles and lumps. 2. having an even surface without lumps. **smoothed, smooth ing; smooth er, smooth est.**

smooth ly　*The engine ran smoothly.*

snail　a small animal that crawls slowly.

snake　a long, thin, crawling reptile without legs.

snap　1. *The box shut with a snap.* 2. *A snap on my dress is broken.* 3. *This wood snaps as it burns.* 4. *Please snap my dress.* **snapped, snap ping.**

snatch　take suddenly. **snatched, snatch ing.**

sneeze　1. *They heard a sneeze in the next room.* 2. *The pepper made her sneeze.* **sneezed, sneez ing.**

sniff　1. *She took one sniff of the rose.* 2. draw air through the nose in short, quick breaths that can be heard. 3. smell with sniffs: *The dog sniffed at the kitten.* **sniffed, sniff ing.**

snor kel　1. a tube for taking air or breathing under water. 2. a moving platform on a fire truck used by firemen to get near fires.

snow　1. water frozen in white flakes: *Snow falls in winter.* 2. *It snowed all day.* **snowed, snow ing.**

snug　1. warm; safe. 2. fitting closely: *That coat is a little too snug on her.* **snug ger, snug gest.**

snug ly　*Father tucked us snugly in bed.*

so　1. *Do not walk so fast.* 2. *Is that so?* 3. *The fire is so big I can't put it out.* 4. *The dog seemed hungry, so we fed him.* 5. *So! Late again!*

soap   something used for washing.

soar   fly to a great height.   **soared, soar ing.**

sob   **1.** a catching of short breaths when you are crying.   **2.** cry with short breaths: *The baby sobbed until I picked her up.*   **sobbed, sob bing.**

so cial   **1.** *We are having an ice-cream social next Friday.*   **2.** *Ten of us have formed a social club.*

sock   a short stocking; a covering for the foot.

so da   **1.** a powder used in cooking and in medicine. **2.** a sweet drink: *We stopped for a soda.*

soft   **1.** not hard; not stiff; giving way easily to touch.   **2.** gentle.   **soft er, soft est.**

soft ly   *The mother sang softly to her child.*

soil¹   ground; earth; dirt: *Our garden has rich soil.*

soil²   make or become dirty.   **soiled, soil ing.**

soiled   **1.** See **soil².**   **2.** *The soiled clothing is washed.*

sold   See **sell.**   *He sold it a week ago.*

sol dier   **1.** a member of the United States Army. **2.** one who serves in an army.

solve   find the answer to.   **solved, solv ing.**

some   **1.** *Some dogs are large; some are small.* **2.** *May I have some of your milk?*

som er sault   a roll or jump, head over heels.

son   the male child of his parents.

song   **1.** *We learned a new song today.*   **2.** *The canary burst into song.*

soon   **1.** *I will see you again soon.*   **2.** *Why have you come so soon?*   **3.** *As soon as I hear, I will let you know.*   **soon er, soon est.**

sooth ing   *The soothing music put me to sleep.*

sore   **1.** a painful place on the body: *The tight shoe caused a sore on her foot.*   **2.** *He bandaged his sore finger.*   **sor er, sor est.**

sor ry   feeling sad: *I am sorry that you are sick. We are sorry we can't go.*   **sor ri er, sor ri est.**

sound¹   **1.** *We heard the sound of music.*   **2.** *The bell sounds at eight o'clock.*   **3.** *The wind sounds like an animal howling.*   **sound ed, sound ing.**

sound²   **1.** healthy.   **2.** not weak or rotten: *The walls of the old house are sound.*   **sound er, sound est.**

349

sound ly *My brother sleeps soundly.*

soup a liquid food of boiled meat and vegetables.

sour having a taste like vinegar or lemon juice: *This green apple is sour.* **sour er, sour est.**

source 1. the beginning of a river; a spring. 2. *A newspaper gets news from many sources.*

south 1. the direction to your right as you face the rising sun. 2. *Drive south forty miles.* 3. coming from the south: *A south wind was blowing.* 4. *The south windows of the house were broken.* 5. **The South** means the southern part of the United States.

South Amer i ca one of the large masses of land on the earth.

South Car o li na one of the fifty states of the United States.

South Da ko ta one of the fifty states of the United States.

south east 1. the direction halfway between south and east: *We are facing southeast.* 2. toward the southeast. 3. *A southeast wind is often warm.*

south ern 1. toward the south: *The southern road is closed.* 2. from the south: *A southern breeze blew.*

South Pole the point farthest south on the earth.

south ward toward the south.

south west 1. the direction halfway between south and west: *The house faces southwest.* 2. toward the southwest. 3. *A southwest wind was blowing.*

sow scatter seed on the ground; plant seed: *He sows more wheat than oats.* **sowed, sow ing.**

soy bean 1. *Soybeans are used in making foods, oil, and other things.* 2. the plant it grows on.

space 1. *Our earth moves through space.* 2. *Is there space in the car for another person?* 3. *The astronaut put on his space suit.*

space hel met a helmet worn by an astronaut.

space ship a vehicle for traveling in space.

space suit a suit worn by an astronaut.

spade a tool for digging; a kind of shovel.

spa ghet ti a food made of flour and water rolled into long, thin sticks or ribbons.

spare   **1.** *Frost killed some flowers but spared others.*
2. *Father couldn't spare the car.*   **3.** *Have you a spare tire?*   **spared, spar ing.**

spark   a small bit of fire: *The burning wood threw off sparks.*   *Sparks flew from the broken wire.*

spar kle   send out little sparks; shine brightly.   **spar kled, spar kling.**

spar row   a small, brown-gray bird.

speak   **1.** say words; talk.   **2.** make a speech.   **spoke, spo ken, speak ing.**

spear   **1.** a long pole with a sharp, pointed head.
2. catch with a spear.   **speared, spear ing.**

spe cial   of a certain kind; different from others.

spe cial ly   *Mother got dinner specially for you.*

speech   **1.** the act of speaking; manner of speaking:
His speech was slow.   **2.** a public talk.   **speech es.**

speed   **1.** *The speed made the ride exciting.*   **2.** go fast:
The boat is speeding over the water.   **sped, speed ing.**

spell[1]   *We had a spell of rainy weather in August.*

spell[2]   *The witch's spell turned the girls into flowers.*

spell[3]   write or say the letters of a word in order:
Some words are easy to spell.   **spelled, spell ing.**

spell er   a book for teaching spelling.

spell ing   *Spend more time on your spelling lessons.*

spend   **1.** *She will spend ten dollars.*   **2.** *Don't spend more time there.*   **spent, spend ing.**

spent   See **spend.**   *I spent my time fishing.*

spice   a plant used for seasoning: *Pepper is a spice.*

spi der   a small animal with eight legs and no wings.

spike   a large, strong nail.   See the picture.

spill   **1.** *Don't spill the jam.*   **2.** *Water spilled from the pail.*   **spilled, spill ing.**

spin   **1.** *The boy spins his top.*   **2.** *Early settlers had to spin their thread.*   **spun, spin ning.**

spire   the top part of a tower or steeple.

spite   **1.** *She picked his flowers out of spite.*
2. In spite of means not being stopped by.

splash   **1.** the sound of liquid hitting a hard surface.   **2.** cause liquid to fly about.   **splash es; splashed, splash ing.**

spike

351

splen did *It was a splendid sunset.*

split 1. break or cut in layers. 2. separate into parts. 3. *We had split-pea soup.* **split, split ting.**

spoil 1. *The rain spoiled the picnic.* 2. *The fruit spoiled.* 3. *He has been spoiled.* **spoiled, spoil ing.**

spoke[1] one of the bars from the center of a wheel to the edge. See the picture under **wheel.**

spoke[2] See **speak.** *She spoke about that yesterday.*

spo ken 1. See **speak.** *They have spoken to me often.* 2. *My dog obeys spoken commands.*

sponge *We washed the car with a sponge.*

spool a round piece of wood or metal on which thread or wire is wound.

spoon a tool for eating.

sport 1. *Baseball and fishing are sports.* 2. *Did you get a new sport shirt?*

spot 1. *His tie is blue with white spots.* 2. *From this spot you can see the ocean.*

spot ted having spots: *The spotted dog chased me.*

sprain 1. *The sprain was beginning to hurt.* 2. twist a joint or muscle: *He sprained his ankle.* **sprained, sprain ing.**

sprained 1. See **sprain.** 2. *The sprained ankle began to swell.*

sprang See **spring.** *The tiger sprang at the deer.*

spray 1. liquid going through the air in small drops. 2. something that sends a liquid out as spray. 3. sprinkle; scatter spray on. **sprayed, spray ing.**

spread 1. a covering. 2. cover with a thin layer. 3. *Fields of corn were spread out before us.* 4. *He has spread the news.* **spread, spread ing.**

spring 1. something that returns to its shape after being pulled out of shape. See the picture. 2. the season when plants begin to grow. 3. a small stream coming from the earth. 4. a leap or jump. 5. rise or move suddenly and lightly. 6. *A bent branch will spring back into place.* 7. *We like to pick spring flowers.* **sprang, sprung, spring ing.**

sprin kle 1. scatter in drops or tiny bits. 2. rain a little bit. **sprin kled, sprin kling.**

1

spring

sprinkler a thing that sprinkles.

sprout **1.** a young plant or a new part of an old plant. **2.** begin to grow. **sprout ed, sprout ing.**

spruce **1.** a kind of evergreen tree: *The Blue Spruce is the State Tree of Utah; the Black Hills Spruce is the State Tree of South Dakota; the Colorado Blue Spruce is the State Tree of Colorado.* **2.** *Spruce trees have leaves shaped like needles.*

sprung See **spring.** *The branch has sprung back.*

spun See **spin.** *The princess spun all the thread.*

spur a pointed object worn on the heel: *Poke a horse lightly with your spurs to make it run.*

spy **1.** a person who secretly watches what others do. **2.** keep a secret watch. **spies; spied, spy ing.**

square **1.** a figure with four equal sides and four equal corners. **2.** *The town square has a playground and a pool.* **3.** *I need a square piece of paper.* **squar er, squar est.**

squawk make a loud, coarse sound: *Hens and ducks squawk when frightened.* **squawked, squawk ing.**

squeak make a short, sharp, shrill sound: *A mouse squeaks.* **squeaked, squeak ing.**

squeal make a long, sharp, shrill cry: *A pig squeals when it is hurt.* **squealed, squeal ing.**

squeeze **1.** force by pressing. **2.** press hard. **3.** hug. **squeezed, squeez ing.**

squir rel a small, bushy-tailed animal.

sta ble a building where horses or cattle are kept.

stack **1.** a pile of anything. **2.** pile or arrange in a stack. **stacked, stack ing.**

stage **1.** the raised platform in a theater. **2.** *Frogs pass through a tadpole stage.*

stage coach a vehicle, drawn by horses, used before railroads were built. **stage coach es.**

stair one of a group of steps for going from one level or floor to another: *He went up the stairs fast.*

stake **1.** a pointed stick driven into the ground. **2.** fasten to or with a stake. **3.** *We staked out a garden.* **staked, stak ing.**

stalk[1] the stem of a plant.

stalk[2] **1.** follow without being seen or heard.
2. walk with slow, stiff strides. **stalked, stalk ing.**
stall **1.** a place in a stable for one animal.
2. a small place for selling things. **3.** go slow
or stop. **stalled, stall ing.**
stamp **1.** a small piece of paper with glue on the
back. **2.** a tool that puts a mark on something:
Use the rubber stamp to mark these letters. **3.** put a
stamp on. **4.** put a mark on. **5.** bring down one's
foot with force. **6.** *May I see your stamp
collection?* **stamped, stamp ing.**
stand **1.** *We bought a paper at the newspaper stana.*
2. *Don't stand if you are tired.* **3.** *Stand the box here.*
4. *Those plants cannot stand much
cold.* **stood, stand ing.**
star **1.** *She is a movie star.* **2.** one of the bright
points seen in the sky at night. **3.** a figure with
five or six points. See the pictures.

3

star

stare look long with the eyes wide open: *The girl
stared at the toys in the window.* **stared, star ing.**
star fish a sea animal. **star fish es** or **star fish.**
star ling a bird that is easily tamed.
start **1.** *Let's get an early start.* **2.** *The train starts
on time.* **3.** move suddenly: *She started in surprise.*
4. *At the start I was ahead.* **start ed, start ing.**
starve suffer with hunger. **starved, starv ing.**
state **1.** *What is the state of your health?* **2.** *There
are fifty states.* **3.** *He carried the state flag.*
sta tion **1.** *The policeman took his station at the
corner.* **2.** *She met her father at the station.*
3. *He works at the radio station.*
sta tion ery writing paper, cards, and envelopes.
stay *Stay for a while. Shall I go or stay? She is
staying with her aunt.* **stayed, stay ing.**
stead i ly *The soldiers marched steadily forward.*
steady **1.** make firm; keep from swaying or
shaking: *Steady the ladder while I climb to the roof.*
2. *A steady stream of water came from the
hose.* **stead ied, stead y ing; stead i er, stead i est.**
steak a slice of meat, specially beef.

steal take something that does not belong to you and keep it. **stole, sto len, steal ing.**

steam 1. hot water in the form of gas or a very fine spray. 2. *We have steam heat in our house.*

steel 1. iron made very hard and strong: *Most tools are made from steel.* 2. *An engine has many steel parts.*

steep having a sharp slope; almost straight up and down: *This hill is steep.* **steep er, steep est.**

stee ple the high tower on a church.

steer[1] any male of beef cattle.

steer[2] *Mother steers the car.* **steered, steer ing.**

stem the main part of a plant above the ground.

step 1. lifting the foot and putting it down in a new position. 2. *Take three steps.* 3. a place for the foot in going up or down. 4. move the legs as in walking: *He stepped on a bug.* 5. **Keep step** means move the same leg at the same time that another person does. **stepped, step ping.**

ster i lize make free from germs: *They boiled the water to sterilize it.* **ster i lized, ster i liz ing.**

stew 1. food cooked by slow boiling: *We made beef stew.* 2. cook by slow boiling. **stewed, stew ing.**

stewed 1. See **stew.** 2. *We ate stewed tomatoes.*

stick[1] 1. a long, thin piece of wood. 2. *He was eating a stick of candy.* 3. *We bought stick candy.*

stick[2] 1. *He sticks his fork into the potato.* 2. *Don't stick your head out of the train window.* 3. *Stick a stamp on the letter.* **stuck, stick ing.**

stiff not easily bent; firm. **stiff er, stiff est.**

stiff ly *The old man walked stiffly and slowly.*

still 1. not moving; without noise; quiet. 2. *You can read still better if you will try.* 3. *Was the store still open? Is he still there?*

stilt one of a pair of poles, used to walk on.

sting 1. *He put mud on the sting to take away the pain.* 2. *Bees and hornets sting.* **stung, sting ing.**

stir 1. mix by moving around. 2. move: *The wind stirs the leaves.* 3. move about: *No one was stirring in the house.* **stirred, stir ring.**

stock *This store keeps a large stock of toys.*

stock ade   a high, strong fence.

stock ing   a knitted covering for the foot and leg.

stole[1]   a wrap like a shawl.

stole[2]   See **steal**.   *He stole the money years ago.*

sto len   See **steal**.   *He has stolen the apples.*

stom ach   **1.** the part of the body that receives the food we swallow.   **2.** *He hit me in the stomach.*

stone   **1.** hard mineral matter that is not metal. **2.** a piece of rock.   **3.** *He built a stone wall.*

stood   See **stand**.   *He stood on the corner for an hour.*

stool   a seat without back or arms.

stop   **1.** keep from moving, working, doing, or being. **2.** *The sink is stopped up.*   **stopped, stop ping.**

store   **1.** a place where things are kept for sale. **2.** put away for use later.   **stored, stor ing.**

stork   a large, long-legged bird with a long neck.

storm   a strong wind with rain, snow, or hail.

sto ry[1]   an account of some happening.   **sto ries.**

sto ry[2]   the set of rooms on the same level or floor of a building: *That house has two stories.*   **sto ries.**

stout   **1.** fat and large.   **2.** strongly built; firm; strong: *The fort has stout walls.*   **stout er, stout est.**

stove   an instrument for cooking and heating.

straight   **1.** without a bend or curve.   **2.** *He went straight home.*   **straight er, straight est.**

strange   **1.** unusual; queer.   **2.** not known, seen, or heard of before.   **strang er, strang est.**

strange ly   *She was strangely dressed for a party.*

strap   a narrow strip of leather or other material.

straw   **1.** the dry stalks of grain.   **2.** *We drank sodas through straws.*   **3.** *She wore a straw hat.*

straw ber ry   **1.** a small red fruit that is good to eat.   **2.** *He had a strawberry soda.*   **straw ber ries.**

stray   **1.** lose one's way; wander.   **2.** *A stray cat is crying at the door.*   **strayed, stray ing.**

streak   **1.** a long, thin mark or line.   **2.** go very fast.   **3.** make long, thin marks or lines on.   **streaked, streak ing.**

stream   **1.** running water.   **2.** any steady flow.

street   a road in a city or town.

stretch **1.** draw the body or limbs out to full length. **2.** reach out; hold out. **3.** become longer or wider without breaking. **stretched, stretch ing.**

strid den See **stride.** *He had stridden away fast.*

stride walk with long steps: *The tall man strides down the street.* **strode, strid den, strid ing.**

strike **1.** *The men are on strike.* **2.** in baseball, a swing of the bat without hitting the ball. **3.** hit with the hand or an object. **4.** *Strike a match.* **5.** stop work to get better pay. **6. Strike out** means fail to hit three times in baseball. **struck, strik ing.**

string **1.** small cord or very thin rope. **2.** a special cord for musical instruments. **3.** *The child is stringing beads.* **strung, string ing.**

strip[1] a long, narrow, flat piece of cloth or paper.

strip[2] take off or take away. **stripped, strip ping.**

stripe a long, narrow band of color.

striped *Zebras are striped.*

strode See **stride.** *He strode over the ditch.*

strong having much power and force: *A strong wind blew down the trees.* **strong er, strong est.**

strong ly *I strongly object to what you are doing.*

struck See **strike.** *The man struck a match.*

strug gle **1.** *It was a struggle to finish my lesson.* **2.** *She struggled very hard to keep back the tears.* **strug gled, strug gling.**

strung See **string.** *I strung the beads again.*

stub born **1.** *The stubborn boy refused to eat.* **2.** *He had a stubborn cough that kept him out of school.* **stub born er, stub born est.**

stub born ly *He stubbornly refused help.*

stuck See **stick**[2]. *She stuck out her tongue.*

stu dio a workroom of an artist.

study **1.** a small room for reading and studying; a den. **2.** learn by reading or thinking. **3.** examine carefully. **stud ies; stud ied, study ing.**

stuff **1.** *She bought some white stuff for curtains.* **2.** *Their attic is full of old stuff.* **3.** *She stuffed food in her mouth.* **stuffed, stuff ing.**

stuffed **1.** See **stuff.** **2.** *The stuffed turkey is done.*

stump

stum ble   almost fall by striking the foot against something.   **stum bled, stum bling.**

stump   the lower end of a tree or plant left after the main part is cut off. See the picture.

stung   See **sting.**   *A wasp stung him.*

stunt   an act; a performance.

stu pid   not smart.   **stu pid er, stu pid est.**

stu pid ly   *He looked up stupidly.*

stur dy   strong; stout.   **stur di er, stur di est.**

stut ter   repeat the same beginning sound of a word while trying to speak.   **stut tered, stut ter ing.**

sub ject   *I study reading, writing, and other subjects.*

sub tract   take away: *Subtract two from ten and you have eight.*   **sub tract ed, sub tract ing.**

sub urb   a town or village just outside of a city.

suc ceed   do what you planned to do; turn out well; have success.   **suc ceed ed, suc ceed ing.**

suc cess   the wished-for ending; good fortune: *Success in school comes from hard work.*   **suc cess es.**

such   **1.** *The child had such a cold that he was in bed.* **2.** *The ladies had such drinks as tea and coffee.*

sud den   **1.** not expected.   **2.** quick; rapid. **3. All of a sudden** means quickly.

sud den ly   *Suddenly she screamed.*

suf fer   have pain.   **suf fered, suf fer ing.**

suf fix   a syllable put at the end of a word to change its meaning.   **suf fix es.**

sugar   **1.** a sweet material made from sugar cane or sugar beets.   **2.** *Sugar cookies are good to eat.*

sug gest   bring a thought or plan to a person's mind.   **sug gest ed, sug gest ing.**

suit   **1.** *A man's suit is made up of a coat and trousers and usually a vest.*   **2.** satisfy: *Does this color suit you?*   **suit ed, suit ing.**

suit case   a case or bag to hold or carry clothes.

sulk   be silently angry.   **sulked, sulk ing.**

sum   **1.** an amount of money.   **2.** two or more numbers or things added together.

sum mer   **1.** the warmest season of the year. **2.** *It is time for summer clothes.*

sun **1.** the body around which the earth turns.
2. the light and heat of the sun: *I sat in the sun.*
3. *I sat under a sun lamp.*

sun dae a dish of ice cream with sauce on top.

Sun day the first day of the week.

sun flow er a tall plant with a large yellow flower: *The Sunflower is the State Flower of Kansas.*

sung See **sing.** *Many songs were sung at the party.*

sunk See **sink.** *The ship had sunk to the bottom.*

sun ny **1.** having much sunshine. **2.** lighted or warmed by the sun. **sun ni er, sun ni est.**

sun rise the coming up of the sun; the time when the sun appears in the morning.

sun set the going down of the sun; the time when the sun is last seen in the evening.

su per in tend ent a person who directs or manages: *The superintendent of schools spoke to us.*

su per mar ket a large grocery store.

su per vi sor a person in charge of something.

sup per the evening meal.

sup pose **1.** *Suppose we are late, will he wait?*
2. *I suppose she will come.* **sup posed, sup pos ing.**

sure **1.** *Thunder is a sure sign of rain.*
2. *Are you sure you locked the door?* **sur er, sur est.**

sure ly *By now he is surely taller than his sister.*

sur face a side or face of something; the outside.

sur prise **1.** something not expected. **2.** *The news surprised us all.* **3.** *They planned a surprise party.* **sur prised, sur pris ing.**

sur round shut in on all sides; be around: *A fence surrounds the field.* **sur round ed, sur round ing.**

sus pect **1.** imagine to be so. **2.** believe something to be bad. **sus pect ed, sus pect ing.**

swal low¹ a small bird that can fly very fast.

swal low² take into the stomach through the mouth. **swal lowed, swal low ing.**

swam See **swim.** *The boy swam a mile to shore.*

swamp wet, soft land.

swampy *Some trees grow best in swampy land.* **swamp i er, swamp i est.**

swan   a large bird with a long, thin, curving neck.

sway   **1.** swing back and forth or from side to side.
2. make move from side to side.   **swayed, sway ing.**

sweat   **1.** water coming through the skin.
2. give out water through the skin.   **3.** come out
in drops.   **sweat or sweat ed, sweat ing.**

sweat er   a knit jacket or blouse.

sweep   clean or clear away dust and dirt with a
broom or brush.   **swept, sweep ing.**

sweep er   a thing that sweeps.

sweet   **1.** having a taste like sugar or honey.
2. pleasant.   **3.** fresh; not sour.   **sweet er, sweet est.**

sweet heart   a person who is loved.

sweet ly   *She sang sweetly to the sleeping baby.*

swept   See **sweep.**   *She swept the room.*

swift   able to move very fast.   **swift er, swift est.**

swift ly   *He threw the ball swiftly to first base.*

swim   **1.** move along in the water.   **2.** *He is going
to swim the river.*   **swam, swum, swim ming.**

swim mer   a person or an animal that swims.

swing   **1.** a seat in which one may move back
and forth.   **2.** move back and forth with a steady
motion.   **swung, swing ing.**

swish   **1.** *He heard the swish of her silk skirt.*
2. *The cane swished through the air.*   **3.** *The cow
swished her tail.*   **swish es; swished, swish ing.**

switch   **1.** a thin stick.   **2.** a button or lever that
controls a machine or electric current.   **3.** *He
switched the boys.*   **4.** *Switch on the light.*   **5.** change:
The wind switched.   **6.** *He rode on the switch
engine.*   **switched, switch ing.**

swoop   come down with a rush; plunge rapidly
down upon something.   **swooped, swoop ing.**

swum   See **swim.**   *He had never swum before.*

swung   See **swing.**   *The door swung open.*

syl la ble   a group of letters that can be
pronounced as one sound in a word.

syn a gogue   a building used for worship.

sy rin ga   a bush with sweet-smelling white flowers:
The Mock Orange Syringa is the State Flower of Idaho.

T

tab er nac le   **1.** a place of worship.   **2.** a temple.
3. a container used in some churches.

ta ble   **1.** a piece of furniture with a flat top on legs.
2. a list of facts or figures.   **3.** *That table leg is scratched.*

tab let   **1.** sheets of writing paper fastened together
at one edge.   **2.** a small, flat sheet.   **3.** a pill.

tack   **1.** a short nail with a broad, flat head.   See
the picture.   **2.** fasten with tacks.   **3.** sail in a
zigzag course.   **4.** *Where did you put the tack
hammer?*   **tacked, tack ing.**

tad pole   a very young frog or toad, at the stage
when it has a tail and lives in water.

tag[1]   **1.** a piece of paper fastened to something.
2. a small, hanging piece; a loose piece.   **3.** put on a
tag or tags.   **4.** follow closely.   **tagged, tag ging.**

tag[2]   **1.** a children's game.   **2.** touch or tap with
the hand.   **tagged, tag ging.**

tail   **1.** the part of an animal's body farthest to the
rear.   **2.** the hind part of anything.

take   **1.** lay hold of: *Take my hand.*   **2.** accept:
Take some candy.   **3.** *It takes time to learn
arithmetic.*   **4.** subtract: *If you take two from seven,
you have five.*   **took, tak en, tak ing.**

tak en   See **take.**   *I have taken away his toy.*

tale   **1.** a story.   **2.** a lie.   **3. Tell tales** often means
tell something about a person to get him into trouble.

talk   **1.** the use of words in speaking; a short speech.
2. use words; speak.   **talked, talk ing.**

tall   **1.** high.   **2.** *The tree is a hundred feet tall.*
3. hard to believe.   **tall er, tall est.**

tal low   hard fat from sheep and cows.

tam bou rine   a small drum with metal plates.

tame   **1.** make something wild become gentle
and ready to obey.   **2.** *This is a tame
bear.*   **tamed, tam ing; tam er, tam est.**

tan   **1.** make a hide into leather.   **2.** make or
become brown by being in the sun.   **3.** *He wore tan
shoes.*   **tanned, tan ning; tan ner, tan nest.**

tack

tank   1. a large container for liquid or gas.   **2.** a vehicle, covered with steel and with a gun in front.

tan ner y   a place where animal hides are tanned.   **tan ner ies.**

tap   strike lightly.   **tapped, tap ping.**

tape   1. a strip of cloth or paper.   **2.** fasten or wrap with tape: *Some athletes tape their ankles.*   **3.** *Where is the tape measure?*   **taped, tap ing.**

tar   1. a black, sticky material taken from wood or coal.   **2.** *I saw a tar pit at the history museum.*

tar dy   behind time; late.   **tar di er, tar di est.**

tar pon   a large fish: *The Tarpon is the State Fish of Alabama.*

task   work to be done; a piece of work; a duty.

tas sel   a bunch of cords, fastened at one end.

taste   1. the one of the five senses that shows the difference between things when you put them in your mouth.   **2.** *She has very good taste in books.*   **3.** try by taking a little into the mouth.   **tast ed, tast ing.**

taught   See **teach.**   *He taught her to swim.*

tax   1. money paid by the people to run a government: *We pay a tax on money we earn.*   **2.** put a tax on.   **tax es; taxed, tax ing.**

taxi   an automobile you can hire.

tea   1. a drink made by pouring boiling water over a certain kind of dried leaves.   **2.** the leaves.   **3.** a meal in the afternoon.   **4.** *Here's a tea bag.*

teach   help learn; show how to do; make understand; give lessons.   **taught, teach ing.**

teach er   a person who teaches.

team   1. *Our team won.*   **2.** two or more animals hitched together.   **3.** *Baseball is a team sport.*

tear¹   1. *There's a tear in your coat.*   **2.** *It is easy to tear cloth.*   **tore, torn, tear ing.**

tear²   a drop of salty water coming from the eye.

tease   1. *Don't be a tease.*   **2.** *Don't tease the dog.*   **3.** beg: *That child teases for candy.*   **teased, teas ing.**

teeth   1. more than one tooth.   **2.** anything like teeth.   See the pictures.

tel e gram   a message sent over wires.

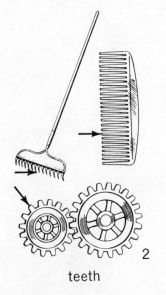

teeth

tel e phone 1. an instrument for talking over a distance. 2. talk by telephone. 3. *Did I hear the telephone bell?* **tel e phoned, tel e phon ing.**

tel e scope an instrument for making distant objects appear nearer and larger.

tel e vi sion *We often call television TV.*

tell 1. *Tell us a story.* 2. *I can't tell which house is yours.* 3. *Do as I tell you.* **told, tell ing.**

tem per a ture 1. the amount of heat or cold in something. 2. more heat in your body than usual.

tem ple a building used for worship; a church.

ten 1. one more than nine. 2. *Wait ten minutes.*

ten der 1. not hard; soft: *The meat is tender.* 2. kind; loving. **ten der er, ten der est.**

ten e ment a building to live in.

Ten nes see one of the fifty states of the United States.

ten nis a game played on a special court indoors or outdoors by two or four players who hit a ball back and forth over a net.

ten sion 1. *When you pull back the bow string, the bow has tension.* 2. *A mother feels tension when her baby is sick.*

tent a shelter made of canvas or skins.

tenth 1. next after the ninth. 2. *On the tenth day it rained.*

ter mi nal 1. *A railroad terminal is a station at the end of the line.* 2. *A battery has two terminals.*

ter ri ble causing great fear; awful.

ter ri bly *He looked terribly frightened.*

ter ri fied 1. See **terrify.** 2. *The terrified dog ran away from the noise.*

ter ri fy frighten very much: *The sight of the bear will terrify him.* **ter ri fied, ter ri fy ing.**

test 1. *We had a test in arithmetic.* 2. try out: *We can test the rope by pulling it.* 3. *Here are your test papers.* **test ed, test ing.**

Tex as one of the fifty states of the United States.

than 1. *He is taller than his sister.* 2. *You know better than I do.*

thank   say that one is pleased for something given or done.   **thanked, thank ing.**

Thanks giv ing   the fourth Thursday in November in most states; a day set apart every year to give thanks for the good things we have received.

that   **1.** *Look at that.*   **2.** *Do you see that boy?*   **3.** *I know that six and four are ten.*   **4.** *He ran so that he would not be late.*   **5.** *He ran so fast that he was early.*   **6.** *Use the box that is open.*   **7.** *I can't stay that long.*

thatch   straw or grass, used as a roof.

thatched   *The house had a thatched roof.*

that's   that is.

thaw   **1.** a time of melting.   **2.** melt ice, snow, or anything frozen.   **thawed, thaw ing.**

the   *The dog I saw had no tail.   The boys on the horses are my brothers.   You are the one to do it.*

the a ter or **the a tre**   a place where plays are acted or movies are shown.

their   *They like their new school.   They raised their heads as we passed.*

them   *Look at them.   Ask them to go along.*

them selves   **1.** *The teachers themselves said the test was too hard.*   **2.** *The boys hurt themselves.*

then   **1.** *Prices were lower then.*   **2.** *The noise stopped and then began again.*   **3.** *First comes spring, then summer.*   **4.** *If he broke the window, then he'll pay for it.*

there   **1.** *Sit there.*   **2.** *You are mistaken there.*   **3.** *There is a new house on our street.*   **4.** *There, there!*

there's   there is.

ther mom e ter   an instrument for measuring the temperature of something.

these   *These two problems are hard.   These are my books.   Shall I take these with me?*

they   **1.** *I put three books here; where are they? They are on the table.*   **2.** *They say we need a new school.*

they'd   **1.** they had: *They'd wanted to go for a long time.*   **2.** they would: *They'd go if they could.*

they'll   they will.

they're   they are.

they've   they have.

thick   **1.** far from one side to the opposite side; not thin.   **2.** *This brick is two inches thick.* **3.** *She has thick hair.*   **4.** like glue; not like water.   **thick er, thick est.**

thick ly   *Weeds grow thickly in the rich soil.*

thigh   the part of the leg between the hip and the knee.   See the picture under **leg.**

thin   **1.** not far from one side to the opposite side; not thick.   **2.** *He is a thin man.*   **3.** *He has thin hair.* **4.** like water; not like glue.   **thin ner, thin nest.**

thing   **1.** any object or material you can see, hear, touch, taste, or smell.   **2.** *A strange thing happened.*

think   **1.** have ideas; use the mind: *I want to think.* **2.** *Do you think it will rain?*   **thought, think ing.**

thin ly   *The coat was thinly lined.*

third   **1.** next after the second.   **2.** *Mother arrived on the third of January.*

thirsty   needing water.   **thirst i er, thirst i est.**

thir teen   **1.** three more than ten.   **2.** *I'll be ready in thirteen minutes.*

thir teenth   **1.** next after the twelfth.   **2.** *The thirteenth of May is my sister's birthday.*

thir ti eth   **1.** next after the twenty-ninth.   **2.** *The last day of September is the thirtieth.*

thir ty   **1.** three times ten.   **2.** *In thirty minutes we'll be there.*   **thir ties.**

this   **1.** *This is mine; that is yours.*   **2.** *This morning we are late.*   **3.** *Come this way.*   **4.** *Stop it this minute.*

thorn   a sharp point on a tree or plant.

those   **1.** *Those are my books.*   **2.** *Do you own those dogs?*

though   **1.** in spite of the fact that.   **2.** even so.

thought   **1.** an idea; thinking about something. **2.** See **think.**   *We thought it would snow yesterday.*

thought ful   **1.** *He was thoughtful for a while and then replied.*   **2.** *She is always thoughtful of her mother.*

thought ful ly   *She looked at him thoughtfully.*

thou sand   ten hundred.

thou sandth   last one of a thousand.

thrash er   a bird somewhat like a thrush: *The Brown Thrasher is the State Bird of Georgia.*

thread   1. *You sew with thread.*   2. *She threaded a needle.*   **thread ed, thread ing.**

three   1. one more than two.   2. *In three days my sister will be home.*

threw   See **throw.**   *He threw a stone and ran away.*

thrill   1. a shivering, excited feeling.   2. have a shivering, excited feeling.   **thrilled, thrill ing.**

throat   the front of the neck.

throne   the chair on which a king or queen sits.

through   1. *The soldiers marched through town.*   2. *She read the book through.*   3. *I am through school at noon.*

throw   make something move through the air by force.   **threw, thrown, throw ing.**

thrown   See **throw.**   *She has thrown out her old toys.*

thrush   a common songbird: *The Hermit Thrush is the State Bird of Vermont.*   **thrush es.**

thumb   1. the short, thick finger.   See the picture under **arm.**   2. any part that covers the thumb.

thump   1. strike with something heavy.   2. make a low sound.   **thumped, thump ing.**

thun der   1. the noise that often follows a flash of lightning.   2. any noise like thunder.   3. make a noise like thunder.   **thun dered, thun der ing.**

Thurs day   the fifth day of the week.

tick et   a card or piece of paper that gives its holder a right to do something.

tick le   touch lightly, causing little thrills and shivers; amuse.   **tick led, tick ling.**

tide   the rise and fall of the ocean about every twelve hours, caused by the moon and the sun.

ti dy   neat and in order.   **ti di er, ti di est.**

tie   1. a necktie.   2. a thing that fastens.   3. a heavy timber.   4. *The game ended in a tie.*   5. fasten with string; bind.   6. *The two teams tied.*   **tied, ty ing.**

ti ger   a fierce, striped animal like a cat.

tight   1. firm.   2. stretched.   3. fitting closely or too closely.   **tight er, tight est.**

tight ly   *He held on tightly to the handle.*

till   until; up to the time of; up to the time when.

tim ber   **1.** a large piece of wood used in building. **2.** trees; forest: *His land is covered with timber.*

time   **1.** all the days there have been or ever will be. **2.** *It is time to go.*   **3.** *The batter times his swing right.* **4. Times**, in arithmetic, means multiply or multiplied by.   **timed, tim ing.**

tim id   easily frightened.   **tim id er, tim id est.**

tim id ly   *The mouse peeped timidly out of the hole.*

tin   **1.** a metal that shines like silver but is softer. **2.** *We picked up all the old tin cans.*

tin kle   make short, light, ringing sounds: *The sleigh bells tinkled.*   **tin kled, tin kling.**

ti ny   very small; wee.   **ti ni er, ti ni est.**

tip[1]   **1.** the end part.   **2.** a piece put on the end.

tip[2]   **1.** slope; slant.   **2.** overturn.   **tipped, tip ping.**

tip[3]   **1.** a small present of money.   **2.** a useful hint. **3.** give a tip to.   **tipped, tip ping.**

tire[1]   a band of rubber or metal around a wheel. See the picture under **wheel.**

tire[2]   make weak and sleepy.   **tired, tir ing.**

tired   **1.** See **tire**[2].   **2.** *The tired team played hard.*

tire some   making you tired; not interesting: *We had to listen to a tiresome speech.*

ti tle   **1.** the name of a book, poem, picture, or song. **2.** a name showing what you are or do.

to   **1.** *Go to the right.*   **2.** *He was brave to the end.* **3.** *Mother came to the rescue.*   **4.** *She tore the letter to pieces.*   **5.** *Give the book to me.*

toad   a small animal something like a frog.

toast   **1.** slices of bread browned by heat.   **2.** brown or warm by heat.   **toast ed, toast ing.**

toast ed   **1.** See **toast.**   **2.** *I ate a toasted roll.*

toast er   an instrument that toasts.

to day   **1.** *Today is Wednesday.*   **2.** *What are you doing today?*   **3.** *Many girls wear short hair today.*

toe   **1.** one of the five end parts of the foot.   See the picture under **leg.**   **2.** the part of a stocking or shoe that covers the toes.   **3.** anything like a toe.

to geth er **1.** *The girls were walking together.*
2. *She can sew these pieces together to make a dress.*

told See **tell.** *You told me that last week.*

tom a hawk a light ax used by American Indians.

to ma to **1.** a fruit, full of juice, used as a vegetable.
2. *I like tomato soup.* **to ma toes.**

to mor row the day after today.

tone **1.** *You can speak in low, angry, or gentle tones.*
2. in music, the difference between two notes.

tongue *The tongue is used for tasting.*

to night *I am going to bed early tonight.*

ton sil one of the two small, round masses on the
inside of the throat: *He's had his tonsils taken out.*

too **1.** *The dog is hungry and thirsty, too. We, too,
are going away.* **2.** *The summer passed too quickly.*

took See **take.** *She took the car an hour ago.*

tool any instrument used to help in doing work.

tooth **1.** one of the hard white parts in the mouth.
See the picture. **2.** something like a tooth. **teeth.**

top[1] **1.** the highest point or part. **2.** the part
that is up, the end, or the surface. **3.** *It's at the top
of the page.* **4.** *Look on the top shelf.*

top[2] a toy that spins on a point.

torch **1.** a light to be carried or put in a holder.
2. an instrument with a very hot flame, used to
burn off paint or melt metal. **torch es.**

tore See **tear**[1]. *She tore her dress on a nail.*

torn **1.** See **tear**[1]. **2.** *His coat was old and torn.*

tor na do a strong, whirling wind that destroys
whatever it passes over.

tor toise a land turtle.

toss **1.** throw lightly with the palm of the hand up;
cast; fling. **2.** *The ship is tossed by the waves.*
3. *She tossed her head.* **tossed, toss ing.**

touch **1.** the sense by which a person knows things
by feeling, handling, or coming against them.
2. *She touched the hot pan.* **touched, touch ing.**

to ward in the direction of.

tow el a piece of cloth or paper for wiping.

tow er a high building.

tooth

1

town **1.** a community smaller than a city. **2.** *We went to the town hall.*

toy **1.** something for a child to play with; a plaything. **2.** *He had a toy truck.*

track **1.** steel rails for trains to run on. **2.** a mark left. **3.** a path. **4.** follow by marks or smell. **5.** make marks on. **tracked, track ing.**

trac tor a vehicle used for pulling farm machines.

trade **1.** buying and selling. **2.** *He made a good trade.* **3.** buy and sell. **4.** *Will you trade seats with me?* **trad ed, trad ing.**

traf fic people and vehicles coming and going.

trail **1.** anything that follows. **2.** a path. **3.** follow; pull or drag along behind. **4.** look for by track or smell. **trailed, trail ing.**

train **1.** a line of vehicles that move together. **2.** bring up; rear; teach: *She trained her dog.* **3.** become fit by exercise. **4.** *There is a signal at the train crossing.* **trained, train ing.**

tramp **1.** a long, steady walk. **2.** the sound of a heavy step. **3.** walk heavily. **tramped, tramp ing.**

tran som a window, usually on hinges, over a door.

trans por ta tion carrying; being carried: *The railroad offers transportation across the nation.*

trap **1.** a thing for catching animals. **2.** catch in a trap. **3.** *Open the trap door.* **trapped, trap ping.**

trap per a man who traps wild animals for their fur.

trash **1.** stuff of no use; garbage; broken or torn bits. **2.** *Put it in the trash can.*

trav el **1.** *She is traveling in Europe this summer.* **2.** *Sound travels in waves.* **trav eled, trav el ing.**

tray a flat container or plate with a raised edge.

treas ure **1.** money and jewels: *The pirates buried treasure along the coast.* **2.** *We found a treasure map.*

treat **1.** a gift of food, drink, or amusement. **2.** *Father treats us well.* **3.** *The dentist treated my toothache.* **treat ed, treat ing.**

tree **1.** a large plant with a trunk, branches, and leaves. See the picture. **2.** A **family tree** is a chart with branches showing the members of a family.

branch — bark — trunk

tree

1

trem ble   shake because of being excited, afraid, or weak.   **trem bled, trem bling.**

tri an gle   a figure having three sides.

trick   **1.** something done to fool.   **2.** an act of skill.   **3.** *He tricked me into going with him.*   **4.** *I had a trick dog.*   **tricked, trick ing.**

tri cy cle   a three-wheeled vehicle like a bicycle.

trim   **1.** make neat by cutting away parts.   **2.** make beautiful.   **trimmed, trim ming.**

trip   **1.** *We took a trip to Europe.*   **2.** *He tripped on the stairs.*   **tripped, trip ping.**

troll[1]   in stories, an ugly giant or elf.

troll[2]   fish with a moving line.   **trolled, troll ing.**

trom bone   a musical instrument.

troop er   **1.** a soldier in a group that rides horses.   **2.** a mounted policeman.

trot   go as a horse does, lifting one front foot and one hind foot at about the same time.   **trot ted, trot ting.**

trou ble   *That boy makes trouble for his teachers.*

trou sers   a two-legged outer piece of clothing.

trout   a fresh-water fish: *The California Golden Trout is the State Fish of California; the Cutthroat Trout is the State Fish of New Mexico.*

truck   a sturdy vehicle for carrying loads.

trudge   walk in a tired way.   **trudged, trudg ing.**

true   agreeing with fact; correct.   **tru er, tru est.**

tru ly   *Tell me truly what you think.*

trum pet   a musical instrument.

trunk   **1.** the main stem of a tree.   See the picture under **tree.**   **2.** an elephant's nose.   **3.** a big box for carrying clothes.   See the pictures.

trust   **1.** a firm view that a person or thing is honest, fair, and true.   **2.** believe firmly in the honesty, truth, or power of.   **trust ed, trust ing.**

truth   that which is true: *Tell the truth.*

try   **1.** *I'd like a try at it.*   **2.** *You try it.*   **3.** *Try this candy.*   **4.** *The man was tried in court.*   **tries; tried, try ing.**

tub   **1.** a bowl for washing.   **2.** a bathtub.

tu ba   a musical instrument.

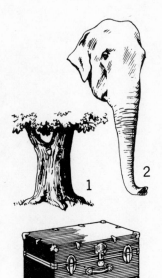

1 2

3

trunk

370

tube　**1.** a long, hollow pipe of metal, glass, rubber, and so on.　**2.** a small container for things like toothpaste.　**3.** *The radio tube was still good.*

tuck　**1.** *Mother took a tuck in my dress.*　**2.** *Tuck your shirt in.*　**3.** *Mother tucks us in bed.*　**4.** *A bird tucks its head under its wing.*　**tucked, tuck ing.**

Tues day　the third day of the week.

tug　pull with force; pull hard.　**tugged, tug ging.**

tu lip　**1.** a spring flower having several colors.　**2.** *Plant the tulip bulbs early.*

tu lip tree　a tall tree with tulip-shaped flowers: *The Tulip Tree is the State Tree of Indiana and of Kentucky; the Tulip Poplar is the State Tree of Tennessee.*

tum ble　**1.** a fall.　**2.** fall; roll or toss about.　**3.** perform leaps, springs, and somersaults usually on a padded mat.　**tum bled, tum bling.**

tu na　a large sea fish.

tune　**1.** a piece of music.　**2.** *This piano is out of tune.*　**3.** put in tune.　**tuned, tun ing.**

tun nel　an underground pass.

tur key　a large American bird raised for food.

turn　**1.** *I made a left turn.*　**2.** *It is his turn to read.*　**3.** *The wheel turned.*　**4.** *I turned the handle.*　**5.** *The road turns.*　**6.** *She turned white.*　**turned, turn ing.**

tur nip　a vegetable with a large, round root.

tur quoise　**1.** a sky-blue or green-blue stone.　**2.** *She wore a turquoise sweater.*

tur tle　an animal having a hard shell.

twelfth　**1.** next after the eleventh.　**2.** *Lincoln's birthday is February twelfth.*

twelve　**1.** one more than eleven.　**2.** *Twelve months ago is the same as one year ago.*

twen ti eth　**1.** next after the nineteenth.　**2.** *May twentieth is his birthday.*

twen ty　**1.** two times ten.　**2.** *Twenty years ago he was born.*　**twen ties.**

twice　**1.** two times: *Twice two is four.*　**2.** *I saw her twice a day.*

twin　one of two children or animals born at the same time of the same mother.

twin kle   shine with quick little flashes: *His eyes twinkled when he laughed.*   **twin kled, twin kling.**

twirl   revolve rapidly; spin; whirl: *Can you twirl a baton?*   **twirled, twirl ing.**

twist   1. *She twisted her ring on her finger.*   2. *The path twists in and out.*   3. *His face twisted with pain.*   4. *Don't twist what I say.*   **twist ed, twist ing.**

twist ed   1. See **twist.**   2. *The twisted rope broke.*

two   1. one more than one: *I'll stay two days.*   2. *Two years ago he left.*   3. *Count the class by twos.*

type writ er   *She wrote her story on a typewriter.*

ty phoon   a terrible storm; a hurricane.

typ ist   a person who operates a typewriter.

U

ug ly   bad to look at.   **ug li er, ug li est.**

um brel la   a folding frame covered with material.

um pire   *The umpire called the man safe.*   See the picture under **baseball.**

un able   not able: *A little baby is unable to walk.*

un buck le   unfasten the buckle of: *Please unbuckle my belt for me.*   **un buck led, un buck ling.**

un but ton   unfasten the button or buttons of a piece of clothing.   **un but toned, un but ton ing.**

un cer tain   not certain; full of doubt.

un chain   let loose; set free: *Be sure to unchain the dog before you go.*   **un chained, un chain ing.**

un cle   the brother of one's father or mother or the husband of one's aunt.

un cov er   1. remove the cover from.   2. *The police uncovered a plot.*   **un cov ered, un cov er ing.**

un der   1. beneath.   2. lower than.   3. less than.

un der neath   *We can sit underneath this tree.*

un der stand   1. *Now I understand her question.*   2. *A good teacher should understand children.*   3. *I understand that he is leaving town in a few days.*   **un der stood, un der stand ing.**

un der stood   See **understand.**   *I understood what he was trying to say.*

un eas y 1. *He had an uneasy feeling about the coming storm.* 2. *He was uneasy when his parents visited school.* **un eas i er, un eas i est.**

un fair not fair; unjust. **un fair er, un fair est.**

un fair ly *We all think you acted unfairly toward us.*

un fas ten undo; loosen; open; take the ties from. **un fas tened, un fas ten ing.**

un friend ly not friendly: *They certainly were an unfriendly group.* **un friend li er, un friend li est.**

un hap pi ly *The girl sighed unhappily.*

un hap py not happy. **un hap pi er, un hap pi est.**

un healthy 1. not having good health. 2. not good for the health. **un health i er, un health i est.**

un hitch unfasten: *Unhitch the horses and let them eat.* **un hitched, un hitch ing.**

uni form 1. clothes, all alike, worn by the members of a group. 2. always the same.

Unit ed States of Amer i ca the United States; the country north of Mexico and south of Canada.

un just not fair: *It is unjust to spread false tales.*

un just ly *She was unjustly accused of wasting time.*

un kind not kind. **un kind er, un kind est.**

un known not known; strange.

un less if not: *We shall go unless it rains.*

un load 1. *Help me unload the groceries.* 2. *Father unloaded the car.* **un load ed, un load ing.**

un lock open the lock of; open anything that is firmly closed. **un locked, un lock ing.**

un lucky not lucky. **un luck i er, un luck i est.**

un pack 1. take things out: *Unpack your clothes right away.* 2. take things out of: *Unpack your trunk.* **un packed, un pack ing.**

un pin take out pins. **un pinned, un pin ning.**

un pleas ant not pleasant; not giving pleasure to. **un pleas ant er, un pleas ant est.**

un roll 1. *He unrolled his blanket.* 2. *The yarn unrolled from the ball.* **un rolled, un roll ing.**

un safe dangerous. **un saf er, un saf est.**

un seal break the seal of. **un sealed, un seal ing.**

un seen not seen.

un stead i ly *Unsteadily the old man stood up.*

un steady not steady; shaky: *He was unsteady standing on one leg.* **un stead i er, un stead i est.**

un tie loosen; unfasten. **un tied, un ty ing.**

un til 1. *It was cold from Christmas until April.* 2. *We waited until the sun had set.* 3. *She did not leave until morning.*

un u su al not in common use; not common; rare.

un will ing not ready to or not wanting to.

un wind 1. *Don't unwind the yarn.* 2. *Thread unwinds from a spool.* **un wound, un wind ing.**

un wise not wise. **un wis er, un wis est.**

un wise ly *She acted unwisely when she didn't obey.*

un wound See **unwind.** *My kite string unwound.*

un wrap remove a wrapping from; open a package. **un wrapped, un wrap ping.**

up 1. *The bird flew up.* 2. *He went up the hill.* 3. *The sun is up.* 4. *Stand up.* 5. *Please get up.*

up on 1. on. 2. *Climb upon the wagon.*

up ward toward a higher place.

urn 1. a kind of vase with a base. 2. a kind of pot for making coffee or tea.

us *Our teacher helps us learn.* *These belong to us.*

use 1. *I have no use for it.* 2. *We use spoons to eat soup.* 3. *Did he use all the milk?* **used, us ing.**

used 1. See **use.** 2. *He works in the used-car lot.*

use ful of use; giving service; helpful.

usu al ly most of the time: *Father is usually right.*

Utah one of the fifty states of the United States.

V

va ca tion 1. time out of school or away from business. 2. *We took a vacation trip.*

vac u um clean er a machine for cleaning carpets.

val en tine a card sent on Valentine's Day.

Val en tine's Day February 14.

val ley low land between hills.

val ue *A dime has a value of ten cents.*

van a covered truck or wagon. See the picture.

van

vase   a holder or container for flowers.

veg e ta ble   **1.** a plant used for food.   **2.** anything that is not an animal or a mineral.   **3.** *Mother made vegetable soup for supper.*

ve hi cle   something people can ride in or on.

vel vet   **1.** thick, soft cloth.   **2.** *I wore a velvet hat.*

verb   a word that tells what we do or did or what we have done.

Ver mont   one of the fifty states of the United States.

verse   **1.** a poem or lines of words that rhyme and have accents at certain places in each line.   **2.** one part of a poem or song.

very   **1.** *The sun is very hot.*   **2.** *He sat in the very same row as I did.*   **3.** *The very thought of it hurts.*

vest   a piece of clothing, short and without sleeves.

vi brate   move rapidly forward and backward; shake very fast.   **vi brat ed, vi brat ing.**

vi bra tion   a rapid moving forward and backward.

view   **1.** *The ship came into view.*   **2.** *The view from here is good.*   **3.** *Children have different views of school.*   **4.** see; look at.   **viewed, view ing.**

vil lage   **1.** a community, usually smaller than a town.   **2.** *The courthouse was on the village square.*

vine   a plant that grows along the ground or climbs.

vin e gar   a sour liquid used in foods.

vi o let   **1.** a small plant that blooms in the spring: *The Violet is the State Flower of Illinois and of Rhode Island; the Purple Violet is the State Flower of New Jersey; the Wood Violet is the State Flower of Wisconsin.*   **2.** *She wore a violet blouse.*

vi o lin   a musical instrument.

Vir gin ia   one of the fifty states of the United States.

vis it   **1.** a call; a short stay.   **2.** go to see; make a call; stay with; be a guest: *I shall visit my aunt next week.*   **vis it ed, vis it ing.**

vis i tor   a person who visits; a guest.

voice   **1.** sounds made through the mouth: *We could hear voices.*   **2.** *He has a bass voice.*

vote **1.** *She got the most votes for president.*
2. *Did you vote for or against me?* **vot ed, vot ing.**
vow el **1.** an open sound made by the voice. **2.** the letter "a," "e," "i," "o," or "u."

W

wade walk through water. **wad ed, wad ing.**
wa fer a thin cracker or cookie.
waf fle a food like a pancake.
wag *A dog wags his tail.* **wagged, wag ging.**
wag on a four-wheeled cart for carrying loads.
wail cry loud and long. **wailed, wail ing.**
wait **1.** stay or stop doing something till something happens. **2.** help serve a meal. **wait ed, wait ing.**
wait er a man who waits on table.
wait ress a woman who waits on table. **wait ress es.**
wake stop sleeping. **waked** or **woke, wak ing.**
walk **1.** *The children went for a walk.* **2.** *Stay on the walk.* **3.** *Walk with me.* **walked, walk ing.**
walk ie-talk ie a small radio set for sending and receiving messages.
wall **1.** the side of a house or room. **2.** a stone or brick fence. **3.** *The flood came in a wall of water.*
wal nut **1.** a large nut. **2.** the tree it grows on. **3.** *We have a walnut tree.*
wal rus a large sea animal. **wal rus es** or **wal rus.**
wand a thin stick or rod: *She has a magic wand.*
wan der *I wandered up and down along the beach.* **wan dered, wan der ing.**
want **1.** wish for. **2.** need. **want ed, want ing.**
war a fight between nations or people.
warm **1.** *She sat in the warm sunshine.* **2.** *We wear warm clothes in winter.* **warm er, warm est.**
warm ly *A warmly dressed child enjoys snow.*
warn give notice of danger. **warned, warn ing.**
was *Once there was a king. I was late to school. The candy was eaten. She was going home.*
wash **1.** *Put your socks in the wash.* **2.** *Wash your dog's face.* **wash es; washed, wash ing.**

wash er   a machine that washes clothes.

Wash ing ton   one of the fifty states of the United States.

Wash ing ton, D.C.   the capital of the United States.

Wash ing ton's Birth day   February 22.

was n't   was not.

wasp   a flying insect with a sharp sting.

waste   **1.** things of no use.   **2.** *Don't waste time.*   **3.** *This is waste paper.*   **wast ed, wast ing.**

waste ful ly   *She wastefully threw away the paper.*

watch   **1.** a small clock.   **2.** *A man keeps watch at night.*   **3.** *Watch when you cross the street.*   **4.** keep guard; protect.   **watch es; watched, watch ing.**

watch ful ly   *The boys turned the corner watchfully.*

wa ter   **1.** the liquid in oceans, rivers, and lakes; rain.   **2.** *We water our lawn every week.*   **3.** *We found a leak in the water pipes.*   **wa tered, wa ter ing.**

wave   **1.** a moving pile of water.   **2.** *Sound moves in waves.*   **3.** *Wave the flag.*   **waved, wav ing.**

wax   **1.** material made by bees.   **2.** anything like this.   **3.** *Wax candles give light.*   **wax es.**

way   **1.** *Scientists are seeking ways to fight germs.*   **2.** *Look this way.*   **3.** *A spoiled child wants his own way.*

we   *We are glad.   We went riding.   We can do it.*

weak   **1.** easily broken or stopped.   **2.** not having strength or power.   **weak er, weak est.**

wear   **1.** have on the body.   **2.** last long; give good service.   **3.** *The paint wears off.*   **wore, worn, wear ing.**

wea sel   a small, quick animal with a thin body.

weath er   **1.** *We have had hot weather for a week.*   **2.** *We looked in the newspaper for the weather report.*

weath er vane   an instrument to show which way the wind is blowing.

weave   form threads or strips into a thing or material.   **wove, wov en, weav ing.**

we'd   **1.** we had: *We'd been there a long time.*   **2.** we would: *We'd like to go there again.*

wed ding   1. *A man and a woman are married in a wedding.*   2. *The wedding cake was beautiful.*

wedge   1. a piece of wood or metal with a thin edge used in splitting.   2. squeeze: *His foot was wedged between two rocks.*   **wedged, wedg ing.**

Wednes day   the fourth day of the week.

wee   very, very small; tiny.   **we er, we est.**

weed   1. a plant without any use.   2. take weeds out of: *Please weed the garden.*   **weed ed, weed ing.**

week   the time from Sunday through Saturday.

week ly   1. lasting a week.   2. once each week.

weep   cry; sob.   **wept, weep ing.**

weigh   find out how heavy a thing is: *I often weigh myself.*   **weighed, weigh ing.**

weight   *The dog's weight is forty pounds.*

wel come   1. greet kindly: *They welcomed me home.*   2. *Welcome home!*   **wel comed, wel com ing.**

well[1]   a hole dug in the ground to get water or oil.

well[2]   1. *The job was well done.*   2. *He is well.*   3. *He knew the lesson well.*   **bet ter, best.**

we'll   we shall; we will.

went   See **go**.   *I went home right after school.*

wept   See **weep**.   *She wept for hours.*

were   1. *We were there yesterday.*   2. *If I were a man, I'd go.*   3. *The flowers were wet by the rain.*

we're   we are.

weren't   were not.

west   1. the direction of the sunset.   2. *Walk west three blocks.*   3. coming from the west: *We enjoyed the west wind.*   4. *Follow the west bank of the river.*   5. **The West** means the western part of the United States.

west ern   1. toward the west: *The western bus leaves at noon.*   2. from the west: *I wrote to my western cousins.*   3. **A Western** is a story of the West.

West Vir gin ia   one of the fifty states of the United States.

west ward   toward the west.

wet   covered with water or other liquid; not dry: *Bring me a wet towel.*   **wet ter, wet test.**

we've we have.

whale a sea animal.

wharf a platform out from the shore, beside which ships can load and unload.

what 1. *What is your name? What time is it?* 2. *I don't know what you mean.* 3. *What a shame!*

what's what is.

wheat 1. a grain from which flour is made. See the picture under **grain.** 2. *Wheat flour is used for bread.*

wheel 1. a round frame that turns on its center. See the picture. 2. move on wheels: *He was wheeling bricks on a cart.* **wheeled, wheel ing.**

when 1. *When does school close?* 2. *Stand up when your name is called.* 3. *When you're ready, start.*

where 1. *Where do you live?* 2. *Where are you going?* 3. *Where did you get that?*

wheth er *It does not matter whether we go or whether we stay. He asked whether he might be excused.*

which 1. *Which boy won the prize? Which seems the best plan?* 2. *Read my book, which you have.*

while 1. *He kept us waiting a long while.* 2. *While I was waiting, I read.* 3. *While I like the color of the hat, I do not like its shape.*

whim per cry with low, broken sounds: *Thunder makes my dog whimper.* **whim pered, whim per ing.**

whine 1. make a low, complaining cry or sound. 2. say with a whining tone. **whined, whin ing.**

whip poor will a bird with a strange call.

whirl turn or swing round and round; spin: *The leaves whirled in the wind.* **whirled, whirl ing.**

whisk er 1. a hair growing on a man's face. 2. **Whiskers** usually means hair on a man's cheeks.

whis per 1. a very soft, spoken sound. 2. speak very softly and low. **whis pered, whis per ing.**

whis tle 1. a clear, shrill sound. 2. an instrument for making such sounds. 3. make a clear, shrill sound. **whis tled, whis tling.**

white the color of snow. **whit er, whit est.**

who 1. *Who goes there? Who is your friend? Who told you?* 2. *The girl who spoke is my best friend.*

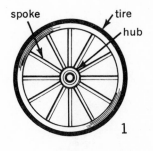

spoke — tire — hub

wheel

1

who'd 1. who had: *He wondered who'd been sitting in his chair.* 2. who would: *Who'd like to go?*

whole 1. *He worked the whole day.* 2. *Three thirds make a whole.* 3. *The dog swallowed the meat whole.*

whole sale 1. *Storekeepers buy their stock wholesale.* 2. *The wholesale price of this dress is ten dollars.*

who'll who will.

whom *Whom do you like best? He does not know whom to believe. The girl to whom I spoke is my cousin.*

who're who are.

who's 1. who is: *Who's going with me?* 2. who has: *Who's got my pencil?*

whose *Whose book is this? Whose are these?*

who've who have.

why 1. *Why did the baby cry? He knows why he failed.* 2. *I'll tell him the reason why.* 3. *Why, yes!*

wick part of a candle. See the picture under **candle.**

wick ed *The wicked old witch frightened everyone.*

wide 1. *This is a wide street.* 2. *The door is three feet wide.* 3. *Open your mouth wide.* **wid er, wid est.**

wide ly *The boys gave two widely different accounts.*

width the distance from side to side.

wie ner a frankfurter.

wife a married woman. **wives.**

wig gle move quickly from side to side: *The child wiggled in his chair.* **wig gled, wig gling.**

wild not tame; fierce. **wild er, wild est.**

wild ly *He rushed wildly out of the burning building.*

will 1. *He will come tomorrow.* 2. *We cannot always do as we will.* 3. *I will do it.* **would.**

will ing ready; wanting to.

wil low 1. a large tree. 2. *Willow trees bend.*

win succeed over others. **won, win ning.**

wind[1] 1. air that is moving. 2. put out of breath: *Walking up the hill winded us.* **wind ed, wind ing.**

wind[2] 1. *Wind your top.* 2. *A brook winds through the woods.* 3. *Wind the clock.* **wound, wind ing.**

win dow 1. an opening in a wall or roof to let in light or air. 2. *Put the vase on the window sill.*

windy *It is a windy day.* **wind i er, wind i est.**

wing **1.** the part of a bird used in flying. See the picture under **bird.** **2.** part of a plane. See the picture under **airplane.**

wink **1.** *Father's wink told us it was time to go.* **2.** *He winked at me.* **winked, wink ing.**

win ter **1.** the coldest of the four seasons. **2.** *It's time for winter clothes.*

wipe rub to clean or take away. **wiped, wip ing.**

wire **1.** metal thread. See the picture under **fence.** **2.** *The house was wired for electricity.* **3.** fasten with wire. **4.** send a telegram. **wired, wir ing.**

Wis con sin one of the fifty states of the United States.

wise knowing much; not stupid. **wis er, wis est.**

wise ly *Be sure to spend your money wisely.*

wish **1.** a desire. **2.** have a desire for; want. **wish es; wished, wish ing.**

witch in stories, a woman said to have magic power, usually an ugly old woman. **witch es.**

with **1.** *Come with me.* **2.** *They will mix with the crowd.* **3.** *The man cut the meat with a knife.*

with in **1.** not beyond. **2.** inside. **3.** not more than.

with out **1.** free from. **2.** leaving out. **3.** outside.

wiz ard in stories, a man said to have magic power.

woke See **wake.** *He woke before we did.*

wolf a wild animal that looks like a dog. **wolves.**

wom an a female human being. **wom en.**

won See **win.** *Which side won yesterday?*

won der **1.** a strange and surprising thing. **2.** feel surprised by a strange thing or event. **3.** wish to know. **won dered, won der ing.**

won der ful *The works of God are wonderful.*

won der ful ly *The sky was wonderfully colored.*

won't will not.

wood **1.** trees cut up for use: *The carpenter uses wood to build things.* **2.** *The ax had a wood handle.*

wood chuck a bushy-tailed, small animal.

wood peck er a bird with a hard, pointed bill.

woods a small forest: *It is fun to walk in the woods.*

wool 1. the soft coat of sheep. 2. *Mother cleans pans with steel wool.* 3. *Wool blankets are very warm.*

word 1. a sound or a group of sounds that has meaning. 2. the writing that stands for a word.

wore See **wear.** *He wore out his shoes in a month.*

work 1. something you do. 2. do something by trying. 3. act; operate. **worked, work ing.**

world 1. the earth. 2. *A bee is part of the insect world.* 3. all people; the public: *The whole world knows it.*

worm a small, thin, crawling or creeping animal.

worn 1. See **wear.** 2. *Throw out the worn shoes.*

wor ry 1. feel uneasy: *Don't worry about me.* 2. annoy: *Don't worry your dad.* **wor ried, wor ry ing.**

worse 1. *The sick man is worse.* 2. *It is raining worse now.*

wor ship *Some people go to a church or a synagogue to worship.* **wor shiped, wor ship ing.**

worst 1. *He's the worst.* 2. *He acts worst.*

worth 1. *That book is worth reading.* 2. *He bought a dollar's worth of stamps.*

would 1. *He would if they would.* 2. *He would go even though we warned him not to.* 3. *He said he would come in ten minutes.*

would n't would not.

wound[1] 1. a hurt caused by cutting or tearing. 2. hurt by cutting or tearing the skin. 3. hurt someone's feelings. **wound ed, wound ing.**

wound[2] See **wind**[2]. *She wound the string into a ball.*

wove See **weave.** *Pioneers wove their own clothes.*

wo ven See **weave.** *She has woven this cloth.*

wrap 1. *Shawls and coats are wraps.* 2. cover by winding or folding something around. **wrapped, wrap ping.**

wreath a ring of flowers or leaves.

wren a small songbird with a short tail: *The Cactus Wren is the State Bird of Arizona; the Carolina Wren is the State Bird of South Carolina.*

wrench 1. a sharp twist. 2. *He gave his ankle a wrench.* 3. a tool to turn nuts. **wrench es.**

wres tle   try to throw or force someone to the ground.   **wres tled, wres tling.**

wres tler   a person who wrestles for fun or money.

wrin kle   *The old man's face has wrinkles.*

wrin kled   *I can't wear this wrinkled dress.*

wrist   the joint connecting the hand and the arm. See the picture under **arm.**

write   make letters or words with pen, pencil, or chalk.   **wrote, writ ten, writ ing.**

writ er   **1.** a person who writes.   **2.** an author.

writ ten   **1.** See **write. 2.** *Written words should be spelled correctly.*

wrong   **1.** not right; bad.   **2.** not true; not correct.

wrote   See **write.**   *He wrote his mother a long letter.*

Wy o ming   one of the fifty states of the United States.

X

X ray   a picture that shows what is inside something.

xy lo phone   a musical instrument.

Y

yard[1]   **1.** *You can play in the yard.*   **2.** ground for special use: *Switch engines work in the railroad yards.*

yard[2]   a measure of length or distance: *Thirty-six inches or three feet are equal to one yard.*

yarn   **1.** any loosely spun thread, usually used for knitting.   **2.** a tale; a story.

yawn   **1.** a deep breath taken with the mouth open. **2.** *He yawns because he is sleepy.*   **3.** open wide: *A big hole yawned at his feet.*   **yawned, yawn ing.**

year   **1.** a period of time twelve months long. **2.** the time from January 1 to December 31.

year ly   **1.** lasting a year.   **2.** once each year.

yeast   a material used in making bread.

yell   **1.** a strong, loud cry.   **2.** cry out with a strong, loud sound.   **yelled, yell ing.**

yel low   having the color of gold or butter.

yel low ham mer   a bird with yellow markings: *The Yellowhammer is the State Bird of Alabama.*

yel low ish   somewhat yellow.

yes   an answer that agrees with something   **yes es.**

yes ter day   the day before today.

yet   **1.** *The work is not yet finished.*   **2.** *Don't go yet.*   **3.** *It was not yet dark.*   **4.** *It is light yet.*

yew   **1.** an evergreen tree.   **2.** the wood of this tree.   **yew.**

yoke   **1.** a frame to hitch oxen.   **2.** the part of a dress fitting the neck and shoulders.   See the picture.

yolk   the yellow part of an egg.

yon der   over there; within sight but not near.

you   *Are you ready?   Then you may go.   I see you.*

you'd   **1.** you had: *I didn't know you'd been here before.*   **2.** you would: *I hoped you'd wait for me.*

you'll   you will.

young   in the early part of life.   **young er, young est.**

your   *Wash your hands.   We enjoyed your visit.*

you're   you are.

yours   **1.** *The red book is yours.*   **2.** *My hands are clean; yours are dirty.   I like ours better than yours.*

your self   **1.** *You yourself know the story is not true.*   **2.** *Did you hurt yourself?*   **your selves.**

you've   you have.

yuc ca   a plant having large white flowers: *The Yucca Flower is the State Flower of New Mexico.*

yoke

Z

ze bra   a striped animal like a horse.

ze ro   **1.** nothing; the figure 0.   **2.** a very low point: *It is so cold it must be below zero.*

zig zag   **1.** move turning sharply from side to side.   **2.** *I took a zigzag path.*   **zig zagged, zig zag ging.**

zip   **1.** a sudden, short hissing sound.   **2.** move quickly.   **3.** fasten with a zipper.   **zipped, zip ping.**

zip per   a sliding fastener for clothing.

zoo   **1.** a place where wild animals are kept.   **2.** *Some zoo animals seem quite tame.*